Kaplan 2016 5 Strategies for the New SAT®

Kaplan Test Prep

PUBLISHING

New York

SAT® is a trademark registered and/or owned by the College Board, which was not involved in the production of, and does not endorse, this product.

Published by Kaplan Publishing, a division of Kaplan, Inc.
395 Hudson Street
New York, NY 10014

ISBN-13: 978-1-62523-587-9

Table of Contents

How to Use This Book

This book has been designed to use in preparation for the new SAT and PSAT. In it you will find information about the format of the new SAT, *The New SAT Challenge*, 5 essential test-taking strategies for the new SAT, and an additional full-length practice test complete with answers and explanations.

In addition to providing a general overview and answering some Frequently Asked Questions regarding the test changes, we have outlined what to do and think about depending on your graduating class.

The New SAT Challenge is a great place to start since it provides a sample of the kinds of questions that will be on the new SAT. When taking *The New SAT Challenge*, make sure you are in a quiet place where you can concentrate.

Once you complete the test and review your results using the New SAT Challenge Correlation Chart provided, go right into learning score-increasing methods with the 5 Strategies for the New SAT chapter. Put all five strategies to good use by completing the full-length practice test at the end of this book to prepare yourself for Test Day.

The content of this book reflects the most up-to-date information. To stay updated, please check out our Test Change Resource center at www.kaptest.com/sat/kaplan-sat-prep/sat-test-change.

— Kaplan Test Prep

KAPLAN

Chapter One: **Overview of Changes**

The SAT is changing, but there is no need to worry; Kaplan is here to help! We're here to guide you through the changes and explain what you need to know about the new SAT.

TIMING

The 2016 SAT will be 3 hours long, or 3 hours and 50 minutes long if you choose to complete the optional Essay Test. The current SAT, which is offered through January 2016, is 3 hours and 45 minutes long and includes a required essay.

2016 SAT Overview		
Subject	**Length**	**Questions**
Reading	65 minutes	52 questions
Writing and Language	35 minutes	44 questions
Math	80 minutes	58 questions
Essay (optional)	50 minutes	1 question
Total	180 minutes OR 230 minutes (w/ essay)	153 OR 154 (w/ essay)

SCORING

The 2016 SAT will have no wrong-answer penalty. It will be scored on a 1600-point scale, which includes 800 possible points for Math and 800 possible points for Evidence-Based Reading and Writing. There are many different kinds of scores you'll receive after taking the 2016 SAT.

COMPOSITE SCORE

The Composite Score is comprised of the sum of your Evidence-Based Reading and Writing score and Math score, each of which is out of 800 points. Each section score will range from 200-800 points, so the Composite Score will range from 400 to 1600 points.

AREA SCORES (ALSO KNOWN AS DOMAIN SCORES)

You will receive two Area Scores on the new SAT: an Evidence-Based Reading and Writing score and a Math score. Each score will range from 200 to 800 points. The Evidence-Based Reading and the Writing Area score is the sum of the Reading Test score and Writing and Language Test score.

TEST SCORES

The 2016 SAT will have Test Scores, each ranging from 10 to 40: A Reading Test score, a Writing and Language Test score, and a Math Test score.

CROSS-TEST SCORES

The new SAT will also include two Cross-Test Scores: Analysis in History/Social Studies and Analysis in Science. These two scores, each on a scale of 10 to 40, will be based on specific questions across the SAT Evidence-Based Reading and Writing and SAT Math sections related to these fields.

SUBSCORES

Each new SAT test will have its own set of Subscores. Each Subscore is scored on a scale of 1 to 15.

EVIDENCE-BASED READING AND WRITING TEST SUBSCORES

The Evidence-Based Reading and Writing Test will have a Command of Evidence subscore and a Relevant Words in Context subscore. The Writing and Language Test will have two additional subscores of Expression of Ideas and Standard English Conventions.

MATH TEST SUBSCORES

The 2016 SAT Math Test will have three subscores corresponding to the three major content areas on the revised exam: Heart of Algebra, Problem Solving and Data Analysis, and Passport to Advanced Math.

ESSAY

The 50-minute-long Essay Test will be optional and scored separately from the 1600-point Composite Score. You will be asked to analyze a source document and write an essay in which you explain how the author builds his or her argument. The Essay will be graded on your abilities to read, analyze, and write. Each of these components (Reading, Analysis, Writing) will be scored on a scale of 1 to 4 by two graders, which will result in three essay subscores ranging from 2 to 8 for each component.

For more detailed information about the Essay, please see the Essay Test section on page 16.

MATH

The 2016 SAT Math Test has an increased emphasis on algebraic reasoning, problem-solving, and data analysis questions that describe real-world situations. Questions may involve analyzing sets or data and/or interpreting charts and graphs.

In addition to the multiple-choice and student-produced response (grid-in) questions that have been carried over from the existing SAT, the 2016 exam includes a new question type: the Extended-Thinking question. These questions involve multiple steps and necessitate making connections among a variety of topics. The Extended-Thinking question set is worth 4 raw-score points on the exam.

The 2016 Math test is scored between 200 and 800 and is broken down into a calculator and a no-calculator section as shown in the table below.

Calculator vs. No-Calculator Math Sections		
Calculator Section	55 minutes	38 questions
No-Calculator Section	25 minutes	20 questions

For more detailed information about the calculator and no-calculator Math sections, please see the Math Test section on page 13.

EVIDENCE-BASED READING AND WRITING

The current Critical Reading and Writing sections are being combined into an Evidence-Based Reading and Writing test on the 2016 SAT. Rather than Sentence Completions that test obscure vocabulary, the new SAT will test "real world" vocabulary-in-context and your ability to revise and edit passages, which will span Literature, Social Studies, and Science. One passage on every exam will be an excerpt from a primary source from United States and/or World History (e.g. Thomas Paine's "Common Sense"). The Evidence-Based Reading and Writing section will be scored on a scale of 200 to 800.

For more detailed information about the Evidence-Based Reading and Writing section, please see the Evidence-Based Reading and Writing Test section on page 8.

Chapter Two: Grade Level Guide to Preparing for the New SAT

CLASS OF 2016

The new PSAT that will be administered in the Fall of 2015 and the new SAT that will be administered in the Spring of 2016 will NOT affect you! By the time these new tests are administered, you will have already taken the PSAT, SAT, and/or ACT and be well into the college application process.

What you can do now, however, is study for any Advanced Placement or college-level courses in which you've enrolled. A well-rounded course of study and strong GPA are top college admissions factors. Scoring well on AP tests can earn you college credit, allowing you to either graduate from college early or place out of introductory-level classes.

CLASS OF 2017+

As you begin to think about preparing for college, be aware that the changes the College Board has announced to the PSAT and SAT will affect you!

You will take the new PSAT during your junior year in October 2015. This will be the first time the new PSAT is administered.

If you are a member of the Class of 2017, you will have the option to take the current version of the 2400-point SAT in November 2015, December 2015, and/or January 2016. We do not recommend taking the SAT before the PSAT in October 2015. If you want to see if the 2400-point SAT is right for you, check out one of our free online practice tests. After January 2016, the current SAT will no longer be offered.

The new SAT will first be given in March 2016. March is usually the first time juniors take the test. Make sure if you are taking the test in or after March 2016 you prep using resources designed for the new test. Materials for the old 2400-point test will no longer apply.

Don't worry, even though the PSAT and SAT are changing, we still have plenty of tools to help you prepare for the new tests! Start by downloading your own copy of our KapMap (http://www.kaptest.com/college-prep/planning/get-kapmap), which outlines what you should be doing to prepare for college, starting at the beginning of your freshman year of high school. Then, use the resources in this book to get a better understanding of your strengths and weaknesses, and to decide which test—the current SAT, the ACT, or the new SAT—is best for you.

UNDERSTANDING PRACTICE TEST SCORES

There are three different scores associated with standardized tests. For the current SAT, the **raw score** is the number of questions you answered correctly, minus one-fourth of a point for each question you answered incorrectly. The **raw score** for the ACT is just a sum of the number of questions you answered correctly.

Each test has its own formula to convert a raw score into a **scaled score**. On the current SAT, your total scaled score is out of 2400 points (800 each for Math, Critical Reading, and Writing). On the ACT, your total scaled score is calculated by averaging your four subject tests (English, Math, Reading, Science), each scored on a scale of 0 to 36 points. If you choose to take the optional ACT Writing test (a 30-minute essay), you will receive a separate Combined English/Writing score that sums your English test score (out of 36) and your essay score (out of 12).

The new SAT will also have a **raw score**, **scaled score**, and a series of other scores. Like the ACT, the new SAT raw score will be calculated only by the number of questions you answered correctly; there will be no wrong answer penalty on the new SAT. Just like on the current SAT and ACT, the new SAT's raw score will be converted into a scaled score. The total scaled score on the new SAT will be out of 1600 points—a total of 800 for Math and 800 for Evidence-Based Reading and Writing. The new SAT also has an optional Essay Test, which will receive a separate score out of 24.

Percentile is the number that compares your score to others who took the test. For example, if you score in the 75th percentile, you achieved a higher score than 75% of those who took the same test you did.

Chapter Three: **Inside the New SAT**

INSIDE THE STRUCTURE OF THE NEW SAT

Structure of the New SAT				
	Test	**Content**	**Timing**	**Questions**
Evidence-Based Reading and Writing	Reading Test	3,250 words total from 4 single passages and 1 paired set, 500-750 words per passage or paired set drawing from U.S. and World Literature, History/Social Studies, and Science. Two passages will include one or two informational graphics.	65 minutes	52 multiple-choice questions (10-11 per passage or passage set)
	Writing and Language Test	1,700 words total from 4 passages of 400-450 words each, drawing from Careers, History/Social Studies, Humanities, or Science. 1-2 passages will be Argumentative, 1-2 passages will be Informative/Explanatory, and 1 passage will be a Nonfiction Nnarrative.	35 minutes	44 multiple-choice questions (11 questions per passage)

Structure of the New SAT				
	Test	**Content**	**Timing**	**Questions**
Math	Calculator Section	Questions are drawn from the Heart of Algebra, Problem Solving and Data Analysis, Passport to Advanced Math, and Additional Topics in Math content areas.	55 minutes	30 multiple-choice questions + 6 student-produced response questions + 2 extended-thinking questions = 38 total questions
	No-Calculator Section	Questions draw from the Heart of Algebra, Passport to Advanced Math, and Additional Topics in Math content areas. No Problem Solving or Data Analysis questions.	25 minutes	15 multiple-choice questions + 5 student-produced response questions = 20 total questions
Essay (optional)		You will be asked to analyze a 650-750 word document and draft an essay. This essay question tests reading, analysis, and writing skills, and requires you to analyze a source document and explain how the author builds an argument.	50 minutes	1 prompt

EVIDENCE-BASED READING AND WRITING SECTION

The Evidence-Based Reading and Writing section of the redesigned SAT will be broken into two sections: the **Reading Test** (65 minutes, 52 multiple-choice questions) and the **Writing and Language Test** (35 minutes, 44 multiple-choice questions).

Your scores from each of these two tests will range from 10 to 40. These scores will be summed and then scaled to a 200-800 score.

The **Reading Test** will focus on your comprehension and reasoning skills when faced with challenging prose passages ranging in text complexity across a range of content areas.

The **Writing and Language Test** will focus on your ability to revise and edit when presented with extended prose passages, also across a range of content areas.

THE READING TEST

OVERVIEW

SAT Reading Test Overview	
Timing	65 minutes
Questions	52 passage-based multiple-choice questions
Passages	4 single passages; 1 set of paired passages
Passage Length	500-750 words each

PASSAGES

Passages will draw from **U.S. and world literature**, **history/social studies**, and **science**. One set of history/social studies or science passages will be a pair of shorter passages instead of one longer passage. History/social studies and science passages can also be accompanied by graphical representations of data such as charts, graphs, tables, etc. All passages will be taken from previously-published sources. Graphics accompanying passages can be taken from published sources as well but may also be created for the exam.

SAT Reading Test Passage Distribution	
U.S. and World Literature	1 passage; 10-11 questions
History/Social Studies	2 passages OR 1 passage and 1 paired passage set; 10-11 questions each
Science	2 passages OR 1 passage and 1 paired passage set; 10-11 questions each

Two of the passages on the 2016 SAT Reading Test will include **1–2 informational graphics** that portray information related to the content of the passage. You will be asked to interpret this data and combine it with the information presented in the text.

Passages will also range in **text complexity,** meaning that the reading material on the SAT ranges in difficulty level from high school to college-level texts.

QUESTIONS

The multiple-choice questions for each passage will be arranged in order from the more general to the more specific so you can actively engage with the entire passage before answering questions about details.

WORDS IN CONTEXT QUESTIONS

Some multiple-choice questions will ask about **relevant words in context**. These questions will test your comprehension of how a word or phrase is used in the context of a

500-750 word prose passage in any of the aforementioned subjects. These words will be neither particularly obscure nor specific to a certain field of study. Rather, you will be asked to figure out the meaning of the word or phrase based on the context in which it is used.

COMMAND OF EVIDENCE QUESTIONS

Other multiple-choice questions will test your **command of evidence**. These questions will be secondary to conclusions you reach in preceding questions; they will ask you to find the best support for your interpretation of the passage by citing the most relevant textual evidence listed in the answer choices. Questions that measure your command of evidence will be phrased along the lines of *Which choice best supports the answer to the previous question?*

ANALYSIS OF HISTORY/SOCIAL STUDIES OR SCIENCE

The remaining questions will be strict **analysis of History/Social Studies or Science passages**. These questions test a variety of skills.

Reading Test Questions	
Information and Ideas	Close reading (determining explicit/implicit meanings and using analogical reasoning); citing textual evidence; determining main ideas and themes
Summarizing	Understanding relationships; interpreting words and phrases in context
Rhetoric	Analyzing word choice; assessing overall text structure; assessing part-whole relationships; analyzing point of view; determining purpose; analyzing arguments (claims and counterclaims, reasoning, evidence)
Synthesis	Analyzing multiple texts (i.e., paired passages); analyzing quantitative information

THE WRITING AND LANGUAGE TEST

OVERVIEW

SAT Writing and Language Test Overview	
Timing	35 minutes
Questions	44 passage-based multiple-choice questions
Passages	4 single passages with 11 questions each
Passage Length	400-450 words each

PASSAGES

The SAT Writing and Language Test will have **four passages** that are written specifically for the test. There will be one passage from each of the following subject areas: **Careers**, **History/Social Studies**, **Humanities**, and **Science**.

SAT Writing and Language Passage Breakdown	
Careers	Hot topics in "major fields of work" like information technology and health care
History/Social Studies	Discussion of historical or social sciences topics such as anthropology, communication studies, economics, education, human geography, law, linguistics, political science, psychology, and sociology
Humanities	The arts and letters
Science	Exploration of concepts, findings, and discoveries in the natural sciences, including Earth science, biology, chemistry, and physics

Passages will also range in the type of text. A passage can be an argument, an informative or explanatory text, or a nonfiction narrative.

Passage Text Type Distribution	
Argument	1-2 passages
Informative/Explanatory Text	1-2 passages
Nonfiction Narrative	1 passage

Some passages and/or questions will refer to one or more informational graphics such as tables, charts, graphs, etc. Questions associated with these graphical representations will ask you to revise and edit the passage based on the data presented in the graphic. These questions will not require computation, only analysis of existing data.

QUESTIONS

The most prevalent question format on the SAT Writing and Language Test will ask you to choose the best of three alternatives to an underlined portion of the passage, or to decide that the current version is the best option. You will be asked to improve the development, organization, and diction in the passages in order to ensure they conform to conventional standards of English grammar, usage, and style. While you will be able to answer some of these multiple-choice questions by looking only at a phrase, clause, or sentence, many of the questions must be answered by considering the passage as a whole.

EXPRESSION OF IDEAS QUESTIONS

24 questions on the Writing and Language Test will be **Expression of Ideas** questions. These questions can include sub-question types such as **words in context**, **command of evidence**, and **analysis of history/social studies or science**.

These questions are further broken down into three categories: **development**, **organization**, and **effective language use**.

Expression of Ideas Questions	
Development	Edit the text in terms of rhetorical purpose by assessing:
	Proposition: Do the main ideas, central claims, counterclaims, and topic sentences appropriately structure the text? Do they clearly and effectively convey arguments, information, and ideas?
	Support: Do the information and ideas like details, facts, and statistics accurately support claims or ideas in the text?
	Focus: Are certain information and ideas relevant to the topic and purpose of the overarching text?
	Quantitative Information: How do graphs, charts, and tables representing quantitative information relate to the text?
Organization	Improve the logic and coherence of text at the level of sentence, paragraph, or entire passage by assessing:
	Logical Sequence: Are the information and ideas presented in the most logical order?
	Introductions, Conclusions, and Transitions: Are transition words, phrases, and sentences used effectively to connect the information and ideas of the text?
Effective Language Use	Improve language use to make sure it reinforces rhetorical purposes by assessing:
	Precision: Are the words chosen (diction) exact and appropriate for the text?
	Concision: Is the text wordy or redundant?
	Style and Tone: Are tone and style consistent throughout the text? Does the text's style and tone match its purpose?
	Syntax: Does the text's sentence structure accurately reflect its rhetorical purposes?

STANDARD ENGLISH CONVENTIONS QUESTIONS

20 questions on the Writing and Language Test will be **Standard English Conventions** questions. These questions focus on editing the passage's text to conform to standard written English conventions of **sentence structure**, **usage**, and **punctuation**.

Issues Tested in Standard English Conventions Questions	
Sentence Structure	run-ons and fragments, coordination and subordination, parallelism, modifiers, verb tenses, mood, voice, pronouns
Conventions of Usage	pronouns, possessives vs. contractions, pronoun-antecedent agreement, subject-verb agreement, noun agreement, frequently-confused words, comparisons, idioms
Conventions of Punctuation	colons, semicolons, dashes, possessive nouns and pronouns, series, parenthetical elements, unnecessary punctuation

THE MATH TEST

OVERVIEW

SAT Math Overview		
	Question Types	**Content Categories**
Calculator Section (55 minutes)	30 multiple-choice + 6 student-produced response (grid-in) + 1 extended-thinking question set (grid-in) = 38 questions	Heart of Algebra, Problem-Solving and Data Analysis, Passport to Advanced Math, and Additional Topics in Math
No-Calculator Section (25 minutes)	15 multiple-choice + 5 student-produced response (grid-in) = 20 questions	Heart of Algebra, Passport to Advanced Math, Additional Topics in Math

All math questions will be worth one point except for the **Extended-Thinking** question set in the Calculator section, which will be worth **four raw-score points**.

HEART OF ALGEBRA

The phrase "Heart of Algebra" encompasses Linear Equations and Functions, skills you will need in a variety of college classes—even those that fall outside the realms of math and science. There will be a total of **21 Heart of Algebra** questions (13 on the Calculator section and 8 on the No-Calculator section) on the Math Test.

The Heart of Algebra content category will assess your ability to fluently apply and conceptually understand the following topics:

1. Linear equations and expressions with one variable

2. Linear inequalities with one variable

3. Linear equations with two variables

4. Functions and function notation

5. Systems of inequalities with two variables

6. Systems of linear equations with two variables

7. Solving systems of equations or inequalities with one variable

8. Solving systems of two linear equations with two variables

9. Interpreting variables and constants in linear function expressions within a real-world context

10. Making connections between algebraic and graphical representations

PROBLEM SOLVING AND DATA ANALYSIS

Problem Solving and Data Analysis questions will ask you to solve single and multistep problems involving percents, ratios, and unit conversions, as well as interpret information presented in graphs and charts.

There will be **15 Problem Solving and Data Analysis questions** on the Math Test, all of which will appear in the Calculator section. In addition, the **Extended-Thinking Grid-In question set** (worth 4 raw-score points) will be a Problem Solving and Data Analysis question.

The Problem Solving and Data Analysis content category will assess your ability to fluently apply and conceptually understand the following topics:

1. Ratios, rates, and proportions

2. Scale drawings

3. Percentages

4. Unit conversion and calculating density

5. Using scatterplots and linear, quadratic, or exponential models to describe how variables are related

6. Using graphs to identify a value or set of values

7. Interpreting graphs based on the relationship between variables

8. Analyzing linear vs. exponential growth

9. Probability

10. Summarizing categorical data

11. Estimating population parameters

12. Averages

13. Standard Deviation

14. Evaluating reports in order to infer, justify conclusions, and determine appropriateness of data collection methods

PASSPORT TO ADVANCED MATH

Passport to Advanced Math includes a variety of topics that cover content found in courses beyond introductory algebra. Most involve working with functions and parts of functions algebraically and graphically.

There will be **16 Passport to Advanced Math questions** on the redesigned SAT Math Test (7 on the Calculator section and 9 on the No-Calculator section).

The Passport to Advanced Math content category will assess your ability to fluently apply and conceptually understand the following topics:

1. Quadratic and exponential functions

2. Determining the most suitable form of an expression or equation based on context

3. Radicals and rational exponents

4. Algebraic expressions and operations

5. Quadratic equations

6. Polynomials

7. Radical and rational equations (sometimes with extraneous solutions)

8. Systems of linear and quadratic equations

9. Rewriting rational expressions

10. Interpreting parts of nonlinear expressions in context

11. Zeros and factors of polynomials

12. Sketching graphs

13. Understanding nonlinear relationships between two variables by making connections between algebraic and graphical representations

14. Function notation

15. Rearranging equations or formulas to isolate a single variable

ADDITIONAL TOPICS IN MATH

Some questions on the redesigned SAT Math Test do not fall into the aforementioned categories. Most of the Additional Topics will come from Geometry and Trigonometry topics.

There will be **6 Additional Topics in Math questions** on the new SAT Math Test (3 in the Calculator section and 3 in the No-Calculator section).

The Additional Topics in Math content category will assess your ability to fluently apply and conceptually understand the following topics:

1. Application of volume formulas

2. Trigonometric ratios

3. The Pythagorean Theorem

4. Right triangles

5. Arithmetic operations on complex numbers

6. Conversion between degrees and radians

7. Circles (including arc length, angle measures, chord lengths, and sector areas)

8. Plane geometry (lines, angles, triangles)

9. Similar triangles

10. Sine and cosine

11. The coordinate plane

THE ESSAY TEST (OPTIONAL)

The Essay Test is undergoing major changes. The Essay has been moved to the end of the exam, as its own test, and has been made optional. In addition, the length of time allotted for essay writing has doubled from 25 minutes to **50 minutes**.

The redesigned SAT Essay Test will assess your college and career readiness by testing your abilities to read, write, and analyze a high-quality source document and write a coherent analysis of the source supported with critical reasoning and evidence from the given text.

THE PASSAGE

The **one passage** featured on the SAT Essay Test, a source text of **650-750 words**, will be argumentative and aimed toward a large audience. Passages will examine ideas, debates, and shifts in the arts and sciences as well as civic, cultural, and political life. Rather than having a simple for/against structure, these passages will be nuanced and will relate views on complex subjects. These passages will also be logical in their structure and reasoning.

It is important to note that **prior knowledge is not required**.

THE PROMPT

The redesigned SAT Essay prompt will ask you to explain how the presented passage's author builds an argument to convince an audience. In writing your essay, you may analyze elements such as the author's use of evidence, reasoning, style, and persuasion; you will not be limited to those elements listed, however.

Rather than writing about whether you agree or disagree with the presented argument, you will write an essay in which you analyze *how* the author makes an argument.

The redesigned SAT Essay Test expects you to demonstrate:

- Careful analysis/comprehension of the passage

- Discerning use of textual evidence to develop and support your own points

- Clear organization and expression of ideas

SCORING

The redesigned SAT Essay Test will be broken down into three categories for scoring: **Reading**, **Analysis**, and **Writing**.

Each of these elements will be scored on a scale of **1 to 4** by two graders, for a total score of 2 to 8 for each category.

READING

The Reading subscore measures your abilities to:

- Understand the source text

- Comprehend main ideas, important details, and how they function together

- Correctly interpret the text

- Use textual evidence like quotations and paraphrases to demonstrate your understanding

ANALYSIS

The Analysis subscore measures your abilities to:

- Analyze the given passage and understand the prompt

- Evaluate the author's use of evidence, reasoning, and stylistic/persuasive elements or other elements of your choosing

- Support your own claims or points

- Highlight the aspects of the text most relevant to the prompt

WRITING

The Writing subscore measures your abilities to:

- Construct a thesis

- Effectively organize and transition between ideas

- Use varied sentence structure

- Use appropriate diction (word choice)

- Maintain a consistent (and appropriate) style and tone

- Utilize the conventions of standard written English

Chapter Four: **Frequently Asked Questions**

WHY IS THE SAT CHANGING?

In a live webcast on March 5, 2014, the College Board—administrators of the SAT—shared more detailed information about their plans for the redesigned SAT.

According to the College Board web site, *"The redesigned SAT will ask students to apply a deep understanding of the few skills and content areas most important for college and career readiness,"* with the goal of supporting *"college readiness and success for more students."* The new SAT is being designed to reinforce what students learn in the classroom.

This does not mean, however, that simply going to class will ensure a high score on the new SAT. Test-specific preparation will still be a factor in ensuring Test Day success. As the College Board releases specifics pertaining to the new SAT, Kaplan will continue to update students with the most up-to-date information.

SHOULD I TAKE THE SAT OR ACT?

While the SAT is an older test, the ACT has gained popularity over the past decade. In 2013, 1.8 million students took the ACT and 1.6 million students took the SAT. However, both tests have the same aim: to level the playing field for college admissions, regardless of background.

All U.S. colleges and universities accept both the SAT and ACT. The best way to determine which test you should study for is to take one of our free practice tests for each exam and determine which test you feel more comfortable with and on which test you scored in a higher percentile. Once you figure out which exam you want to take, start prepping!

WHAT ABOUT THE NEW PSAT/NMSQT, PSAT 10, AND PSAT 8/9?

The new PSAT/NMSQT (National Merit Scholarship Qualifying Test) and PSAT suite of assessments will help students, parents, and educators identify skill-gaps early so students can better prepare for the SAT. The PSAT/NMSQT will be available for 11th graders in the fall of their junior year. 10th grade students may also take the PSAT/NMSQT, but they will not be eligible for National Merit. PSAT 10 is designed for 10th grade students and will be available during the spring of sophomore year. PSAT 8/9 is for 8th and 9th grade students and will be available in either the spring or fall. Because all of these tests are scaled on the same vertical scale as the new SAT, student, parents, and educators will be able to easily see a student's strengths and weaknesses. The PSAT, like the SAT, will test Math, Reading, and Writing and Language, but does not include an essay portion. The redesigned PSAT/NMSQT will contain 4 sections—2 Math, 1 Reading, and 1 Writing and Language—and will last 2 hours and 45 minutes. A high score on the PSAT/NMSQT can qualify you for participation in the National Merit Scholarship Competition, as well as a host of other scholarship opportunities. The first administration of the new PSAT suite of assessments will take place in October 2015.

WHEN SHOULD I TAKE THE SAT OR ACT? HOW MANY TIMES?

Most students take the SAT/ACT tests for the first time during their junior year so they have time to retake it if needed. You can take these tests more than once and, in fact, probably should! Students generally see an increase in scores the second time they take the test. Furthermore, SAT and ACT score reporting options let you choose which scores get sent to colleges, so if you didn't score as high as you wanted to on your first try, the colleges you're applying to don't have to see it! But before taking the SAT or ACT, make sure you've practiced with a Kaplan Practice Test or two (or three or four)!

WHAT ARE SAT SUBJECT TESTS AND AP EXAMS? DO I NEED TO TAKE THEM?

SAT Subject Tests are designed to measure what you know about specific subjects, including History, Math, Science, English, and Foreign Languages, and help your strengths stand out on your college application. SAT Subject Tests are offered throughout the year, typically taken in the spring, and are an hour long. Some colleges also use Subject Tests to place students into appropriate courses. Some schools require one or more Subject Tests, so be sure to check your target college's website to find out. If you are doing well in an AP class, consider taking the Subject Test related to it. Studying for your AP exams is a great way to start studying for Subject Tests.

Take the AP exam as soon as you complete your course, and have the scores sent to your college. Look online or call your target college's Admissions Department to find out how your AP credits can be applied at your college. Scoring well on an AP exam can earn you college credit that may allow you to graduate early or place out of an introductory-level course.

Chapter Five: **Free Online Resources**

The best things in life are free, as are these Kaplan resources. We're determined to provide as much support as we can as you move through the college application process. In Kaplan's more than 75 years of providing test preparation, we have successfully supported students through many test changes, and we continue to do that now. Check out the links below to learn more about the current SAT and ACT, the new SAT and PSAT, and the college application process.

SAT CHANGE RESOURCE CENTER

http://www.kaptest.com/college-prep/test-information/sat-test-change

For the most up-to-date information regarding the changes to the SAT and PSAT, make sure to visit our SAT Change Resource Center website.

THE KAPMAP

http://www.kaptest.com/college-prep/planning/get-kapmap

The KapMap is a college planner that breaks down what you should be doing and thinking about during each month of all four years of high school. It's a useful tool to make sure you stay on track and get into the college of your choice!

COLLEGE APPLICATION TOOLS AND TIPS

http://www.kaptest.com/college-prep/planning/admissionszone

Getting into the college of your choice takes a strong college application, which showcases your strongest grades, extracurricular activities, and personal essay! Every college has different criteria for determining which students to admit. The best tip during this process is to stay organized and pay close attention to the many details. This link is home to several essential tools to help you through this process, including FAQs about the Common

Application, tips for acing your college interviews, and a step-by-step guide on how to begin the college application process.

FINANCIAL AID & SCHOLARSHIP INFORMATION

http://www.kaptest.com/college-prep/financial-aid/financial-aid-resource-center

As college costs rise, so does the opportunity and need to get funding through federal aid, grants, low-interest loans, and scholarships. Doing your financial aid homework can really pay off. Use this link to learn about FAFSA (Free Application for Federal Student Aid) and how you can ensure you successfully obtain a scholarship.

ONLINE EVENTS AND PRACTICE TESTS

http://www.kaptest.com/college-prep

Find a free event near you by entering your zip code, or take a look at the online ACT, SAT, and PSAT events at this link via our Classroom Anywhere® platform. Events range from workshops to sample lessons from our courses to practice tests.

THE SAT/ACT INSIDER

http://blog.kaplansatact.com/

With posts aimed at students, parents, and guidance counselors, Kaplan's SAT/ACT Insider blog is a great source of information about the college admissions process, financial aid, and walk-throughs of actual test-like questions from our expert Kaplan instructors.

TURBO TESTS

http://www.kaptest.com/sat/kaplan-sat-prep/free-sat-practice-test

Want to see how you'd do on the SAT, PSAT, or ACT? Try one of Kaplan's Turbo Tests, 90-minute adaptive diagnostic exams you can take online to gauge how you will perform on Test Day.

TWITTER

Do you tweet? So does Kaplan! Follow us on Twitter at **@KaplanSATACT** for tips about exams and college admissions, as well as news about special offers and free events and resources!

FACEBOOK

Speaking of social media, you can also follow us on **Facebook.com/KaplanSAT**! Stay up-to-date on the latest SAT, ACT, PSAT, and college admissions news, and take a crack at test-like questions with Test Yourself Tuesdays!

How to Use This Challenge

The *New SAT Challenge* includes the new question types that will be on the 2016 SAT as outlined by the College Board. It does not represent the full SAT experience since it is specially designed to help you determine which new SAT content you need to focus on the most. Use the correlation chart available at the end of this chapter to find out which topics are your greatest areas of opportunity.

Before you begin, find a quiet place where you can concentrate for 2 hours and 10 minutes. Go through the sections and follow the directions for each test. For each multiple-choice question, select an answer and fill in the corresponding oval. For Student-Produced Response questions, or Grid-Ins, write your answer in the boxes, then fill in the corresponding ovals below the boxes. If you decide to take the optional Essay Test, write your response on the lined pages provided after the prompt.

Do not look at the answer key until you have completed the entire test. Once you have finished, go through the answer key and mark which questions you answered correctly and which questions you answered incorrectly. Remember, there will be no wrong-answer penalty on the new SAT, so it's important that you make an educated guess for every question.

After you have marked which questions you answered correctly and incorrectly, take a look at the correlation charts to see what kinds of questions you're great at and which question types were more challenging for you. Thoroughly read through the explanations for the questions you missed to make sure you understand the reasoning behind the correct answer. It's also helpful to read through the explanations for questions you've answered correctly—there might be a more efficient way to get to the answer.

Now it's time to sit up tall, take a deep breath, sharpen your no. 2 pencils, and try the *New SAT Challenge*.

Good luck!

New SAT Challenge
Answer Sheet

Remove (or photocopy) the answer sheet and use it to complete the New SAT Challenge.
See the answer key and explanations following the test when finished.

Start with number 1 for each section.
If a section has fewer questions than answer spaces, leave the extra spaces blank.

SECTION 1

1. Ⓐ Ⓑ Ⓒ Ⓓ Ⓔ   7. Ⓐ Ⓑ Ⓒ Ⓓ Ⓔ   13. Ⓐ Ⓑ Ⓒ Ⓓ Ⓔ   19. Ⓐ Ⓑ Ⓒ Ⓓ Ⓔ
2. Ⓐ Ⓑ Ⓒ Ⓓ Ⓔ   8. Ⓐ Ⓑ Ⓒ Ⓓ Ⓔ   14. Ⓐ Ⓑ Ⓒ Ⓓ Ⓔ   20. Ⓐ Ⓑ Ⓒ Ⓓ Ⓔ
3. Ⓐ Ⓑ Ⓒ Ⓓ Ⓔ   9. Ⓐ Ⓑ Ⓒ Ⓓ Ⓔ   15. Ⓐ Ⓑ Ⓒ Ⓓ Ⓔ   21. Ⓐ Ⓑ Ⓒ Ⓓ Ⓔ
4. Ⓐ Ⓑ Ⓒ Ⓓ Ⓔ   10. Ⓐ Ⓑ Ⓒ Ⓓ Ⓔ   16. Ⓐ Ⓑ Ⓒ Ⓓ Ⓔ   22. Ⓐ Ⓑ Ⓒ Ⓓ Ⓔ
5. Ⓐ Ⓑ Ⓒ Ⓓ Ⓔ   11. Ⓐ Ⓑ Ⓒ Ⓓ Ⓔ   17. Ⓐ Ⓑ Ⓒ Ⓓ Ⓔ
6. Ⓐ Ⓑ Ⓒ Ⓓ Ⓔ   12. Ⓐ Ⓑ Ⓒ Ⓓ Ⓔ   18. Ⓐ Ⓑ Ⓒ Ⓓ Ⓔ

□ # right in Section 1

□ # wrong in Section 1

SECTION 2

1. Ⓐ Ⓑ Ⓒ Ⓓ Ⓔ   5. Ⓐ Ⓑ Ⓒ Ⓓ Ⓔ   9. Ⓐ Ⓑ Ⓒ Ⓓ Ⓕ   13. Ⓐ Ⓑ Ⓒ Ⓓ Ⓔ
2. Ⓐ Ⓑ Ⓒ Ⓓ Ⓔ   6. Ⓐ Ⓑ Ⓒ Ⓓ Ⓔ   10. Ⓐ Ⓑ Ⓒ Ⓓ Ⓔ   14. Ⓐ Ⓑ Ⓒ Ⓓ Ⓔ
3. Ⓐ Ⓑ Ⓒ Ⓓ Ⓔ   7. Ⓐ Ⓑ Ⓒ Ⓓ Ⓔ   11. Ⓐ Ⓑ Ⓒ Ⓓ Ⓔ   15. Ⓐ Ⓑ Ⓒ Ⓓ Ⓔ
4. Ⓐ Ⓑ Ⓒ Ⓓ Ⓔ   8. Ⓐ Ⓑ Ⓒ Ⓓ Ⓔ   12. Ⓐ Ⓑ Ⓒ Ⓓ Ⓔ   16. Ⓐ Ⓑ Ⓒ Ⓓ Ⓔ

17.   18.   19A.   19B.

□ # right in Section 2

□ # wrong in Section 2

SECTION 3

1. Ⓐ Ⓑ Ⓒ Ⓓ Ⓔ   9. Ⓐ Ⓑ Ⓒ Ⓓ Ⓔ   17. Ⓐ Ⓑ Ⓒ Ⓓ Ⓔ   25. Ⓐ Ⓑ Ⓒ Ⓓ Ⓔ
2. Ⓐ Ⓑ Ⓒ Ⓓ Ⓔ   10. Ⓐ Ⓑ Ⓒ Ⓓ Ⓔ   18. Ⓐ Ⓑ Ⓒ Ⓓ Ⓔ   26. Ⓐ Ⓑ Ⓒ Ⓓ Ⓔ
3. Ⓐ Ⓑ Ⓒ Ⓓ Ⓔ   11. Ⓐ Ⓑ Ⓒ Ⓓ Ⓔ   19. Ⓐ Ⓑ Ⓒ Ⓓ Ⓔ   27. Ⓐ Ⓑ Ⓒ Ⓓ Ⓔ
4. Ⓐ Ⓑ Ⓒ Ⓓ Ⓔ   12. Ⓐ Ⓑ Ⓒ Ⓓ Ⓔ   20. Ⓐ Ⓑ Ⓒ Ⓓ Ⓔ   28. Ⓐ Ⓑ Ⓒ Ⓓ Ⓔ
5. Ⓐ Ⓑ Ⓒ Ⓓ Ⓔ   13. Ⓐ Ⓑ Ⓒ Ⓓ Ⓔ   21. Ⓐ Ⓑ Ⓒ Ⓓ Ⓔ   29. Ⓐ Ⓑ Ⓒ Ⓓ Ⓔ
6. Ⓐ Ⓑ Ⓒ Ⓓ Ⓔ   14. Ⓐ Ⓑ Ⓒ Ⓓ Ⓔ   22. Ⓐ Ⓑ Ⓒ Ⓓ Ⓔ   30. Ⓐ Ⓑ Ⓒ Ⓓ Ⓔ
7. Ⓐ Ⓑ Ⓒ Ⓓ Ⓔ   15. Ⓐ Ⓑ Ⓒ Ⓓ Ⓔ   23. Ⓐ Ⓑ Ⓒ Ⓓ Ⓔ
8. Ⓐ Ⓑ Ⓒ Ⓓ Ⓔ   16. Ⓐ Ⓑ Ⓒ Ⓓ Ⓔ   24. Ⓐ Ⓑ Ⓒ Ⓓ Ⓔ

□ # right in Section 3

□ # wrong in Section 3

Remove (or photocopy) the answer sheet and use it to complete the New SAT Challenge.

Start with number 1 for each section. If a section has fewer questions than answer spaces, leave the extra spaces blank.

SECTION 4

1. Ⓐ Ⓑ Ⓒ Ⓓ Ⓔ
2. Ⓐ Ⓑ Ⓒ Ⓓ Ⓔ
3. Ⓐ Ⓑ Ⓒ Ⓓ Ⓔ
4. Ⓐ Ⓑ Ⓒ Ⓓ Ⓔ
5. Ⓐ Ⓑ Ⓒ Ⓓ Ⓔ
6. Ⓐ Ⓑ Ⓒ Ⓓ Ⓔ
7. Ⓐ Ⓑ Ⓒ Ⓓ Ⓔ

8.
9.
10.

right in Section 4

wrong in Section 4

SECTION 5

Section 5 is the Optional Essay test.

WRITING AND LANGUAGE TEST

20 Minutes–22 Questions

Directions In the following two passages, certain words and phrases are underlined and numbered. Beside the passage are alternatives for each underlined portion. Select the one that best conveys the idea, creates the most grammatically correct sentence, or is most consistent with the style and tone of the passage. If you decide that the original version is best, select NO CHANGE. You may also find questions that ask about the entire passage or a section of the passage. These questions will correspond to small, numbered boxes in the text. For these questions, decide which choice best accomplishes the purpose set out in the question stem. For some questions, you'll need to read the context to answer correctly. Be sure to read until you have enough information to determine the correct answer choice.

Questions 1–11 refer to the following passage.

American Jazz

❶ One of the earliest music forms to originate in the United States was Jazz. Known as truly mid-American because of ❷ it's origins in several locations in middle America, the music developed almost simultaneously in New York, New Orleans, Saint Louis, Kansas City, and Chicago.

At the start of the 20th century, musicians all along the Mississippi River familiar with West African folk music blended it with European classical music from the early nineteenth century. This combination was adopted by artists in the region who began to use minor chords and ❸ syncopation, in their own music, ragtime and blues. At the same time, brass bands and gospel choirs adopted Jazz music, and it became a true blend of cultures.

1. (A) NO CHANGE
   (B) One of the most earliest
   (C) The most early
   (D) The earliest

2. (A) NO CHANGE
   (B) its
   (C) its's
   (D) its'

3. (A) NO CHANGE
   (B) syncopation in their own music,
   (C) syncopation, in their own music
   (D) syncopation in their own music

GO ON TO THE NEXT PAGE

Eventually, a different music ❹ <u>style developed; based on</u> a blend of the many different cultures in America at the time. ❺ <u>It was American Jazz and</u> became the first indigenous American style to affect music in the rest of the world. [1] One of the true greats of American Jazz was Cabell "Cab" Calloway III. [2] He was born in New York in 1907, ❻ <u>therefore</u> his family moved to Chicago during his teen years. [3] Growing up, Cab made his living working as a shoe shiner and a waiter. [4] During these years, he also spent time at the racetrack, where he walked horses to keep them in good shape.

4. (A) NO CHANGE
    (B) style developed based on
    (C) style developed based on,
    (D) style, developed based on

5. (A) NO CHANGE
    (B) This style, known as American Jazz,
    (C) Being known as American Jazz, it
    (D) It being American Jazz first

6. (A) NO CHANGE
    (B) and
    (C) but
    (D) also

GO ON TO THE NEXT PAGE

[5] After graduating from high school in Chicago, Cab got his first performance in a revue called "Plantation Days." [6] His strong and impressive voice soon gained him ❼ <u>popularity in the top Jazz circles</u> of the United States. 8

Many others have followed Cab's lead ❾ <u>and have moved from the east coast to middle America</u>. Like other folk music forms, American

7. (A) NO CHANGE
    (B) popularity: in the top Jazz circles
    (C) popularity, in the top Jazz circles,
    (D) popularity in the top Jazz circles,

8. Upon reviewing this paragraph and finding that some information has been left out, the writer composes the following sentence incorporating that information:

    He became widely known as "The man in the zoot suit with the reet pleats."

    This sentence would most logically be placed after sentence:

    (A) 3.
    (B) 4.
    (C) 5.
    (D) 6.

9. Given that all choices are true, which one would most effectively tie together the two main subjects of this essay?

    (A) NO CHANGE
    (B) and have added to the rich tradition of American Jazz.
    (C) such as George Duke and Earl Klugh.
    (D) and have signed large recording contracts.

Jazz has a rich history and unique sound that ❿ <u>means it'll stick around for awhile.</u>

10. (A) NO CHANGE
    (B) causes it to be an enduring institution with a timeless appeal.
    (C) makes many people enjoy it.
    (D) ensures its continued vitality.

11. Suppose the writer's goal was to write a brief essay focusing on the history and development of American Jazz music. Would this essay successfully fulfill this goal?

    (A) Yes, because the essay describes the origins of American Jazz music and one of its important figures.
    (B) Yes, because the essay mentions the contributions American Jazz music has made to other folk music traditions.
    (C) No, because the essay refers to other musical forms besides American Jazz music.
    (D) No, because the essay focuses on only one American Jazz musician, Cab Calloway.

GO ON TO THE NEXT PAGE ⟩

Questions 12–22 refer to the following passage.

Arctic Sea Ice and Global Warming

Polar ice consists of sea-ice formed from frozen seawater as well as ice sheets and glaciers formed from the buildup and compaction of falling snow. The Earth is home to **12** <u>two polar ice caps; high-latitude regions of a planet or natural satellite covered in ice.</u>

The high latitude of polar ice caps causes these **13** <u>domains</u> to receive less energy in the form of **14** <u>solar radiation from the sun</u> than equatorial regions do, which results in lower surface temperatures.

12. (A) NO CHANGE
    (B) two polar ice caps high-latitude regions of a planet or natural satellite covered in ice.
    (C) two polar ice caps: high-latitude regions of a planet or natural satellite covered in ice.
    (D) two polar ice caps. High-latitude regions of a planet or natural satellite covered in ice.

13. (A) NO CHANGE
    (B) areas
    (C) homes
    (D) ranges

14. (A) NO CHANGE
    (B) radiation
    (C) radiation that's from the sun
    (D) solar radiation

GO ON TO THE NEXT PAGE

The Earth's polar ice caps **15** <u>are changing</u> dramatically over the course of the last 12,000 years. Seasonal variations of the ice caps **16** <u>takes place</u> due to varied solar energy absorption as the planet revolves around the sun. Ice caps can also grow or shrink due to climate variation. Global warming is expected to cause more ice to melt, reducing the energy reflected back to space and **17** <u>to increase</u> the energy absorbed at the surface. This would cause the affected portions of the Earth to warm.

If the most dire of the widespread global warming theories is accurate, the polar ice caps should be receding significantly. Recent studies, **18** <u>too</u>, have demonstrated that **19** <u>the Arctic ice shelf is not just maintaining its mass, it is increasing</u>. In addition, satellite temperature readings,

15. (A) NO CHANGE
     (B) change
     (C) have changed
     (D) will change

16. (A) NO CHANGE
     (B) took place
     (C) take place
     (D) takes places

17. (A) NO CHANGE
     (B) to increasing
     (C) increasing
     (D) increase

18. (A) NO CHANGE
     (B) however
     (C) furthermore
     (D) especially

19. (A) NO CHANGE
     (B) the Arctic ice shelf is not just maintaining its mass, but it is increasing also
     (C) the Arctic ice shelf is not just maintaining its mass, but increasing
     (D) the Arctic ice shelf is not just maintaining its mass, but it is experiencing an increase

20 considered by many to be more reliable than surface temperatures taken by humans under varying conditions, indicate no global warming of the lower atmosphere, and scientific reports confirm an increase in the arctic sea-ice extent. However, upon careful review of a 20-year span of data, environmental organizations determined that **21** the increase occurred steadily over the twenty-year period, suggesting the reported increases were the result of **22** errors rather than a growing trend.

20. (A) NO CHANGE
    (B) which many consider more reliable than humans taking surface temperatures
    (C) considered by many to be more reliable than humans taking surface temperatures
    (D) which are always more reliable than surface temperatures taken by humans

21. Which choice completes the sentence with accurate data based on the line graph?

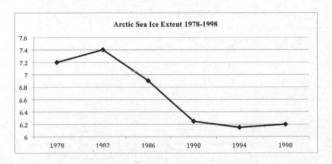

Arctic Sea Ice Extent 1978-1998

    (A) NO CHANGE
    (B) the increase occurred during two 4-year segments of the 20-year period
    (C) almost the entirety of this increase occurred during a period of only one year
    (D) the reverse is true

22. (A) NO CHANGE
    (B) mistakes
    (C) oversights
    (D) anomalies

MATH TEST—CALCULATOR

28 Minutes—20 Questions

Directions For this section, solve each problem and decide which is the best of the choices given. Fill in the corresponding oval on the answer sheet. You may use any available space for scratch work.

Notes:

1. Calculator use is permitted.
2. All numbers used are real numbers.
3. All figures used are necessary to solving the problems that they accompany. All figures are drawn to scale EXCEPT when it is stated that a specific figure is not drawn to scale.
4. Unless stated otherwise, the domain of any function f is assumed to be the set of all real numbers x, for which $f(x)$ is a real number.

Information:

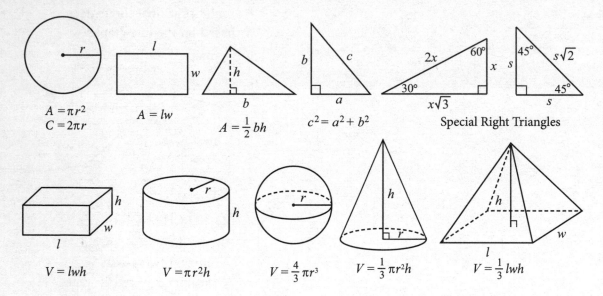

$A = \pi r^2$
$C = 2\pi r$

$A = lw$

$A = \frac{1}{2}bh$

$c^2 = a^2 + b^2$

Special Right Triangles

$V = lwh$

$V = \pi r^2 h$

$V = \frac{4}{3}\pi r^3$

$V = \frac{1}{3}\pi r^2 h$

$V = \frac{1}{3}lwh$

The sum of the degree measures of the angles in a triangle is 180.

The number of degrees of arc in a circle is 360.

The number of radians of arc in a circle is 2π.

GO ON TO THE NEXT PAGE

1. Darnel just started a subscription for satellite radio. The cost for the subscription is $16.99 per month plus 6% tax. There is an additional one-time untaxed activation fee of $25. Which of the following represents Darnel's total charge, in dollars, if he subscribes for x months?

   (A) $1.06(16.99x + 25)$

   (B) $1.06(16.99 + 25)x$

   (C) $1.06(16.99x) + 25$

   (D) $(16.99 + 0.06x) + 25$

2. A system of three equations and their graphs are shown here. How many solutions does the system of equations have?

   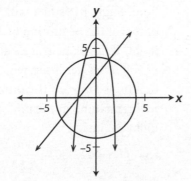

   $$\begin{cases} x^2 + y^2 = 17 \\ 2x^2 + y = 6 \\ 3x - 2y = -5 \end{cases}$$

   (A) none

   (B) one

   (C) two

   (D) three

3. Two objects that had been heated to a temperature of 160°C were removed from a furnace and placed in a room at 20°C. The temperatures of the objects were measured and recorded each hour. The data for each object was modeled using a smooth curve as shown in the following graph.

   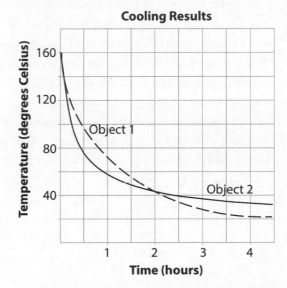

   Cooling Results

   Which of the following does <u>not</u> accurately describe the data?

   (A) Between 2 and 3 hours, the temperature of Object 2 decreased at a faster rate than the temperature of Object 1.

   (B) For the first 15 minutes, the temperature of Object 2 decreased at a faster rate than the temperature of Object 1.

   (C) At 0 hours and at 2 hours, the temperatures of the two objects were the same.

   (D) As long as the temperature of the room does not change, the graphs for each data set will remain above $y = 20$.

GO ON TO THE NEXT PAGE

4. Pure silver is a very soft metal and is easily damaged, so it is usually mixed with another metal to form a metal alloy before being molded into jewelry settings. A jeweler is making one batch of ring settings from a metal alloy composed of silver and copper and another batch from an alloy composed of silver and nickel. The jeweler's cost for making the first batch is $38 per setting and the cost for making the second batch is $46 per setting. During a two-week period, the jeweler makes 75 ring settings and uses a total of $3,122 worth of silver, copper, and nickel. Solving which system of equations yields the number of silver-copper settings, x, and the number of silver-nickel settings, y, that the jeweler made?

(A) $\begin{cases} x + y = 3,122 \\ 38x + 46y = 75 \end{cases}$

(B) $\begin{cases} x + y = 75 \\ 38x + 46y = 3,122 \end{cases}$

(C) $\begin{cases} x + y = 75 \\ 38x + 46y = \dfrac{3,122}{2} \end{cases}$

(D) $\begin{cases} x + y = 75 \\ 38x + 46y = 3,122 \times 2 \end{cases}$

5. A typical song downloaded from the Internet is 4 megabytes in size. Lindy has satellite Internet and her computer downloads music at a rate of 256 kilobytes per second. If 1 megabyte equals 1,024 kilobytes, about how many songs can Lindy download in 2 hours?

(A) 128 songs

(B) 450 songs

(C) 1,800 songs

(D) 1,920 songs

6. If (x, y) is a solution to the system of equations below, what is the value of y^2?

$$\begin{cases} x^2 + y^2 = 160 \\ y = 3x \end{cases}$$

(A) 12

(B) 16

(C) 120

(D) 144

7. A commercial airline has calculated that the approximate fuel mileage for its 600-passenger airplane is 0.2 miles per gallon when the plane travels at an average speed of 500 miles per hour. Flight 818's fuel tank has 42,000 gallons of fuel at the beginning of an international flight. If the plane travels at an average speed of 500 miles per hour, which of the following functions f models the number of gallons of fuel remaining in the tank t hours after the flight begins?

(A) $f(t) = 42,000 - \dfrac{500t}{0.2}$

(B) $f(t) = 42,000 - \dfrac{0.2}{500t}$

(C) $f(t) = \dfrac{42,000 - 500t}{0.2}$

(D) $f(t) = \dfrac{42,000 - 0.2t}{500}$

GO ON TO THE NEXT PAGE

8. In 1978, the bald eagle was listed as an endangered species throughout the lower 48 states (not in Alaska or Hawaii). Since that time, the number of nesting pairs of bald eagles has recovered to the point that they no longer need to be protected by the Endangered Species Act and as a result, were removed from the list in June of 2007. The scatter plot below shows approximate counts of bald eagles in Florida from 1986 to 2006. Based on the line of best fit shown, which of the following values is closest to the average yearly increase in the number of nesting pairs between 1986 and 2006?

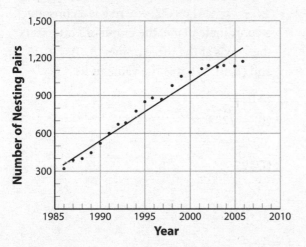

(A) 0.021

(B) 0.48

(C) 21

(D) 48

9. A property management company handles an apartment complex with 120 two-bedroom units. When the monthly rent is $725 per unit, all 120 units are occupied. When the rent is $800 per month, the average number of occupied units drops to 105. If the number of units rented decreases at a constant rate as the rent increases, which of the following linear models best describes the number of units rented, n, at a monthly rent of d dollars?

(A) $n = -5d + 265$

(B) $n = -5d + 1,325$

(C) $n = -\dfrac{1}{5}d + 265$

(D) $n = -\dfrac{1}{5}d + 749$

GO ON TO THE NEXT PAGE

Questions 10–11 refer to the following information.

A survey was conducted among a randomly-chosen sample of people who owned a cell phone in 2013. The following table shows a summary of the survey results.

	Owned a Smart Phone	Did Not Own a Smart Phone	No Response	Total
15- to 29-year-olds	28,542	19,116	11,223	58,881
30- to 44-year-olds	33,116	24,308	9,414	66,838
45- to 59-year-olds	11,960	21,405	6,549	39,914
60-year-olds and over	1,023	1,897	862	3,782
Total	74,641	66,726	28,048	169,415

10. According to the survey results, for which age group did the greatest percentage of people report that they owned a Smart Phone?

(A) 15- to 29-year-olds

(B) 30- to 44-year-olds

(C) 45- to 59-year-olds

(D) 60-year-olds and over

11. Of the 15- to 29-year-olds who reported owning a Smart Phone, 500 people were selected at random to do a follow-up survey in which they were asked whether they watched streaming videos on their phones. There were 302 people in this follow-up survey who responded *Yes* to the question and 198 who responded *No*. Using the data from both the follow-up survey and the initial survey, which of the following is most likely to be an accurate statement?

(A) About 45,083 people 15 to 29 years old would report watching streaming videos on their Smart Phones.

(B) About 35,564 people 15 to 29 years old would report watching streaming videos on their Smart Phones.

(C) About 17,239 people 15 to 29 years old would report watching streaming videos on their Smart Phones.

(D) About 102,327 people 15 to 29 years old would report watching streaming videos on their Smart Phones.

12. The polynomial function f is defined by $f(x) = 4x^3 + bx^2 + 41x + 12$, where b is a constant. On a coordinate plane, the graph of f intersects the x-axis at the three points $(3, 0)$, $(-0.25, 0)$, and $(k, 0)$. What is the value of b?

(A) -27

(B) $-\sqrt{207}$

(C) 4

(D) 27

GO ON TO THE NEXT PAGE

13. If k is a rational number such that $k > 1$, which of the following could be the graph of the equation $y = ky + kx + x + 5$?

(A)

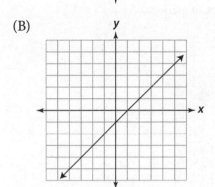

(B)

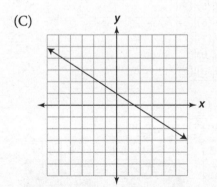

(C)

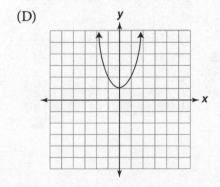

(D)

14. If the expression $\dfrac{9x^2}{3x-2}$ is rewritten in the equivalent form $\dfrac{4}{3x-2} + A$, what is A in terms of x?

(A) $\dfrac{9x^2}{4}$

(B) $3x + 2$

(C) $3x - 2$

(D) $9x^2 - 4$

15. Priya is buying a used car. She has narrowed her search down to two cars. The following table shows the information about each car.

Car	Purchase Price	Gas Mileage (miles per gallon)	Tax, Registration, and Repairs
A	$3,500	20	$800
B	$5,000	25	$400

Priya likes Car B better, because it is newer and gets better gas mileage, but she has calculated that it will cost her less to buy and use Car A based on the following criteria:

- Priya estimates that she will drive approximately 400 miles per month.

- The average cost of gasoline per gallon for her area is $3.80.

- Priya plans on owning the car for 3 years.

Based on the data, how much less will it cost Priya to buy and use Car A?

(A) $552.80

(B) $952.80

(C) $1,054.40

(D) $1,084.80

Directions: For questions 16–19, solve the problem and enter your answer in the grid, as described below, on the answer sheet.

1. Although not required, it is suggested that you write your answer in the boxes at the top of the columns to help you fill in the circles accurately. You will receive credit only if the circles are filled in correctly.

2. Mark no more than one circle in any column.

3. No question has a negative answer.

4. Some problems may have more than one correct answer. In such cases, grid only one answer.

5. **Mixed numbers** such as $3\frac{1}{2}$ must be gridded as 3.5 or $\frac{7}{2}$. (If $3\frac{1}{2}$ is entered into the grid as $\boxed{1\,|\,1\,|\,/\,|\,4}$, it will be interpreted as $\frac{31}{2}$, not $3\frac{1}{2}$).

6. **Decimal answers:** If you obtain a decimal answer with more digits than the grid can accommodate, it may be either rounded or truncated, but it must fill the entire grid.

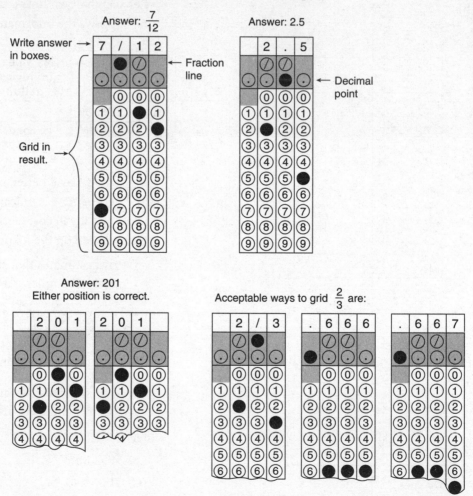

GO ON TO THE NEXT PAGE ⟶

16. If $-\dfrac{2}{3} < 6x - 4 < -\dfrac{2}{5}$, what is one possible value of $-3x + 2$?

17. A locking pin is often made using a cylinder-cylinder pair in which a narrow cylinder fits tightly inside a wider cylinder. The inner cylinder protrudes from the outer cylinder, usually by equal amounts on both ends. In the following diagram, the radius of the inner cylinder is half the radius of the outer cylinder, and it protrudes from the outer cylinder by 4 centimeters on each end.

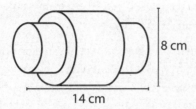

What is the volume of the locking pin, to the nearest cubic centimeter?

18. Find the value of x that is between 90° and 180° such that $\sin x° = \cos 30°$.

19. Eli left his home in New York and traveled to Brazil on business. On Monday, he used his credit card to purchase these pewter vases as a gift for his wife.

For daily purchases totaling less than 200 U.S. dollars, Eli's credit card company charges a 2% fee. If the total charge on his credit card for the vases was $126.48, and no other purchases were made, what was the foreign exchange rate on Monday in Brazilian reais (R$) per U.S. dollar? If necessary, round your answer to the nearest hundredth.

20. On Wednesday, Eli bought a tourmaline ring that cost R$ 763. For daily purchases over $200, his credit card company charges the same 2% fee on the first $200 of the converted price and 3% on the portion of the converted price that is over $200. If the total charge on his credit card for the ring was $358.50, what was the amount of decrease, as a percentage, in the foreign exchange rate between Monday and Wednesday? Round your answer to the nearest whole percent.

READING TEST

45 Minutes–30 Questions

Directions: Choose the best answer for each question.

Questions 1–10 are based on the following passage.

This passage is from a speech delivered in 1873 by Susan B. Anthony, a key leader in the women's rights movement of the 19th century. In 1872, Anthony, along with her sisters and several other women, had voted in the presidential election. At the time, it was illegal for women to vote.

Friends and fellow citizens: I stand before you tonight under indictment for the alleged crime of having voted at the last Presidential election,

Line without having a lawful right to vote. It shall be my

(5) work this evening to prove to you that in thus voting, I not only committed no crime, but, instead, simply exercised my citizen's rights, guaranteed to me and all United States citizens by the National Constitution, beyond the power of any State to deny.

(10) The preamble of the Federal Constitution says:

"We, the people of the United States, in order to form a more perfect union, establish justice, insure domestic tranquillity, provide for the common defense, promote the general welfare, and

(15) secure the blessings of liberty to ourselves and our posterity, do ordain and establish this Constitution for the United States of America."

It was we, the people; not we, the white male citizens; nor yet we, the male citizens; but we, the

(20) whole people, who formed the Union. And we formed it, not to give the blessings of liberty, but to secure them; not to the half of ourselves and the half of our posterity, but to the whole people—women as well as men. And it is a downright mockery to talk to

(25) women of their enjoyment of the blessings of liberty while they are denied the use of the only means of securing them provided by this democratic-republican government—the ballot.

For any State to make sex a qualification that

(30) must ever result in the disfranchisement of one entire half of the people, is to pass a bill of attainder, or, an *ex post facto* law, and is therefore a violation of the supreme law of the land. By it the blessings of liberty are forever withheld from women and

(35) their female posterity.

To them this government has no just powers derived from the consent of the governed. To them this government is not a democracy. It is not a republic. It is an odious aristocracy; a hateful

(40) oligarchy of sex; the most hateful aristocracy ever established on the face of the globe; an oligarchy of wealth, where the rich govern the poor. An oligarchy of learning, where the educated govern the ignorant, or even an oligarchy of race, where

(45) the Saxon rules the African, might be endured; but this oligarchy of sex, which makes father, brothers, husband, sons, the oligarchs over the mother and sisters, the wife and daughters, of every household—which ordains all men sovereigns, all

(50) women subjects, carries dissension, discord, and rebellion into every home of the nation.

Webster, Worcester, and Bouvier[1] all define a citizen to be a person in the United States, entitled to vote and hold office.

(55) The only question left to be settled now is: Are women persons? And I hardly believe any of our opponents will have the hardihood to say they are not. Being persons, then, women are citizens; and no State has a right to make any

(60) law, or to enforce any old law, that shall abridge their privileges or immunities. Hence, every discrimination against women in the constitutions and laws of the several States is today null and void, precisely as is every one

(65) against Negroes.

[1] Three dictionaries of the time

GO ON TO THE NEXT PAGE ⟶

1. The central idea of the passage is that

   (A) the government has turned into an aristocracy.

   (B) the Consitution established our laws.

   (C) some male citizens are being denied basic rights.

   (D) all citizens should have the right to vote.

2. In lines 18–20 ("It was we, the people . . . the Union."), Anthony's argument rests mainly on the strategy of convincing her audience that

   (A) the preamble to the Constitution established rights for all.

   (B) the writers of the Constitution favored male citizens.

   (C) the preamble to the Constitution did not address voting rights.

   (D) the writers of the Constitution were all aristocrats.

3. Which choice provides the best evidence for the answer to the previous question?

   (A) Lines 1–2 ("I stand . . . indictment")

   (B) Lines 11–17 ("We, . . . Constitution for United States")

   (C) Lines 33–34 ("blessings . . . withheld")

   (D) Line 54 ("entitled to . . . office")

4. The stance Anthony takes in the passage is best described as that of

   (A) a judge accusing lawmakers.

   (B) a politician looking to gain votes.

   (C) a lawyer defending herself.

   (D) a historian explaining past events.

5. As used in line 6, *committed* most nearly means

   (A) made a promise.

   (B) assigned.

   (C) did something wrong.

   (D) entrusted.

6. It can be reasonably inferred from the passage that Anthony thinks

   (A) denying women the right to vote is against the law.

   (B) future generations will find fault with U.S. practices.

   (C) rights granted to women should be determined by states.

   (D) encouraging women to vote illegally will eventually change the law.

7. Which choice provides the best evidence for the answer to the previous question?

   (A) Lines 4–9 ("It shall be . . . to deny.")

   (B) Lines 24–28 ("And it is . . . the ballot.")

   (C) Lines 29–33 ("For any State . . . of the land.")

   (D) Lines 37–38 ("To them . . . democracy.")

8. As used in line 15, *secure* most nearly means

   (A) guarantee.

   (B) fasten.

   (C) strengthen.

   (D) start.

GO ON TO THE NEXT PAGE

9. In lines 55–56 , what is the most likely reason that Anthony poses the question "Are women persons?"

(A) To convince her audience to lobby for her acquittal of wrongdoing

(B) To illustrate the need for a women's rights movement in the United States

(C) To present a logical reason why women should be provided rights

(D) To criticize lawmakers who view women as second-class citizens

10. At the end of the speech (lines 61–65), what is the most likely reason Anthony makes a connection between African Americans and women?

(A) To agree with the common sentiments of the U.S. population at the time

(B) To make the case that both groups are guaranteed rights as citizens

(C) To distinguish between the voting rights of one group versus another

(D) To argue that both groups should work together to secure their rights

Questions 11–20 are based on the following passage.

This passage describes an important process within the human body.

The various biological mechanisms within the human body operate with precision and specificity, guaranteeing our health and, ultimately, our
Line survival. In this essay, we will examine the
(5) physiology of blood, the cardiovascular system's vehicle for conveying vital materials throughout the body.

Classified as a connective tissue, blood is a sticky fluid that is pumped through the body's blood
(10) vessels by the heart, the chief organ of the cardiovascular system. Blood has three major functions: transportation, protection, and regulation.

Transportation

Blood transports gases, specifically oxygen and
(15) carbon dioxide, from the lungs and delivers nutrients from the digestive tract; blood also conveys hormones produced by the body's glands to the appropriate targeted places within the body. Finally, blood transports heat to the skin
(20) in order to help control body temperature.

Protection

Blood helps protect the body in several essential ways. It contributes to the destruction of cancer cells and invading microorganisms and assists in the removal of any other foreign bodies that are
(25) present in the bloodstream. Blood's protective function is ever-present, safeguarding the body when the appropriate conditions present themselves.

Regulation

A third important function of the blood, regula-
(30) tion, works to control the pH of the blood with acids and bases and maintains water balance by transferring water to and from the body's tissues.

Blood Composition

Blood comprises the following main components: plasma, red blood cells, white blood cells,
(35) and platelets.

Plasma, which is a yellowish watery substance, constitutes around 60 percent of our blood and operates as a transport medium for blood cells and platelets; it also serves as a solvent for ions,
(40) such as electrolytes, and molecules, including hundreds of different kinds of plasma proteins.

GO ON TO THE NEXT PAGE

Some of the plasma proteins carry lipids and fat-soluble vitamins through the body, while others have roles in blood clotting or in defense against (45) pathogens. Collectively, the concentration of plasma proteins determines the blood's fluid volume, for it influences the movement of water between blood and interstitial fluid.

Red blood cells, also known as erythrocytes, are (50) biconcave disks, similar to doughnuts with a squashed-in center instead of a hole; they transport the oxygen used in aerobic respiration and carry away some carbon dioxide wastes. When oxygen diffuses into the blood, it binds with (55) hemoglobin, the iron-containing pigment that gives red blood cells their color. Like all blood cells, red blood cells are produced in bone marrow. By far the most abundant type of solid found in blood, more than 250 million red blood cells are (60) contained in a single drop of blood.

Leukocytes, or white blood cells, originate from a certain type of bone marrow cell called stem cells. Leukocytes function in the daily housekeeping and defense of the body. Many patrol tissues, where (65) they target or engulf damaged or dead cells and anything chemically recognized as foreign to the body. Many other leukocytes are massed together in the lymph nodes and spleen, where they divide to produce armies of cells that battle viruses, (70) bacteria, and other invaders.

White blood cells differ in size, nuclear shape, and staining traits, and consist of five categories: neutrophils, eosinophils, basophils, monocytes, and lymphocytes. The neutrophils and monocytes are (75) search-and-destroy cells; the monocytes follow chemical trails to inflamed tissues, where they develop into macrophages that can engulf invaders and debris. Two classes of lymphocytes, B cells and T cells, exhibit highly-specific defense (80) responses.

Some stem cells in bone marrow give rise to giant cells called megakaryocytes; these shed fragments of cytoplasm enclosed in a bit of plasma membrane and are referred to as platelets, another

(85) important component of blood. Platelets, which initiate blood clotting and help to minimize blood loss, exist for only five to nine days, but hundreds of thousands of platelets are constantly circulating in the bloodstream.

(90) Mature red blood cells do not have a nucleus, nor do they require it; they have enough hemoglobin, enzymes, and other proteins to adequately function for about 120 days, or approximately four months. Macrophages then break down and engulf (95) these mature red cells in the same way that they attack invading microorganisms or cancer cells. Despite this seemingly destructive process, however, the system maintains itself involuntarily; new red blood cell replacements are generated regularly (100) and keep the cell count fairly stable.

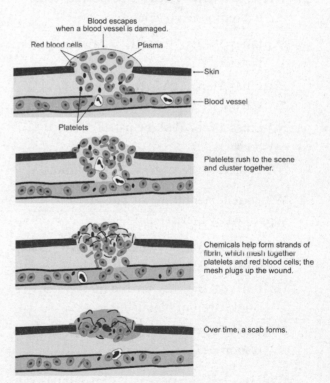

The Clotting Process

Blood escapes when a blood vessel is damaged.

Red blood cells — Plasma

Skin

Blood vessel

Platelets

Platelets rush to the scene and cluster together.

Chemicals help form strands of fibrin, which mesh together platelets and red blood cells; the mesh plugs up the wound.

Over time, a scab forms.

GO ON TO THE NEXT PAGE

11. The central idea of the passage is primarily concerned with

  (A) blood function.

  (B) the cardiovascular system.

  (C) blood clotting.

  (D) the immune system.

12. The passage most strongly suggests that which of the following plays a major role in protecting the body?

  (A) Erythrocytes

  (B) Leukocytes

  (C) Blood vessels

  (D) Plasma proteins

13. Which choice provides the best evidence for the answer to the previous question?

  (A) Lines 36–39 ("Plasma, . . . and platelets")

  (B) Lines 51–53 ("they transport . . . wastes")

  (C) Lines 64–67 ("Many patrol . . . to the body.")

  (D) Line 98 ("the system . . . involuntarily")

14. Which statement from the passage is supported by the graphic?

  (A) Lines 94–96 ("Macrophages then break down . . . or cancer cells.")

  (B) Lines 58–60 ("By far the most . . . a single drop of blood.")

  (C) Lines 78–80 ("Two classes of . . . defense responses.")

  (D) Line 98 ("the system . . . involuntarily")

15. As used in line 54, *diffuses* most nearly means

  (A) softens.

  (B) spreads.

  (C) disappears.

  (D) separates.

16. The author's use of words such as *patrol* and *battle* implies that white blood cells

  (A) differ in size, shape, and purpose.

  (B) can invade the body.

  (C) are like the body's personal army.

  (D) can be highly specific.

17. Which choice provides the best evidence for the answer to the previous question?

  (A) Lines 5–7 ("the cardiovascular . . . throughout the body.")

  (B) Lines 25–26 ("Blood's . . . ever-present")

  (C) Lines 63–64 ("Leukocytes . . . of the body.")

  (D) Lines 81–82 ("Some stem cells . . . megakaryocytes")

18. As used in line 100, *stable* most nearly means

  (A) settled.

  (B) long-lived.

  (C) reliable.

  (D) consistent.

19. The passage most strongly suggests that which of the following is true of plasma?

  (A) It is the liquid substance of blood.

  (B) It is the most important blood component.

  (C) It is produced by bone marrow.

  (D) It is normally at a pH of 7.4.

20. It can be reasonably inferred from the passage and graphic that a platelet deficiency could cause

  (A) formation of fibrin threads.

  (B) excessive blood loss.

  (C) destruction of red blood cells.

  (D) limited bone marrow.

GO ON TO THE NEXT PAGE ⟶

Directions: Choose the best answer for each question.

Questions 21–30 are based on the following passage.

In this passage, American author Mark Twain recalls his boyhood in a small town along the Mississippi River.

My father was a justice of the peace, and I supposed he possessed the power of life and death over all men and could hang anybody that offended him.
Line
(5) This was distinction enough for me as a general thing; but the desire to be a steamboatman kept intruding, nevertheless. I first wanted to be a cabin boy so that I could come out with a white apron on and shake a tablecloth over the side, where all my old comrades could see me. Later I thought I would

(10) rather be the deck hand who stood on the end of the stage plank with a coil of rope in his hand, because he was particularly conspicuous. But these were only daydreams—too heavenly to be contemplated as real possibilities. By and by one of

(15) the boys went away. He was not heard of for a long time. At last he turned up as an apprentice engineer or "striker" on a steamboat.

This thing shook the bottom out of all my Sunday-school teachings. That boy had been noto-

(20) riously worldly, and I had been just the reverse—yet he was exalted to this eminence, and I was left in obscurity and misery. There was nothing generrous about this fellow in his greatness. He would always manage to have a rusty bolt to scrub while

(25) his boat was docked at our town, and he would sit on the inside guard and scrub it, where we could all see him and envy him and loathe him.

He used all sorts of steamboat technicalities in his talk, as if he were so used to them that he forgot

(30) common people could not understand them. He would speak of the "labboard" side of a horse in an easy, natural way that would make you wish he was dead. And he was always talking about "St. Looy" like an old citizen. Two or three of the boys

(35) had long been persons of consideration among us because they had been to St. Louis once and had a

vague general knowledge of its wonders, but the day of their glory was over now. They lapsed into a humble silence and learned to disappear when the

(40) ruthless "cub" engineer approached. This fellow had money, too, and hair oil, and he wore a showy brass watch chain, a leather belt, and used no suspenders. No girl could withstand his charms. He "cut out" every boy in the village. When his boat

(45) blew up at last, it diffused a tranquil contentment among us such as we had not known for months. But when he came home the next week, alive, renowned, and appeared in church all battered up and bandaged, a shining hero, stared at and

(50) wondered over by everybody, it seemed to us that the partiality of Providence for an undeserving reptile had reached a point where it was open to criticism.

This creature's career could produce but one

(55) result, and it speedily followed. Boy after boy managed to get on the river. Four sons of the chief merchant and two sons of the county judge became pilots, the grandest position of all. But some of us could not get on the river—at least our

(60) parents would not let us.

So by and by I ran away. I said I would never come home again till I was a pilot and could return in glory. But somehow I could not manage it. I went meekly aboard a few of the boats that lay

(65) packed together like sardines at the long St. Louis wharf and very humbly inquired for the pilots but got only a cold shoulder and short words from mates and clerks. I had to make the best of this sort of treatment for the time being, but I had comfort-

(70) ing daydreams of a future when I should be a great and honored pilot, with plenty of money, and could kill some of these mates and clerks and pay for them.

GO ON TO THE NEXT PAGE

21. The central idea of the passage is that

    (A) becoming a justice of the peace commanded the respect of others.

    (B) the author eventually found work on a steamboat.

    (C) working on a steamboat was the best thing a boy could imagine.

    (D) the engineer didn't deserve the sympathy of others.

22. The passage most strongly suggests that which of the following is true of the author?

    (A) He thinks that the engineer's success is an injustice.

    (B) He thinks a person must have deep religious beliefs.

    (C) He thinks being a deck hand pays the highest wages.

    (D) He thinks that steamboat work will make him famous.

23. Which choice provides the best evidence for the answer to the previous question?

    (A) Lines 9–12 ("Later I thought . . . conspicuous.")

    (B) Lines 18–22 ("This thing shook me . . . and misery.")

    (C) Lines 54–55 ("This creature's career . . . followed.")

    (D) Lines 58–60 ("But some of us . . . would not let us. ")

24. The author makes the statement that "I supposed he . . . offended him" (lines 1–3) primarily to suggest the

    (A) power held by a justice of the peace in a frontier town.

    (B) respect in which the townspeople held his father and how that influenced his thinking.

    (C) somewhat naïve point of view he held about his father's importance.

    (D) harsh environment in which he was brought up and how that influenced his point of view.

25. As used in line 4, *distinction* most nearly means

    (A) difference.

    (B) feature.

    (C) clarity.

    (D) prestige.

26. It can be reasonably inferred from the passage that the boys in the town

    (A) had all gone to St. Louis before.

    (B) had all gone to Sunday school.

    (C) were relieved when the boat blew up.

    (D) were in competition with one another.

27. Which choice provides the best evidence for the answer to the previous question?

    (A) Lines 12–14 ("But these . . . real possibilities.")

    (B) Lines 44–46 ("When his boat . . . for months.")

    (C) Lines 47–49 ("But when he . . . a shining hero")

    (D) Lines 56–58 ("Four sons . . . grandest position of all.")

GO ON TO THE NEXT PAGE

28. As used in line 35, *consideration* most nearly means

    (A) generosity.

    (B) reputation.

    (C) contemplation.

    (D) unselfishness.

29. In lines 28–30 ("He used . . . understand them."), what is the most likely reason the author refers to "steamboat technicalities"?

    (A) To emphasize the engineer's desire to appear sophisticated

    (B) To convey the engineer's strong interest in steamboat work

    (C) To show the engineer's inability to communicate effectively

    (D) To reveal the engineer's fascination with trivial information

30. Based on the passage, which choice best describes the relationship between the engineer and the other boys in town?

    (A) The engineer is envious of the other boys.

    (B) The other boys are envious of the engineer.

    (C) The engineer thinks he is better than the other boys.

    (D) The other boys think they are better than the engineer.

IF YOU FINISH BEFORE TIME IS CALLED, YOU MAY CHECK YOUR WORK ON THIS SECTION ONLY. DO NOT TURN TO ANY OTHER SECTION IN THE TEST.

STOP

MATH TEST—NO-CALCULATOR

13 Minutes—10 Questions

Directions: For this section, solve each problem and decide which is the best of the choices given. Fill in the corresponding oval on the answer sheet. You may use any available space for scratch work.

Notes:

1. Calculator use is NOT permitted.
2. All numbers used are real numbers.
3. All figures used are necessary to solving the problems that they accompany. All figures are drawn to scale EXCEPT when it is stated that a specific figure is not drawn to scale.
4. Unless stated otherwise, the domain of any function f is assumed to be the set of all real numbers x, for which $f(x)$ is a real number.

Information:

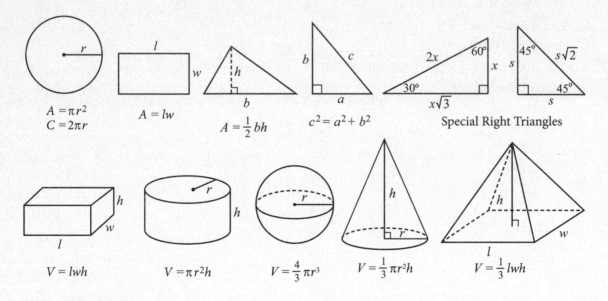

The sum of the degree measures of the angles in a triangle is 180.

The number of degrees of arc in a circle is 360.

The number of radians of arc in a circle is 2π.

GO ON TO THE NEXT PAGE

1. In the following equation, what is the value of n?

$$\frac{3(n+4)-8}{5} = \frac{11-(6-2n)}{2}$$

(A) $-\dfrac{33}{4}$

(B) $-\dfrac{17}{4}$

(C) $\dfrac{17}{16}$

(D) $\dfrac{33}{16}$

2. The following figure shows the graph of $f(x)$ from $x = -6$ to $x = 6$. If $f(3) = a$, what is $f(a)$?

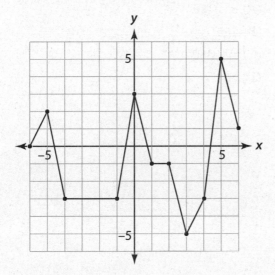

(A) -6

(B) -5

(C) 0

(D) 2

3. In the system of linear equations shown, a is a constant. If the system has no solution, what is the value of a?

$$\begin{cases} \dfrac{1}{3}x - \dfrac{1}{2}y = 5 \\ ax - 6y = 15 \end{cases}$$

(A) $\dfrac{1}{3}$

(B) 1

(C) 4

(D) 12

4. A pool restoration company is emptying a swimming pool for a client using two submersible sump pumps. One of the pumps removes water three times as fast as the other, and together the pumps can completely empty the pool in 4 hours. The following equation represents the scenario:

$$\frac{1}{x} + \frac{3}{x} = \frac{1}{4}$$

Which of the following describes what the expression $\dfrac{1}{x}$ represents in this equation?

(A) The portion of the pool that the slower pump is able to empty in 1 hour

(B) The portion of the pool that the faster pump is able to empty in 3 hours

(C) The time, in hours, that it would take the slower pump to empty the pool if it were working alone

(D) The time, in hours, that it would take the slower pump to empty $\dfrac{1}{4}$ of the pool if it were working alone

GO ON TO THE NEXT PAGE ⟩

5. Segment *DB* in the diagram shown is tangent to Circle *C* at *A*. What is the area, in square units, of triangle *ABC*?

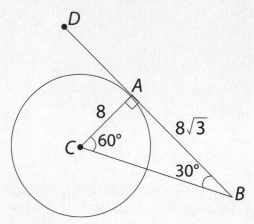

(A) $8\sqrt{3}$

(B) $32\sqrt{3}$

(C) 64

(D) $64\sqrt{3}$

6. Based on the following system of equations, what is the value of the quotient $\dfrac{x}{y}$?

$$\begin{cases} \dfrac{1}{3}x - \dfrac{1}{2}y = 5 \\ ax - 6y = 15 \end{cases}$$

(A) $\dfrac{1}{2}$

(B) $\dfrac{3}{2}$

(C) 3

(D) 6

7. It is given that $\sin x = -a$, where *x* is the measure of an angle, in degrees, and $270° < x < 360°$. If $\sin w = a$, which of the following could be the value of *w*?

(A) $x - 180°$

(B) $180° - x$

(C) $x - 360°$

(D) $360° + x$

GO ON TO THE NEXT PAGE

Directions: For questions 8–10, solve the problem and enter your answer in the grid, as described below, on the answer sheet.

1. Although not required, it is suggested that you write your answer in the boxes at the top of the columns to help you fill in the circles accurately. You will receive credit only if the circles are filled in correctly.

2. Mark no more than one circle in any column.

3. No question has a negative answer.

4. Some problems may have more than one correct answer. In such cases, grid only one answer.

5. **Mixed numbers** such as $3\frac{1}{2}$ must be gridded as 3.5 or $\frac{7}{2}$. (If $3\frac{1}{2}$ is entered into the grid as $\boxed{1\;1\;/\;4}$, it will be interpreted as $\frac{31}{2}$, not $3\frac{1}{2}$).

6. **Decimal answers:** If you obtain a decimal answer with more digits than the grid can accommodate, it may be either rounded or truncated, but it must fill the entire grid.

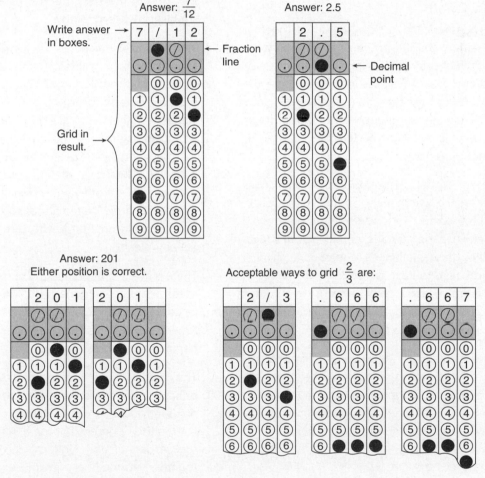

8. If $\frac{2}{5}x + \frac{1}{2}y = 3$, what is the value of $4x + 5y$?

9. If $x^2 + 10x = 24$ and $x > 0$, what is the value of $x + 5$?

10. What is one possible solution to the rational equation $\frac{1}{x} - \frac{2}{x-2} = 3$?

ESSAY TEST (OPTIONAL)

50 Minutes–1 Prompt

Directions: As you read the passage below, consider how President Clinton uses:

- evidence, such as facts or examples, to support claims.

- reasoning to develop ideas and to connect claims and evidence.

- stylistic or persuasive elements, such as word choice or appeals to emotion, to add power to the ideas expressed.

Adapted from President Bill Clinton's 1993 speech to Congress, endorsing health care reform.

My fellow Americans, tonight we come together to write a new chapter in the American story. We are in a time of profound change and opportunity. The end of the Cold War, the information age, the global economy have brought us both opportunity and hope and strife and uncertainty. Our purpose in this dynamic age must be to make change our friend, not our enemy.

To achieve that goal, we must face all our challenges with confidence, whether we're reducing the deficit, creating tomorrow's jobs and training our people to fill them, expanding trade, or making our streets safer. All of these challenges require us to change. If Americans are to have the courage to change in a difficult time, we must first be secure in our most basic needs. This health care system of ours is badly broken and it is time to fix it.

Despite the dedication of literally millions of talented health care professionals, our health care is too uncertain and too expensive, too bureaucratic and too wasteful. At long last, after decades of false starts, we must make this our most urgent priority: giving every American health security, health care that can never be taken away.

On this journey, there will be rough spots in the road and honest disagreements about how we should proceed. This is a complicated issue. But if we can agree on some basic values and principles, we will reach this destination together. We all know

what's right. We're blessed with the best health care professionals on earth, the finest health care institutions, the best medical research, the most sophisticated technology.

Yet millions of Americans are just a pink slip away from losing their health insurance, and one serious illness away from losing all their savings. Millions more are locked into the jobs they have now because someone in their family had once been sick. And on any given day, over 37 million Americans—most of them working people and their little children—have no health insurance at all. And in spite of all this, our medical bills are growing at over twice the rate of inflation, and the United States spends over a third more of its income on health care than any other nation on earth.

There is no excuse for this kind of system. We know other people have done better. We know people in our own country are doing better. My fellow Americans, we must fix this system, and it has to begin with Congressional action.

The proposal I will describe borrows many of the principles and ideas that have been embraced in plans introduced by both Republicans and Democrats in this Congress. For the first time in this century leaders of both political parties have joined together around the principle of providing universal, comprehensive health care. It is a magic moment, and we must seize it.

I have been deeply moved by the spirit of this debate, by the openness of all people to new ideas and argument and information. Both sides

GO ON TO THE NEXT PAGE

understand the ethical imperative of doing some-thing about the system we have now. Rising above our past differences will go a long way toward defining who we are and who we intend to be as a people in this challenging era.

And so tonight let me ask all of you: let us keep this spirit and let us keep this commitment until this job is done. We owe it to the American people. Over the coming months, you'll be bombarded with information from all kinds of sources. There will be some who will disagree with what I have proposed and with all other plans, for that matter. Some of the arguments will be genuinely sincere and enlightening. Others may be scare tactics by those motivated by self-interest in the waste the

system now generates because that waste is pro-viding jobs and money for some people. I ask you only to think of this: when you hear all of these arguments ask yourself whether the cost of staying on this same course isn't greater than the cost of change, and ask whether the arguments are in your interest or someone else's.

Everything about America's past tells us we will do this. Let us guarantee every American comprehen-sive health benefits that can never be taken away. This is our chance. And when our work is done, we will know that we have met the challenge of our time.

Write an essay in which you explain how President Clinton builds an argument to persuade his audience that health care reform is possible and should be pursued. In your essay, analyze how Clinton uses one or more of the features listed above the essay (or features of your own choice) to strengthen the logic and persuasiveness of his argument. Be sure that your analysis focuses on the most relevant features of the speech.

Your essay should not explain whether you agree with Clinton's argument, but rather explain how Clinton builds an argument to persuade his audience.

IF YOU FINISH BEFORE TIME IS CALLED, YOU MAY CHECK YOUR WORK ON THIS SECTION ONLY. DO NOT TURN TO ANY OTHER SECTION IN THE TEST.

STOP

Answer Key
WRITING AND LANGUAGE TEST

1.	**A**	9.	**B**	17.	**C**
2.	**B**	10.	**D**	18.	**B**
3.	**B**	11.	**A**	19.	**C**
4.	**B**	12.	**C**	20.	**A**
5.	**B**	13.	**B**	21.	**B**
6.	**C**	14.	**D**	22.	**D**
7.	**A**	15.	**C**		
8.	**D**	16.	**C**		

ANSWERS AND EXPLANATIONS

WRITING AND LANGUAGE TEST

1. A

Choice (A) is the best answer because this sentence needs NO CHANGE. "Earliest" is the correct superlative adjective to refer to all "music forms."

Choice (B) is not the best answer because using "most" with "earliest" is grammatically incorrect.

Choice (C) is not the best answer because "most early" is incorrect; "most" is only used with words that do not have an – *est* superlative form.

Choice (D) is not the best answer because although it uses the right adjective, it creates a subject-verb agreement error; "The earliest . . . forms" does not agree with the singular verb form "was."

The superlative adjective form will use –*est* or *most*— not both.

2. B

Choice (A) is not the best answer because it doesn't make sense to say "because of it is (or has) having."

Choice (B) is the best answer because this answer choice substitutes the correct singular possessive adjective, "its," meaning that the "origins" belong to American Jazz.

Choice (C) is not the best answer because "its's" is never correct; it's not a word.

Choice (D) is not the best answer because "its'" is never correct.

"It's" is a contraction of *it is* or *it has*. If neither of these makes sense when substituted for the contraction, the contraction is incorrect.

3. B

Choice (A) is not the best answer because removing the phrase set off by commas does not result in a logical sentence.

Choice (B) is the best answer because the phrase "ragtime and blues" should be set of from the rest of the sentence with a comma because it is not essential to the meaning of the sentence.

Choice (C) is not the best answer because it incorrectly separates a prepositional phrase from the rest of the sentence.

Choice (D) is not the best answer because it eliminates the commas, making the sentence difficult to understand.

If a phrase is set off by a comma or commas, the sentence must make sense without it.

4. B

Choice (A) is not the best answer because this sentence incorrectly places a semicolon between an independent and a dependent clause.

Choice (B) is the best answer because it eliminates the incorrect semicolon.

Choice (C) is not the best answer because it incorrectly inserts a comma between a preposition and its object.

Choice (D) is not the best answer because it separates a subject from its verb with a comma, which is incorrect.

If a semicolon is used to combine clauses, the clauses must be independent.

5. B

Choice (A) is not the best answer because there are several singular nouns in the sentence previous to this one ("style," "blend," "America," "the time") that could be antecedents for the pronoun "It."

Choice (B) is the best answer because it replaces the pronoun with the appropriate noun.

Choice (C) is not the best answer because it does not address the ambiguity issue; that is, there are several singular nouns in the sentence that could be the antecedent for the pronoun "It."

Choice (D) is not the best answer because it does not address the ambiguity issue; that is, there are several singular nouns in the sentence that could be the antecedent for the pronoun "It."

When an underlined selection includes a pronoun, make sure its antecedent is clear and unambiguous.

6. C

Choice (A) is not the best answer because "therefore" indicates a cause-and-effect relationship.

Choice (B) is not the best answer because it neither makes sense logically nor works grammatically, as it creates a run-on sentence.

Choice (C) is the best answer because "but" correctly connects the contrasting parts of the sentence.

Choice (D) is not the best answer because it is grammatically incorrect in that it creates a comma splice error, which is also indicative of a run-on sentence.

When a transition word is underlined, make sure it accurately and correctly represents the relationship between the ideas it connects.

7. A

Choice (A) is the best answer because no punctuation is needed here.

Choice (B) is not the best answer because it inserts a colon, which is generally used to introduce a brief explanation, definition, or list.

Choice (C) is not the best answer because it treats the phrase "in the top Jazz circles" as nonessential information, but the sentence does not make sense without it.

Choice (D) is not the best answer because it inserts an unneeded comma before a prepositional phrase.

8. D

Choice (A) is not the best answer because it doesn't make sense that he was well known when he was a shoe shiner and waiter.

Choice (B) is not the best answer because it doesn't make sense that he was well known when he was walking racehorses.

Choice (C) is not the best answer because it doesn't make sense that he was well known when he first began performing.

Choice (D) is the best answer because this is the most logical placement of the sentence.

Because NO CHANGE is not an answer choice, the sentence must be relevant; you'll need to determine its most logical placement. "Widely known" is a good context clue.

9. B

Choice (A) is not the best answer because it does not mention American Jazz, which is the second main subject (and title) of the essay.

Choice (B) is the best answer because it creates a sentence that mentions both Cab Calloway and American Jazz and relates them to one another.

Choice (C) is not the best answer because these people are mentioned, but only as minor details.

Choice (D) is not the best answer because this has nothing to do with the main subjects of the passage.

Your Reading skills will be helpful in answering questions like this one. The two topics of this essay are Cab Calloway and American Jazz.

10. D

Choice (A) is not the best answer because the phrase "it'll stick around for a while" is too informal and slangy for the rest of this passage.

Choice (B) is not the best answer because it is unnecessarily wordy.

Choice (C) is not the best answer because it doesn't provide a logical conclusion to the passage; it concerns Jazz's popularity rather than its endurance.

Choice (D) is the best answer because it matches the tone of the essay and provides a logical conclusion.

In addition to following the rules of grammar, style, and usage, the correct answer choice must also be consistent with the tone of the passage.

11. A

Choice (A) is the best answer because the passage does focus on the history and development of American Jazz music by focusing on one of its important figures.

Choice (B) is not the best answer because it misstates the information in the passage, which tells us that Jazz developed from folk music, not the other way around.

Choice (C) is not the best answer because the essay focuses on American Jazz, not other musical forms.

Choice (D) is not the best answer because the essay does focus on only one American Jazz musician but the writer is successful in his goal.

Once you determine whether or not the passage satisfies the conditions in the question stem, you can immediately eliminate two of the four choices.

12. C

Choice (A) is not the best answer because semicolons are used to combine independent clauses in order to avoid run-ons, but the second part of this sentence is not an independent clause.

Choice (B) is not the best answer because it is a run-on sentence.

Choice (C) is the best answer because the second part of the sentence is an explanation of what polar ice caps are.

Choice (D) is not the best answer because replacing the comma with a period creates a fragment.

Determine how parts of a sentence relate to each other to determine what punctuation to use.

13. B

Choice (A) is not the best answer because while "domains" can be used to indicate territories, it is more often used to indicate a sphere of influence.

Choice (B) is the best answer because "areas" indicates actual physical portions of the Earth.

Choice (C) is not the best answer because while "domains" can indicate "homes," this does not make sense in the context of the passage.

Choice (D) is not the best answer because this relates to the math context of the word "domains."

Determine which word makes the most sense in context.

14. D

Choice (A) is not the best answer because "solar" implies from or of the sun, so it's unnecessary to use both "sun" and "solar" to describe the radiation.

Choice (B) is not the best answer because while it is the shortest answer, it eliminates both "sun" and "solar," thereby eliminating the modifier for "radiation" and losing the intended meaning.

Choice (C) is not the best answer because it just rewords the underlined portion without fixing the error.

Choice (D) is the best answer because it eliminates "from the sun," fixing the wordiness error.

Identify redundancy and make the sentence concise.

15. C

Choice (A) is not the best answer because the sentence states that this has happened "over the course of the last 12,000 years," so the present tense is incorrect.

Choice (B) is not the best answer because it is still in the present tense, which is incorrect for the sentence.

Choice (C) is the best answer because it changes the verb tense to the present perfect, which indicates something that happened in the past and continued to happen.

Choice (D) is not the best answer because the future tense is incorrect in this sentence.

When a verb or verb phrase is underlined, make sure it reflects the time period of the sentence.

16. C

Choice (A) is not the best answer. What takes place? Seasonal variations. The verb does not agree with its subject.

Choice (B) is not the best answer because it unnecessarily changes the verb to the past tense.

Choice (C) is the best answer because the verb should be plural to agree with "seasonal variations."

Choice (D) is not the best answer because it unnecessarily makes "place" plural, which does not make sense.

When a verb is underlined, make sure it agrees with its subject.

17. C

Choice (A) is not the best answer because as written, this sentence reads, ". . . reducing the energy . . . and to increase." These items are not parallel.

Choice (B) is not the best answer because it mixes the gerund and infinitive verb forms.

Choice (C) is the best answer because "reducing" and "to increase" are joined by "and," so "to increase" should be "increasing" to maintain parallel structure.

Choice (D) is not the best answer because it removes the preposition before the verb but does not correct the error.

Verbs joined by a conjunction must be parallel in form.

18. B

Choice (A) is not the best answer because the sentence to which the underlined portion belongs—which says that the arctic ice shelf's mass is increasing—contrasts with the preceding sentence, which informs the reader that the ice caps should be receding, or losing mass, according to certain global warming theories. Therefore, a contrast transition is needed. "Too" indicates continuation.

Choice (B) is the best answer because "however" appropriately indicates the contrast relationship between the two ideas.

Choice (C) is not the best answer because "furthermore" is a continuation transition.

Choice (D) is not the best answer because "especially" is a continuation transition.

When a transition is underlined, determine the relationship between the ideas it connects.

19. C

Choice (A) is not the best answer because as written, this sentence has a comma splice error because two independent clauses are combined using only a comma.

Choice (B) is not the best answer because although it corrects the comma splice error, it is overly wordy.

Choice (C) is the best answer because it uses the FANBOYS conjunction *but* to make the second clause dependent.

Choice (D) is not the best answer because while it corrects the comma splice error, it is overly wordy.

The most obvious way to correct a run-on will not always be correct.

20. A

Choice (A) is the best answer because the passive voice is appropriately used.

Choice (B) is not the best answer because it introduces a parallelism error.

Choice (C) is not the best answer because it introduces a parallelism error.

Choice (D) is not the best answer because it changes the intended meaning of the sentence by including the word "always."

Some underlined portions will be correct as written.

21. B

Choice (A) is not the best answer because as written, the text and the chart do not match. A steady 20-year increase would be a straight upward sloping line while the line featured on the graph includes a major decrease after a slight increase and an even smaller increase within the last four years of the reported data.

Choice (B) is the best answer because it is the most accurate description of the graph.

Choice (C) is not the best answer because the graph is broken up into four-year periods, so it is impossible to see the increase during a single year.

Choice (D) is not the best answer because a steady 20-year decrease would be a straight downward sloping line rather than a non-linear drawing that includes both slight increases and major decreases.

Make sure the underlined text in the passage accurately reflects what is portrayed in the featured graph or chart.

22. D

Choice (A) is not the best answer because nowhere in the passage does the author mention errors in taking measurements (a human task), so as written, *error* is out of scope. Furthermore, an exception to a "growing trend" would indicate an anomaly rather than a human mistake.

Choice (B) is not the best answer because *mistake* is a synonym of *error*, which is reflective of a human mistake.

Choice (C) is not the best answer because the word *oversights* is a synonym of *errors*, which is reflective of a human mistake.

Choice (D) is the best answer because the word *anomalies* removes the human element and fits appropriately within the context.

Treat the underlined word as if it were a blank and predict a word to best fit the context of the sentence and passage. As we know from the preceding text and graph, the temperature change was not a steady 20-year increase but occurred during two specific 4-year periods.

Answer Key
MATH TEST—CALCULATOR

1. **C**
2. **B**
3. **A**
4. **B**
5. **B**
6. **D**
7. **A**
8. **D**
9. **C**

10. **B**
11. **C**
12. **A**
13. **A**
14. **B**
15. **A**

16. **Any value greater than $\frac{1}{5}$ and less than $\frac{1}{3}$ is correct.**

17. **402**
18. **120°**
19. **2.25**
20. **3 or .03**

ANSWERS AND EXPLANATIONS

MATH TEST – CALCULATOR

1. C

Choice (A) is not correct because the expression includes tax on the activation fee.

Choice (B) is not correct because the expression includes tax on the activation fee, and the activation fee is being multiplied by the number of months.

Choice (C) is correct. The total charge that Darnel will pay is the monthly rate, the 6% tax on the monthly rate, and the fixed activation fee. If Darnel subscribes for x months, then the total charge is $16.99x + 0.06(16.99x) + 25$, which can be rewritten as $1.06(16.99x) + 25$.

Choice (D) is not correct because the expression includes only one month of the subscription cost and does not accurately account for the tax on the monthly rate.

2. B

Choice (A) is not correct. All three graphs intersect at (1, 4) and therefore the system does have a solution.

Choice (B) is correct. The solution to the system of equations is the point where all three graphs intersect. This point is (1, 4) and is the only solution to the system.

Choice (C) is not correct. All three graphs intersect in only one point, not two points, so the system has only one solution.

Choice (D) is not correct. All three graphs intersect in only one point, not three points, so the system has only one solution.

3. A

Choice (A) is correct. Between $x = 2$ and $x = 3$, the slope of the graph representing the temperature of Object 1 (the dashed line) is steeper than the slope of the graph representing Object 2 (the solid line). This means the temperature of Object 1, not Object 2, decreased at a faster rate between 2 and 3 hours, so this statement does <u>not</u> accurately describe the data.

Choice (B) is not correct. This statement *does* accurately describe the data because, for the first 15 minutes (between $x = 0$ and $x = \frac{1}{4}$), the slope of the graph representing the temperature of Object 2 is steeper than the slope of the graph representing Object 1. This means the temperature of Object 2 decreased at a faster rate than Object 1 for the first 15 minutes.

Choice (C) is not correct. This statement *does* accurately describe the data because the problem states that both objects started at the same temperature (160°C), and because the graphs intersect at $x = 2$, which indicates that the temperatures of the objects were again the same at time = 2 hours.

Choice (D) is not correct. This statement *does* accurately describe the data because the temperatures of the objects cannot cool to less than the temperature of the room. The y-values of the graphs represent temperature, so the graphs will remain above $y = 20$.

4. B

Choice (A) is not correct. If x is the number of silver-copper settings and y is the number of silver-nickel settings, then $x + y$ represents the total number of settings the jeweler made. The jeweler made 75 settings, so $x + y$ must equal 75, not 3,122.

Choice (B) is correct. If x is the number of silver-copper settings and y is the number of silver-nickel settings, then $x + y$ represents the total number of settings the jeweler made, 75. This means that one of the equations in the system must be $x + y = 75$. The second equation in the system (the cost equation) can be written in words as: the cost to make each silver-nickel setting ($38) times the number of silver-nickel settings (x) plus the cost to make each silver-copper setting ($46) times the number of silver-copper settings (y) equals the total cost ($3,122). Translating this sentence into numbers and symbols yields the equation $38x + 46y = 3,122$.

Choice (C) is not correct because the second equation in the system is wrong. The student may have tried to use the information that the jeweler made the settings over a two-week period of time, but this information is not needed in setting up the system of equations.

Choice (D) is not correct because the second equation in the system is wrong. The student may have tried to use the information that the jeweler made the settings over a two-week period of time, but this information is not needed in setting up the system of equations.

5. B

Choice (A) is not correct because the student did not synthesize all of the information. This answer may result from multiplying 256 (the download rate in kilobytes per second) by 2 (the number of hours downloading) and dividing by 4 (the size of an average song in megabytes), neglecting to convert 256 kilobytes per second into megabytes per hour.

Choice (B) is correct. Lindy's computer can download 1,843,200 kilobytes in 2 hours $\left(\dfrac{256 \text{ kb}}{\text{sec}} \times \dfrac{60 \text{ sec}}{1 \text{ min}} \times \dfrac{60 \text{ min}}{1 \text{ hr}} \times 2 \text{ hr} \right)$. This is equivalent to 1,800 megabytes $\left(1,843,200 \text{ kb} \times \dfrac{1 \text{ mb}}{1,024 \text{ kb}} \right)$. If each song is about 4 megabytes in size, then the number of songs she can download in 2 hours is $1,800 \div 4 = 450$ songs.

Choice (C) is not correct because the student did not synthesize all of the information. This answer may result from converting 2 hours into seconds (7,200), then multiplying the result by the rate in kilobytes per second (256), then dividing by the number of kilobytes in 1 megabyte (1,024), neglecting to utilize the size of a typical song (4 mb).

Choice (D) is not correct because the student did not synthesize all of the information. This answer may result from converting the number of megabytes in a song to kilobytes ($4 \times 1,024 = 4,096$), dividing by the rate of 256 kilobytes per second, and then converting 2 hours to minutes (120) instead of seconds and multiplying.

6. D

Choice (A) is not correct. This answer may result from finding the value of y, not y^2.

Choice (B) is not correct. This answer may result from finding the value of x^2, not y^2.

Choice (C) is not correct. This answer may result from neglecting to square the coefficient, 3, when substituting $3x$ into the first equation, resulting in $x^2 = 40$ and subsequently $y^2 = 160 - 40 = 120$.

Choice (D) is correct. The second equation gives that y is equal to $3x$. Substituting this value for y into the first equation yields the following:

$$x^2 + (3x)^2 = 160$$
$$x^2 + 9x^2 = 160$$
$$10x^2 = 160$$
$$x^2 = 16$$

Substituting 16 for x^2 into the first equation again, yields:

$$16 + y^2 = 160$$
$$y^2 = 144$$

7. A

Choice (A) is correct. Because the airplane is traveling at an average speed of 500 miles per hour and the plane's fuel mileage is 0.2 miles per gallon, the number of gallons of fuel used each hour can be found by $\dfrac{500 \text{ miles}}{1 \text{ hour}} \times \dfrac{1 \text{ gallon}}{0.2 \text{ miles}} = \dfrac{500}{0.2}$ gallons per hour. This means that in t hours, the plane uses $\dfrac{500}{0.2} \times t$, or $\dfrac{500t}{0.2}$, gallons of fuel. The plane's tank has 42,000 gallons of fuel at the beginning of the flight, so after t hours the amount of fuel remaining is $f(t) = 42,000 - \dfrac{500t}{0.2}$.

Choice (B) is not correct because the number of gallons of fuel used each hour should be found by

dividing the average speed by the airplane's fuel mileage, not the reverse as it is in this equation.

Choice (C) is not correct because the number of gallons of fuel used each hour $\dfrac{500}{0.2}$ must be multiplied by time t *before* it is subtracted from the amount of fuel in the tank at the beginning of the flight (42,000).

Choice (D) is not correct because the number of gallons of fuel used each hour is misrepresented as $\dfrac{0.2}{500}$. Also, the number of gallons of fuel used each hour must be multiplied by time t *before* it is subtracted from the amount of fuel in the tank at the beginning of the flight.

8. D

Choice (A) is not correct. To arrive at this answer, the student may have reversed the independent and dependent variables, using the points (350, 1986) and (1,300, 2006) to calculate the slope. Students could also arrive at this answer by incorrectly calculating the slope using the formula $m = \dfrac{x_2 - x_1}{y_2 - y_1}$, rather than $m = \dfrac{y_2 - y_1}{x_2 - x_1}$.

Choice (B) is not correct. To arrive at this answer, the student may have disregarded the scale of the plot when finding the slope and interpreted the scale as if each tick mark along both axes represented one unit.

Choice (C) is not correct. To arrive at this answer, the student may have reversed the variables and disregarded the scale of the plot.

Choice (D) is correct. The slope of the line of best fit represents the average increase in the number of nesting pairs of bald eagles per year. Using approximate values found at the endpoints of the line of best fit (350 nesting pairs in 1986 and 1,300 pairs in 2006), the approximate slope is $\dfrac{1,300 - 350}{2006 - 1986} = \dfrac{950}{20} = 47.5 \approx 48$.

9. C

Choice (A) is not correct because the slope in the equation is wrong. The student may have calculated the rate of change using the formula $m = \frac{x_2 - x_1}{y_2 - y_1}$, rather than $m = \frac{y_2 - y_1}{x_2 - x_1}$.

Choice (B) is not correct because both the slope and the y-intercept in the equation are wrong. The student may have calculated the rate of change using the formula $m = \frac{x_2 - x_1}{y_2 - y_1}$, rather than $m = \frac{y_2 - y_1}{x_2 - x_1}$, and incorrectly used the ordered pair (120, 725), rather than (725, 120), to find the y-intercept.

Choice (C) is correct. To determine the linear model, students must first determine the rate at which the number of units occupied decreases as a result of the increase in the monthly rent. Calculating this using the ordered pairs (725, 120) and (800, 105) gives $\frac{105 - 120}{800 - 725} = \frac{-15}{75} = -\frac{1}{5}$, so the linear model looks like $y = -\frac{1}{5}x + b$, or in this case, $n = -\frac{1}{5}d + b$. Substituting the ordered pair (725, 120) into the equation and solving for b yields $120 = -\frac{1}{5}(725) + b \rightarrow b = 265$. Therefore, the model that can be used to relate the number of units occupied to the monthly rent is $n = -\frac{1}{5}d + 265$.

Choice (D) is not correct because the y-intercept in the equation is wrong. The student may have incorrectly used the ordered pair (120, 725), rather than (725, 120), to find the y-intercept.

10. B

Choice (A) is not correct. Another age group had a greater percentage of people report that they owned a Smart Phone.

Choice (B) is correct. To answer this question, students must select the relevant information from the table and compute the percentage for each age group. The relevant information consists of the number of people in the age group that reported owning a Smart Phone (first column of numbers) and the total number of people that were surveyed in that age group (last column of numbers). The calculations are as follows:

15- to 29-year-olds: $\frac{28,542}{58,881} \oplus 48.5\%$

30- to 44-year-olds: $\frac{33,116}{66,838} \oplus 49.5\%$ (the highest)

45- to 59-year-olds: $\frac{11,960}{39,914} \oplus 30.0\%$

60- year-olds and over: $\frac{1,023}{3,782} \oplus 27.0\%$

Choice (C) is not correct. Another age group had a greater percentage of people report that they owned a Smart Phone.

Choice (D) is not correct. Another age group had a greater percentage of people report that they owned a Smart Phone.

11. C

Choice (A) is not correct. This answer may result from multiplying the fraction of the sample by the total number of people who owned a Smart Phone, which is an incorrect application of the information.

Choice (B) is not correct. This answer may result from multiplying the fraction of the sample by the total number of 15- to 29-year-olds in the initial survey, which is an incorrect application of the information.

Choice (C) is correct. To answer this question, extrapolate from a random sample to estimate the number of 15- to 29-year-olds who watch streaming videos on their Smart Phones. This is done by multiplying the fraction of people in the follow-up survey who responded *Yes* by the total population of 15- to 29-year-olds that own a Smart Phone which yields $\frac{302}{500} \times 28,542 = 17,239$.

Choice (D) is not correct. This answer may result from multiplying the fraction of the sample by the entire population, which is an incorrect application of the information.

12. A

Choice (A) is correct. To find the value of b, students can use either of the two given zeros to set up an equation and solve for b. Substituting 3 for x and 0 for $f(x)$ yields the following:

$$
\begin{aligned}
0 &= 4(3)^3 + b(3)^2 + 41(3) + 12 \\
0 &= 108 + 9b + 123 + 12 \\
0 &= 243 + 9b \\
-243 &= 9b \\
-27 &= b
\end{aligned}
$$

Choice (B) is not correct. This represents incorrectly using the order of operations when simplifying the terms containing exponents.

Choice (C) is not correct. This is the value of k, not c.

Choice (D) is not correct. This represents a sign error in the final step in determining the value of b.

13. A

Choice (A) is correct. Rearranging the equation to solve for y results in the following:

$$
\begin{aligned}
y &= ky + kx + x + 5 \\
y - ky &= kx + x + 5 \\
y(1-k) &= x(k+1) + 5 \\
y &= \frac{(k+1)}{(1-k)}x + \frac{5}{1-k}
\end{aligned}
$$

This manipulation reveals a linear equation with a slope of $\dfrac{k+1}{1-k}$ and a y-intercept of $\dfrac{5}{1-k}$. It is given in the problem that $k > 1$, so the quantity $k + 1$ is positive, and $1 - k$ is negative, resulting in a negative slope and a negative y-intercept. Of the choices given, only this graph satisfies these conditions.

Choice (B) is not correct because the slope of the line is positive, not negative.

Choice (C) is not correct because the y-intercept of the line is positive, not negative.

Choice (D) is not correct because the graph is not that of a linear equation. The graph is a parabola, which represents a quadratic equation.

14. B

Choice (A) is not correct. To arrive at this answer, the student may have incorrectly manipulated the expression as follows:

$$
\frac{9x^2}{3x-2} = \frac{4 \cdot \dfrac{9x^2}{4}}{3x-2} = \frac{4}{3x-2} + \frac{9x^2}{4}.
$$

Choice (B) is correct. The expression is written in improper rational form, which suggests that long division can be used to rewrite it as follows:

$$
\begin{array}{r}
3x + 2 + \dfrac{4}{3x-2} \\
3x-2 \,\overline{)\, 9x^2 } \\
-\underline{\;9x^2 - 6x\;} \\
6x \\
-\underline{\;6x - 4\;} \\
4
\end{array}
$$

Because the remainder 4 matches the numerator in $\dfrac{4}{3x-2}$, it is clear that the value of A is $3x + 2$.

As an alternate method, students might write the equation, $\dfrac{9x^2}{3x-2} = \dfrac{4}{3x-2} + A$, and then solve for A as follows:

$$
\begin{aligned}
\frac{9x^2}{3x-2} - \frac{4}{3x-2} &= A \\
\frac{9x^2 - 4}{3x-2} &= A \\
\frac{(3x-2)(3x+2)}{3x-2} &= A \\
3x + 2 &= A
\end{aligned}
$$

Choice (C) is not correct. To arrive at this answer, the student may have made a sign error during the long division process.

Choice (D) is not correct. To arrive at this answer, the student may have incorrectly manipulated the expression as follows:

$$
\frac{9x^2}{3x-2} = \frac{4 + 9x^2 - 4}{3x-2} = \frac{4}{3x-2} + 9x^2 - 4.
$$

15. A

Choice (A) is correct. Finding the difference in the costs requires that students analyze the units involved, attend to the meaning of quantities, and know and use different properties of operations. The cost analysis is:

Car A:

$$\$3,500+\$800+\frac{400\text{ m}}{\text{mo}}\times36\text{ mo}\times\frac{1\text{ gal}}{20\text{ m}}\times\frac{\$3.80}{\text{gal}}=\$7,036$$

Car B:

$$\$5,000+\$400+\frac{400\text{ m}}{\text{mo}}\times36\text{ mo}\times\frac{1\text{ gal}}{25\text{ m}}\times\frac{\$3.80}{\text{gal}}=\$7,588.80$$

It will cost Priya $7,588.80 – $7,036 = $552.80 less to buy and use Car A.

Choice (B) is not correct. The student may have neglected to include the amounts for the tax, registration, and repairs in the calculations.

Choice (C) is not correct. When determining the cost for gas, the student may have multiplied by 3 years (instead of 36 months).

Choice (D) is not correct. When determining the cost for gas, the student may have neglected to factor in the length of time that Priya planned to own the car.

16. Any value greater than $\frac{1}{5}$ and less than $\frac{1}{3}$ is correct.

To solve this problem, students must examine the relationship between $-3x+2$ and $6x-4$ and recognize that $-3x+2=-\frac{1}{2}(6x-4)$. Multiplying all parts of the inequality by $-\frac{1}{2}$ reverses the inequality signs, which yields $\frac{1}{3}>-3x+2>\frac{1}{5}$, or written with increasing values from left to right, $\frac{1}{5}<-3x+2<\frac{1}{3}$. This means that any value greater than $\frac{1}{5}$ and less than $\frac{1}{3}$ is correct.

17. 402

Finding the total volume of the locking pin requires several steps. First, students should think of the locking pin as one wide cylinder (the outer ring and what's inside of it) and two smaller cylinders (the protruding ends), which are the same size. Students can then use the information given in the problem and the dimensions provided in the diagram to determine the measures of each cylinder.

The volume of a cylinder is the area of the base (πr^2) multiplied by the height. The total volume of the locking pin is $V = \pi(4)^2(6) + 2[\pi(2)^2(4)] = 96\pi + 32\pi = 128\pi$ cubic centimeters. When the value for π is substituted and the result is rounded to the near cubic centimeter, the answer is 402 cubic centimeters. Note that students must attend to the precision of their calculations when solving this problem, and not apply any intermediate rounding until the final answer is reached. The use of a calculator provides the ability to attend to precision more effectively, so students should be encouraged to use one when solving this type of problem.

18. 120

To find the value of x, students should start by evaluating cos 30°, which is $\frac{\sqrt{3}}{2}$, and then solve the equation $\sin x° = \frac{\sqrt{3}}{2}$ for x. To solve the equation, students may do either of the following:

- Recall from memory that $\sin 60° = \frac{\sqrt{3}}{2}$, indicating that the reference angle for x is 60°. Because it is given that x is between 90° and 180° (i.e., in Quadrant II), use the formula 180° − (reference angle) to find the value of x, which yields 180° − 60° = 120°.

- Use a graphing calculator and an inverse trig function to find the reference angle for x, as follows:

$$\sin^{-1}(\sin x°) = \sin^{-1}\frac{\sqrt{3}}{2}$$

$$x = 60$$

Then, use the formula 180° − (reference angle) to find the value of x, which yields 180° − 60° = 120°.

19. 2.25

The charge amount of $126.48 represents the conversion of $128 + 66 + 85 = 279$ Brazilian reais plus the 2% fee that Eli's credit card company charged him. To find the original cost, c, of the vases in U.S. dollars (before the 2% fee), write and solve the equation, $1.02c = 126.48$. Dividing both sides of the equation by 1.02 results in a cost of $c = \$124$.

To find the foreign exchange rate, r, in Brazilian reais per U.S. dollar, let units guide you:

$$124 \text{ dollars} \times \frac{r \text{ reais}}{1 \text{ dollar}} = 279 \text{ reais} \;\rightarrow\; r = \frac{279}{124} = 2.25$$

The exchange rate on Monday was 2.25 Brazilian reais per U.S. dollar.

20. 3 or .03

Break this problem into parts, solving one piece at a time. Find the original converted price, use the result to calculate the exchange rate for Wednesday, and then use the two exchange rates from Monday and Wednesday to find the net change in the rates as a percentage.

If p represents the original price in U.S. dollars, then the total charge of $358.50 represents $1.02(200) + 1.03(p - 200)$. Setting the total charge equal to this expression and solving for p yields:

$$358.5 = 1.02(200) + 1.03(p - 200)$$
$$358.5 = 204 + 1.03p - 206$$
$$358.5 = -2 + 1.03p$$
$$360.5 = 1.03p$$
$$350 = p$$

To calculate the exchange rate on Wednesday:

$$350 \text{ dollars} \times \frac{r \text{ reais}}{1 \text{ dollar}} = 763 \text{ reais} \;\rightarrow\; r = \frac{763}{350} = 2.18$$

To find the amount of decrease, as a percentage, in the exchange rates from Monday to Wednesday:

$\frac{2.18 - 2.25}{2.25} = \frac{-0.07}{2.25} \approx -0.031$, which represents a decrease of about 3%.

Answer Key
READING TEST

1. **D**
2. **A**
3. **B**
4. **C**
5. **C**
6. **A**
7. **C**
8. **A**
9. **C**
10. **B**

11. **A**
12. **B**
13. **C**
14. **D**
15. **B**
16. **C**
17. **C**
18. **D**
19. **A**
20. **B**

21. **C**
22. **A**
23. **B**
24. **C**
25. **D**
26. **C**
27. **B**
28. **B**
29. **A**
30. **B**

ANSWERS AND EXPLANATIONS

READING TEST

1. D

Choice (A) is not the best answer. Though Anthony argues that "this government is not a democracy . . . It is an odious aristocracy" (lines 38–39), this does not represent the most important idea of her speech. Rather, she uses this statement, along with many others, to help develop her argument.

Choice (B) is not the best answer. Though Anthony refers to the Constitution to help set the stage for her argument (lines 10–17), this does not represent the most important idea of her speech. Rather, it is a statement that helps her prove her argument.

Choice (C) is not the best answer. Anthony does not argue that some male citizens are being denied basic rights, so this could not be the central idea of the passage.

Choice (D) is the best answer because it reflects the most important idea presented by the author over the course of the passage.

2. A

Choice (A) is the best answer. In lines 18–20, Anthony points to the wording of the preamble to the Constitution to convince her audience that the founding fathers already established rights for all citizens.

Choice (B) is not the best answer. Anthony does not make the argument that the writers of the Constitution favored male citizens.

Choice (C) is not the best answer. Though it might be true that the preamble to the Constitution does not specifically address voting rights, this is not the point Anthony is making.

Choice (D) is not the best answer. Anthony does not make the argument that the writers of the Constitution were all aristocrats.

3. B

Choice (A) is not the best answer because in lines 1–2, Anthony is stating the reason for her speech, not giving evidence of what the Constitution provides for. These lines therefore do not serve as the best evidence for the answer to the previous question.

Choice (B) is the best answer because lines 11–17 provide a direct quote from the preamble to the Constitution, the strongest kind of evidence to prove the point that the Constitution did not establish rights for only some of its citizens.

Choice (C) is not the best answer because in lines 33–34, Anthony is describing the result of denying rights to women, not evidence of what the Constitution provides for. These lines therefore do not serve as the best evidence for the answer to the previous question.

Choice (D) is not the best answer because in line 54, which occurs much later in the speech, Anthony is giving the dictionary definition of a citizen. Though this is a convincing rhetorical device in Anthony's overall argument, it does not serve as the best evidence for the answer to the previous question.

4. C

Choice (A) is not the best answer. Though Anthony views the inability of women to vote as a "downright mockery" (line 24) and accuses the government of being "an odious aristocracy" (line 39), her stance does not resemble that of a judge in a court of law accusing lawmakers.

Choice (B) is not the best answer. Anthony does not present herself as a politician running for office; therefore, she is not looking to gain votes by delivering her speech.

Choice (C) is the best answer because in lines 1–9, Anthony presents her "case" as a person who is being indicted, or accused of committing a crime, in the way a lawyer presents a case to prove a person's innocence.

Choice (D) is not the best answer. Though Anthony refers to the historic document of the preamble to the Constitution, her stance in this speech cannot be described as that of a historian explaining past events. She uses the intent of the preamble to help present her case.

5. C

Choice (A) is not the best answer because while *committed* sometimes means "made a promise," it would make little sense in context for Anthony to say that she did or did not make a promise in her attempt to vote.

Choice (B) is not the best answer because while *committed* sometimes means "assigned," it would make little sense in context for Anthony to say that she assigned no crime in her attempt to vote.

Choice (C) is the best answer because in lines 4–9, Anthony explains that she is not guilty of a crime, or wrongdoing, in her attempt to vote.

Choice (D) is not the best answer because while *committed* sometimes means "entrusted," it would make little sense in context for Anthony to say that she entrusted no crime in her attempt to vote.

6. A

Choice (A) is the best answer. Though Anthony does not directly state this opinion, it can be inferred that she views any denial of the right to vote as going against the law.

Choice (B) is not the best answer. Though Anthony refers to future generations in her use of the term "posterity" (lines 23 and 35), it cannot be inferred from the passage that Anthony thinks future generations will find fault with U.S. practices.

Choice (C) is not the best answer. In the last paragraph of her speech (lines 59–61), Anthony is critical of states that make their own laws or enforce old laws.

Choice (D) is not the best answer. Though Anthony herself, along with a few others, chose to vote when it was technically illegal to do so, it cannot be inferred from the passage that Anthony thinks encouraging women to vote illegally will eventually change the law.

7. C

Choice (A) is not the best answer. In lines 4–9, Anthony is establishing the reason for her speech. These lines do not serve as the best evidence for inferring that Anthony thinks the denial of the right to vote is illegal.

Choice (B) is not the best answer. In lines 24–28, Anthony says it is wrong to speak of women's "enjoyment of the blessings of liberty" when they are denied the ability to vote. However, these lines do not serve as the best evidence for inferring that Anthony thinks the denial of the right to vote is illegal.

Choice (C) is the best answer. In lines 29–33, Anthony argues that for a government to deny rights on the basis of gender "is to pass a bill of attainder, or, an *ex post facto* law, and is therefore a violation of the supreme law of the land." This strongly supports the inference that Anthony thinks denying women the right to vote is against the law.

Choice (D) is not the best answer. In lines 37–38, Anthony states that the deprival of rights makes women feel that their government is not a democracy. However, these lines do not serve as the best evidence for inferring that Anthony thinks the denial of the right to vote is illegal.

8. A

Choice (A) is the best answer because lines 11–17 describe several goals that the writers of the preamble to the Constitution set out to achieve for the good of the people of the United States. In this context, to "guarantee" liberty makes the most sense.

Choice (B) is not the best answer because while *secure* sometimes means "fasten," it would make no sense in context for the writers of the preamble to have the goal of fastening the blessings of liberty.

Choice (C) is not the best answer because while *secure* sometimes means "strengthen," it would make little sense in context for the writers of the preamble to have the goal of strengthening the blessings of liberty when these blessings had not yet been established.

Choice (D) is not the best answer. While *secure* sometimes means "start," in this context there is another answer that more precisely reflects the goals of the writers of the preamble.

9. C

Choice (A) is not the best answer. Though Anthony had been accused of voting illegally the year before, this is not the most likely reason she poses the question.

Choice (B) is not the best answer. Though Anthony's entire speech might have inspired some to establish a women's rights movement, this is not the most likely reason she poses the question.

Choice (C) is the best answer. Throughout her speech, Anthony focuses on the Constitution's reference to "the people." Immediately prior to her posing the question, she refers to the dictionary definition of a citizen as a "person of the United States, entitled to vote and hold office" (lines 53–54). By posing this question, she brings her logical argument full circle by stating the obvious: women are persons.

Choice (D) is not the best answer. Though Anthony is critical of lawmakers and the government in general for their denial of rights to women, this does not explain specifically why she poses the question.

10. B

Choice (A) is not the best answer. Anthony does not describe the common sentiments of the U.S.

population at that time, nor is there evidence that she necessarily would have agreed with them.

Choice (B) is the best answer. In lines 61–65, Anthony most likely makes a connection between African Americans and women because both groups were often denied the rights guaranteed by the Constitution.

Choice (C) is not the best answer. Anthony's purpose in mentioning African Americans is not to distinguish, or contrast, their rights with those of women. Rather, she argues that there is a strong connection between the two groups and the rights they are guaranteed.

Choice (D) is not the best answer. Within the context of the passage, it is a leap to conclude that Anthony thinks both groups should work together to secure their rights.

11.

Choice (A) is the best answer. In the second paragraph, the passage introduces the three main functions of blood and then proceeds with a discussion of how these functions specifically work. Therefore, the central idea of the passage is primarily concerned with blood function.

Choice (B) is not the best answer. Though the cardiovascular system is mentioned in the first paragraph, it is too broad a topic to be considered the central focus of the passage.

Choice (C) is not the best answer. Though blood clotting is discussed in the passage and is the subject of the graphic, it is too narrow a topic to be considered the central focus of the entire passage.

Choice (D) is not the best answer. Though various references are made to the body's natural defenses, the immune system is not mentioned nor described thoroughly enough to be considered the central focus of the passage.

12. B

Choice (A) is not the best answer because the passage does not indicate that erythrocytes play a major role in protecting the body. Rather, a major role of erythrocytes is the transport of oxygen to help nourish the body and remove carbon dioxide as a waste (lines 51–53).

Choice (B) is the best answer. The passage states that leukocytes "function in the daily housekeeping and defense of the body" (lines 63–64), which indicates their major role in protecting the body.

Choice (C) is not the best answer. Blood vessels are the veins and arteries through which blood is pumped to various parts of the body. They do not play a specific role in protecting the body.

Choice (D) is not the best answer. Though some plasma proteins "have roles in blood clotting or in defense against pathogens" (lines 44–45), it cannot be said that they play a major role in protecting the body.

13. C

Choice (A) is not the best answer because lines 36–39 describe plasma, the liquid medium that makes up around 60 percent of blood. Plasma does not have a direct role in the protection of the body. These lines therefore do not serve as the best evidence for the answer to the previous question.

Choice (B) is not the best answer because lines 51–53 describe the major role of red blood cells, or erythrocytes, not leukocytes. These lines therefore do not serve as the best evidence for the answer to the previous question.

Choice (C) is the best answer. Lines 64–67 provide strong evidence that leukocytes play a major role in protecting the body by targeting dead cells and anything foreign to the body.

Choice (D) is not the best answer, because lines 97–98 describe the process by which the number of red blood cells is maintained. These lines therefore

do not serve as the best evidence for the answer to the previous question.

14. D

Choice (A) is not the best answer. Lines 94–96 describe the process by which mature red blood cells are destroyed. The graphic does not contain information that relates to this process.

Choice (B) is not the best answer. Lines 58–60 describe the abundance of red blood cells in the body. The graphic does not contain information that relates to this fact.

Choice (C) is not the best answer. Lines 78–80 describe two types of lymphocytes that have highly-specific defense responses. The graphic does not contain information that relates to this process.

Choice (D) is the best answer. Lines 85–89 describe the process by which platelets "initiate blood clotting and help to minimize blood loss," a statement supported by the graphic depiction of platelets rushing to the scene of a wound.

15. B

Choice (A) is not the best answer because while *diffuses* sometimes means "softens," it would make little sense in context to say that oxygen softens into the blood. The sentence is describing the movement of oxygen, not its texture.

Choice (B) is the best answer because the context makes clear that oxygen "spreads," or moves, into the blood.

Choice (C) is not the best answer because while *diffuses* sometimes means "disappears," it would make little sense in context to say that oxygen disappears into the blood. As a gas, oxygen is not visible; therefore, "disappears" is not a good description of what happens.

Choice (D) is not the best answer because while *diffuses* sometimes means "separates," it would make little sense in context to say that oxygen separates, or divides into parts, in the blood.

16. C

Choice (A) is not the best answer. While the passage states that white blood cells differ in size, shape, and purpose (lines 71–80), this information is not implied by the author's use of words such as *patrol* and *battle*.

Choice (B) is not the best answer because the passage never states that white blood cells can invade the body. They are part of the body.

Choice (C) is the best answer. The use of *patrol* and *battle*, along with other words such as *target*, *engulf*, and *armies* (lines 64–69), helps the reader infer that the work of white blood cells resembles the body's personal army.

Choice (D) is not the best answer. While the passage states that white blood cells can be highly specific (lines 78–80), this information is not implied by the author's use of words such as *patrol* and *battle*.

17. C

Choice (A) is not the best answer. As part of the introductory paragraph of the passage, lines 5–7 simply define what blood is and have little to do with the idea of the body having its own personal army. These lines therefore do not serve as the best evidence for the answer to the previous question.

Choice (B) is not the best answer. Though lines 25–26 describe the blood's protective function, there is another answer that better supports the author's idea of white blood cells as the body's personal army. These lines therefore do not serve as strong evidence for the answer to the previous question.

Choice (C) is the best answer. The battle-related words found in lines 63–64 provide strong evidence that white blood cells can be thought of as the body's personal army.

Choice (D) is not the best answer. Though lines 80–82 describe one of the body's defense mechanisms,

there is another answer that better supports the author's idea of white blood cells as the body's personal army.

18. D

Choice (A) is not the best answer. *Stable* sometimes means "settled" or established, but in this context there is another answer that reflects the description of this process more accurately.

Choice (B) is not the best answer because while *stable* sometimes means "long-lived," it would make little sense in context to say that the red blood cell count is long-lived.

Choice (C) is not the best answer. *Stable* sometimes means "reliable," or "dependable," but in this context there is another answer that reflects the description of this process more accurately.

Choice (D) is the best answer because the context makes clear that through an involuntary process of destruction and replacement, the red blood cell count is kept "consistent," or steady and constant.

19. A

Choice (A) is the best answer. The passage states that plasma is a "yellowish watery substance" that "constitutes around 60 percent of our blood" (lines 36–37).

Choice (B) is not the best answer because the passage does not indicate that plasma is the most important blood component.

Choice (C) is not the best answer. Though the passage states that "all blood cells" are produced in bone marrow (lines 56–57), and this would include plasma cells, there is another answer that is more strongly suggested by the passage.

Choice (D) is not the best answer because though the passage mentions the pH of blood, it never states what the normal pH is.

20. B

Choice (A) is not the best answer. According to one of the graphic captions, fibrin threads help mesh together platelets and red blood cells. However, there is no evidence in either the passage or the graphic that a platelet deficiency would cause the formation of fibrin threads.

Choice (B) is the best answer. Lines 86–87 indicate that platelets "initiate blood clotting and help to minimize blood loss." The graphic illustrates this clotting process, leading to the inference that a deficiency, or lack, of platelets could cause excessive blood loss.

Choice (C) is not the best answer. The last paragraph of the passage describes the process by which red blood cells are destroyed as they age. However, there is no evidence in either the passage or the graphic that a platelet deficiency would cause the destruction of red blood cells.

Choice (D) is not the best answer. Lines 81–85 describe a connection between bone marrow and platelets. However, there is no evidence in either the passage or the graphic that a platelet deficiency would cause limited bone marrow.

21. C

Choice (A) is not the best answer because it deals only with the author's father and does not reflect the most important idea of the entire passage.

Choice (B) is not the best answer. The passage does not say that the author eventually found work on a steamboat.

Choice (C) is the best answer because it reflects the most important idea presented by the author over the course of the passage.

Choice (D) is not the best answer because the central idea of a passage must reflect the most important idea of the entire passage. Also, based on the passage, it is debatable whether the engineer did or did not deserve the sympathy of others.

22. A

Choice (A) is the best answer because it describes the author's outrage that a boy known for being less than an upstanding individual had landed a steamboat job as an apprentice engineer.

Choice (B) is not the best answer. Though the author refers to his "Sunday-school teachings" (line 19), there is no mention of the idea that a person must have deep religious beliefs.

Choice (C) is not the best answer. Though the author thinks he'd rather be a deck hand than a cabin boy (lines 9–12), there is no mention in the passage about one job paying the highest wages.

Choice (D) is not the best answer. Though the author mentions a desire to be seen and to be "conspicuous" as a deck hand (line 12), this does not provide evidence that the author thinks steamboat work will make him famous.

23. B

Choice (A) is not the best answer because lines 9–12 describe what job the author thought he might want on a steamboat and have little to do with the author's sense of injustice. These lines therefore do not serve as the best evidence for the answer to the previous question.

Choice (B) is the best answer because in lines 18–22, the author conveys his sense of injustice that the boy who became a steamboat engineer did not deserve the privilege. The boy had been "notoriously worldly," implying he had not always acted properly; the author, on the other hand, had been "just the reverse."

Choice (C) is not the best answer because, though lines 54–55 relate to the boys' response to the engineer's success, they show the boys' desire to be like the engineer, not the boys'—nor the author's—sense of injustice. These lines therefore do not serve as the best evidence for the answer to the previous question.

Choice (D) is not the best answer. Lines 58–60 describe some parents' refusal to let their sons "get on the river," and though it might be inferred that the author would view this as unjust, this is not well developed in the passage. These lines therefore do not serve as the best evidence for the answer to the previous question.

24. C

Choice (A) is not the best answer because this would mean that lines 1–3 are to be interpreted literally—that the author is describing how much power a justice of the peace held in a frontier town.

Choice (B) is not the best answer. The author's intention in lines 1–3 is to suggest his own feelings about his father's stature and power, not to suggest how the townspeople truly felt about his father's importance.

Choice (C) is the best answer. Lines 1–3 convey the author's boyish, naïve belief that his father was all-powerful in his role as justice of the peace; they help establish that all events described in the passage will reflect the point of view of a child.

Choice (D) is not the best answer because this would mean that lines 1–3 are to be interpreted as a true reflection of the author's town environment. These lines are instead included by the author to suggest his perspective as a boy.

25. D

Choice (A) is not the best answer because while *distinction* sometimes means "difference," it would make little sense in context to say that his father's difference as the justice of the peace was "enough for me as a general thing" (lines 4–5).

Choice (B) is not the best answer because while *distinction* sometimes means "feature," it would make no sense in context to say that his father's feature as the justice of the peace was "enough for me as a general thing" (lines 4–5).

Choice (C) is not the best answer because while *distinction* sometimes means "clarity," it would make no sense in context to say that his father's clarity as the justice of the peace was "enough for me as a general thing" (lines 4–5).

Choice (D) is the best answer because the context makes clear that the author thought his father possessed "the power of life and death over all men" (lines 2–3), or great power and prestige as the justice of the peace.

26. C

Choice (A) is not the best answer. The passage states that "two or three of the boys" in the town had gone to St. Louis before, not all (lines 34–37), so this is not a reasonable inference.

Choice (B) is not the best answer. The author makes reference to his own attendance of Sunday school (line 19), but there is no evidence in the passage to infer that all the boys had attended Sunday school.

Choice (C) is the best answer. It can be inferred that the boys were relieved because if the engineer had been killed when the bloat blew up, they would no longer be annoyed by his boasting and bragging.

Choice (D) is not the best answer because there is no mention in the passage that the boys were in competition with one another.

27. B

Choice (A) is not the best answer because lines 12–14 describe the author's early daydreams about working on a steamboat. They have nothing to do with the sense of relief the boys experienced when they heard that the engineer's boat had blown up. These lines therefore do not serve as the best evidence for the answer to the previous question.

Choice (B) is the best answer because in lines 44–46, the author uses the phrase "diffused a tranquil contentment," evidence that the boys felt relieved in their assumption that the engineer had died when the boat blew up.

Choice (C) is not the best answer because lines 47–49 describe how the engineer did indeed survive the explosion of the boat, which would have meant the end of the boys' sense of relief. These lines therefore do not serve as the best evidence for the answer to the previous question.

Choice (D) is not the best answer because lines 56–58 describe the fact that several boys in the town went to work on the river. The lines have nothing to do with the sense of relief the boys experienced when they heard that the engineer's boat had blown up. These lines therefore do not serve as the best evidence for the answer to the previous question.

28. B

Choice (A) is not the best answer. While *consideration* sometimes means "generosity," it would make little sense in context to say that the boys had long been persons of generosity; it is the boys' knowledge of St. Louis, not their behavior, that is being described.

Choice (B) is the best answer because the context makes clear that the author is describing the boys as having a "reputation" for knowing a good deal about St. Louis.

Choice (C) is not the best answer because while *consideration* sometimes means "contemplation," it would make little sense in context to say that the boys had long been persons of contemplation, or thought.

Choice (D) is not the best answer because while *consideration* sometimes means "unselfishness," it would make little sense in context to say that the boys had long been persons of unselfishness; it is the boys' knowledge of St. Louis, not their behavior, that is being described.

29. A

Choice (A) is the best answer because it reflects the author's sense that the engineer was determined to impress others with his knowledge of steamboat work.

Choice (B) is not the best answer. There is nothing in the passage to indicate that using "steamboat technicalities" would mean the engineer had a strong interest in steamboat work.

Choice (C) is not the best answer. There is nothing in the passage to indicate that using "steamboat technicalities" would mean the engineer was unable to communicate effectively.

Choice (D) is not the best answer. There is nothing in the passage to indicate that using "steamboat technicalities" would mean the engineer had a fascination with trivial information.

30. B

Choice (A) is not the best answer because the passage does not indicate the engineer's feelings toward the other boys.

Choice (B) is the best answer. Though the author might think he is better than the engineer, the relationship is best described in terms of envy. The author and the other boys wish they could have a job like the engineer does. The last two paragraphs provide evidence of this, as "boy after boy managed to get on the river" (lines 55–56).

Choice (C) is not the best answer. The engineer's ability to get work on a steamboat might make him feel that he is better than the other boys, but the passage does not provide this information.

Choice (D) is not the best answer. The author might think he is a better person than the engineer, evidenced by such descriptions of him as "this creature" (line 54), but it is a leap to think that all the boys in the town viewed themselves as better than the engineer.

Answer Key
MATH TEST—NO-CALCULATOR

1. **B**
2. **D**
3. **C**
4. **A**
5. **B**

6. **D**
7. **A**
8. **30**
9. **7**
10. $\frac{2}{3}$, **1**

ANSWERS AND EXPLANATIONS

MATH TEST—NO-CALCULATOR

1. B

Choice (A) is not correct. This answer may result from not correctly applying the distributive property on the left-hand side of the equation, resulting in the expression $3n + 4 - 8$, instead of $3n + 12 - 8$.

Choice (B) is correct. Simplifying the numerators yields $\dfrac{3n+4}{5} = \dfrac{5+2n}{2}$, and cross-multiplication results in the equation $2(3n + 4) = 5(5 + 2n)$ or $6n + 8 = 25 + 10n$. Solving for n using inverse operations results in $-4n = 17$ or $n = -\dfrac{17}{4}$.

Choice (C) is not correct. This answer may result from not correctly applying the distributive property on the right-hand side of the equation, resulting in the expression $11 - 6 - 2n$, instead of $11 - 6 + 2n$.

Choice (D) is not correct. This answer may result from not correctly applying the distributive property on either side of the equation, resulting in the expressions $3n + 4 - 8$ and $11 - 6 - 2n$, instead of $3n + 12 - 8$ and $11 - 6 + 2n$.

2. D

Choice (A) is not correct. To arrive at this answer, students may have interpreted $f(3)$ to mean finding the x-coordinate when $y = 3$, which is 0, and then finding the x-coordinate when $y = 0$, which is -6.

Choice (B) is not correct. To arrive at this answer, students may have correctly evaluated $f(3)$, but then neglected to incorporate the next part of the question in their answer.

Choice (C) is not correct. To arrive at this answer, students may have interpreted $f(3)$ to mean finding the x-coordinate when $y = 3$, which is 0, and then neglected to incorporate the next part of the question in their answer.

Choice (D) is correct. To answer this problem, students must conceptually understand how function notation relates to a graph. One way to interpret the notation $f(3) = a$ is to say that the graph of the function contains the point $(3, a)$, so a is equal to the y-coordinate of the point whose x-coordinate is 3. Reading from the graph we see that a is equal to -5 because the graph contains the point $(3, -5)$. The question then asks what is $f(a)$, or in this case, what is $f(-5)$? The point on the graph that has an x-coordinate of -5 is $(-5, 2)$, so $f(-5)$ is 2.

3. C

Choice (A) is not correct. This answer may result from the misconception that if each equation in a system has the same x-coefficient, then the system has no solution, which is not necessarily true.

Choice (B) is not correct. This answer may result from attempting to make the second equation a multiple of the first equation by looking at the ratio of the constants on the right-hand sides, $\dfrac{15}{5}$, and wrongly concluding that the second equation must be 3 times the first equation, which gives $a = 3\dfrac{1}{3} = 1$.

Choice (C) is correct. When a system of linear equations has no solution, the graphs of the equations in the system are parallel lines, or in other words, have the same slope. Solving the first equation for y by multiplying through by the common denominator, 6, yields the equation $2x - 3y = 30$, which gives $-3y = -2x + 30$, or $y = \dfrac{2}{3}x - 10$. The slope of this line is $\dfrac{2}{3}$. Solving the second equation for y gives $-6y = -ax + 15$, or $y = \dfrac{a}{6}x - \dfrac{15}{6}$. The lines are parallel if $\dfrac{a}{6} = \dfrac{2}{3}$. Cross-multiplication yields the equation $3a = 12$, or $a = 4$.

Choice (D) is not correct. The student may have found the factor, 12, that when multiplied by the left side of the first equation results in the left side of the second equation, but then neglected to find that $a = 12\dfrac{1}{3} = 4$.

4. A

Choice (A) is correct. Based on the description of the scenario, $\dfrac{1}{4}$ is the portion of the pool that the two pumps, working together, can empty in one hour, and each term in the sum on the left side of the equation is the portion of this $\dfrac{1}{4}$ of the pool that one of the pumps empties. Because one of the pumps is three times as fast as the other, $\dfrac{3}{x}$ describes the portion of the pool that the faster pump is able to empty in one hour and $\dfrac{1}{x}$ describes the portion of the pool that the slower pump is able to empty in one hour.

Choice (B) is not correct. The student may have recognized that $\dfrac{1}{x}$ is the smaller term in the sum, wrongly concluded that the smaller term must apply to the faster pump, and then assumed the 3 in the numerator of the second term implies the equation describes the portion of the pool emptied in 3 hours. In fact, the portion of the pool that the faster pump could empty in 3 hours is $(3)\dfrac{3}{x} = \dfrac{9}{x}$.

Choice (C) is not correct. The student may not have seen that in this context, the rates of the pumps can be added to get the combined rate, but the times it takes each pump to empty the pool cannot be added to get the time for both pumps working together, since the time for the pumps working together is less than, not greater than, the times for each pump alone. This means that the terms in the sum cannot refer to the number of hours that the pumps work.

Choice (D) is not correct. The student may not have seen that in this context, the rates of the pumps can be added to get the combined rate, but the times it takes each pump to empty the pool cannot be added to get the time for both pumps working together, since the time for the pumps working together is less than, not greater than, the times for each pump alone. This means that the terms in the sum cannot refer to the number of hours that the pumps work.

5. B

Choice (A) is not correct. This is the length of segment AB, not the area of the triangle.

Choice (B) is correct. Because segment DB is tangent to the circle at A, and segment CA is a radius of the circle, CA is perpendicular to DB. This means that triangle ABC is a 30-60-90 degree triangle, the sides of which are in the ratio $x : x\sqrt{3} : 2x$, with $x = 8$. Side AB is across from the 60° angle and therefore has length $8\sqrt{3}$, as shown in the following diagram.

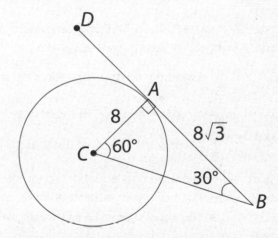

This means that the base of the triangle is 8, the height of the triangle is $8\sqrt{3}$, and the area of the triangle is $\dfrac{1}{2}(8)(8\sqrt{3}) = \dfrac{1}{2}(64\sqrt{3}) = 32\sqrt{3}$ square units. Alternatively, students could use trigonometric ratios to find the length of side AB, and then find the area of the triangle.

Choice (C) is not correct. To arrive at this answer, the student may have incorrectly identified the length of side AB as the part of the ratio represented by $2x$, rather than $8\sqrt{3}$, and as a result calculated the area using a base of 8 and a height of 16.

Choice (D) is not correct. To arrive at this answer, the student may have neglected to multiply by $\frac{1}{2}$ when calculating the area of the triangle.

6. D

Choice (A) is not correct. This is the value of y for the solution to the system, not the value of the quotient, $\frac{x}{y}$.

Choice (B) is not correct. This answer may result from incorrectly dividing 3 by $\frac{1}{2}$. The student may have changed the operation to multiplication but neglected to use the reciprocal of $\frac{1}{2}$ in the calculation.

Choice (C) is not correct. This is the value of x for the solution to the system, not the value of the quotient, $\frac{x}{y}$.

Choice (D) is correct. Rewriting both equations in standard form yields the equivalent system:

$x + 2y = 4$
$2x - 6y = 3$. Multiplying the top equation by

3 and then adding the two equations results in:

$3x + 6y = 12$
$2x - 6y = 3$ $\rightarrow 5x = 15 \rightarrow x = 3$. Substituting 3

for x in the original second equation (one could substitute the value of x into either equation and solve) results in the equation $6 = 3 + 6y$, which gives $y = \frac{3}{6} = \frac{1}{2}$. Finally, the $\frac{x}{y} = \frac{3}{\frac{1}{2}} = 3 \times \frac{2}{1} = 6$.

7. A

Choice (A) is correct. The terminal side of an angle in standard position with degree measure x such that $270° < x < 360°$ is in Quadrant IV of the coordinate plane. Using the information that $\sin x = -a$, it is clear that $-a$ is the y-coordinate of the point P where the terminal side of the angle intersects the unit circle. If $\sin w = a$, a positive value, then the y-coordinate of a point on the terminal side of an angle with degree measure w is positive and the angle measure must be between 0° and 180°, or in other words,

must fall in Quadrant I or Quadrant II. The value of $w = x - 180°$ is in Quadrant II because subtracting 180° from x results in the following: $270° - 180° < x - 180° < 360° - 180°$ or $90° < w < 180°$.

Choice (B) is not correct because $w = 180° - x$ falls in Quadrant III, not Quadrants I or II: $180° - 270° < 180° - x < 180° - 360°$ or $-90° < w < -180°$.

Choice (C) is not correct because adding or subtracting 360° to the initial angle measure will result in an angle whose terminal side is in the same quadrant as it began (e.g., the angle goes full circle and lands where it started), which means that $\sin w$ is still equal to $-a$, not a.

Choice (D) is not correct because adding or subtracting 360° to the initial angle measure will result in an angle whose terminal side is in the same quadrant as it began (e.g., the angle goes full circle and lands where it started), which means that $\sin w$ is still equal to $-a$, not a.

8. 30

To find the solution to this problem, students must examine the structure of the given equation and recognize that multiplying both sides of the equation by 10 to clear the fractions results in the equation $4x + 5y = 30$, so the correct answer is 30.

9. 7

One way to solve this problem is by factoring the equation. To use this method, the equation must first be rewritten in standard form, $x^2 + 10x - 24 = 0$, and then factored to arrive at $(x + 12)(x - 2) = 0$. Using the Zero-Product property to solve for x results in $x = -12$ and $x = 2$. It is given that $x > 0$, so x must equal 2. This means that $x + 5$ is equal to $2 + 5$, or 7.

Alternatively, students could use the quadratic formula to find that the possible values of x are:

$$x = \frac{-10 \pm \sqrt{10^2 - 4(1)(-24)}}{2(1)} = \frac{-10 \pm \sqrt{196}}{2} = \frac{-10 \pm 14}{2} .$$

Simplifying this expression results in $x = -12$ and $x = 2$. Again, it is given that $x > 0$, so x must equal 2, and $x + 5$ is therefore equal to 7.

Some students may also recognize that adding 25 to both sides of the initial equation yields $x^2 + 10x + 25 = 24 + 25$, or $(x + 5)^2 = 49$, which has a perfect square on each side. Because it is given that $x > 0$, the value of $x + 5$ is the positive square root of 49, or 7.

10. $\dfrac{2}{3}$**, 1**

In this problem, multiplying both sides of the equation by the common denominator $(x)(x - 2)$ yields the following:

$$
\begin{aligned}
1(x - 2) - 2(x) &= 3(x)(x - 2) \\
x - 2 - 2x &= 3(x^2 - 2x) \\
-x - 2 &= 3x^2 - 6x \\
0 &= 3x^2 - 5x + 2 \\
0 &= (3x - 2)(x - 1)
\end{aligned}
$$

Using the Zero-Product Property to solve the equation yields $x = \dfrac{2}{3}$ and $x = 1$, both of which must be checked in the original equation to ensure that they are not extraneous solutions. Here, neither value results in a zero denominator, so they are both valid solutions to the equation.

ESSAY TEST (OPTIONAL)

SAMPLE ESSAY

I think Clinton seemed to do a pretty good job saing health care needed to be reformed. People don't have health insurance and I agree they should.

People should have health insurance because if they get sick they could have a lot of financial problems, if they can't pay their medical bills. If they don't have it the government should help them get insurance. Like Clinton said it's bad for the economy if people can't pay their bills, it would hurt the people who can't pay their bills and it would hurt the doctors who don't get payed.

Clinton did good showng me that people should get insurance. He understood how bad it is for the government not to make sure people have it.

The essay above would score a 2 in the three graded areas: Reading, Analysis, and Writing. It is clear the student had read at least some of the prompt, but no mention is made of important facets, like the need for bipartisan support in Congress. No factual errors are presented in the essay, but there is limited use of information and no use of quotation. Analytically, there are missing elements. The student sees that this is a persuasive speech, but rather than focusing on the main question—how effective is the argument, and how is it structured effectively—the student discusses why the author is right. In Writing, this student uses limited vocabulary repetitively, and demonstrates errors of conventions. The overall paragraph structure is appropriate, but used to limited effect, and shows limited development of ideas. This student would need to increase focus on the directions and provide more information about the essay to get a higher score.

SAMPLE ESSAY

In his 1993 speech to Congress, then-President Bill Clinton made highly effective use of his time and his position of leadership to argue for health care reform. While there is more he could have done, for example providing specific examples and ideas, he did a lot to demonstrate why reform was both necessary and possible.

One of the most effective things Clinton did was show the need and possibility for support from Democrats and Republicans. Democrats and Republicans disagree about most things, so talking to both of them like both of their help is necessary is very effective. He even went so far as to say "you'll be bombarded with information from all kinds of sources" which said he knew there would be disagreements, and people like lobbyists giving bad information, and asked that people stay together in what was important. I would definitely have listened to him if I had been there.

He (*Clinton) also did a good job talking about just how bad the situation was. If you don't think a situation needs fixing, nobody's going to want to fix it. But he says how much more

Americans spend on health care than other countries, and how people wind up bankrupt or having to work forever, and how we have the best doctors but most people can't get to them. This sounds terrible; I would definitely have agreed with him if I were in Congress. I would be furious that my own Americans couldn't get the health care they needed.

A big problem with his arguement is the lack of specifics. He is very convincing that something needs to be done, but I don't know what has to be done, other than fixing it. But is it going to cost a lot? Or is it going to take a lot of work? It's so important, why hasn't it already been done? If he knows what to do, he isn't saying, which is confusing. I can't really be convinced without facts.

So overall this is a convincing speech, but it needs more facts.

The essay above would receive a score of 4 in the three graded areas: Reading, Analysis, and Writing. It is very clear that the student read the prompt essay thoroughly, as multiple parts are referenced directly, and quoted. The student understands the passage clearly and the relative importance of its arguments. The Analysis topic is handled well, with the substantial majority of the essay being focused on why arguments are or are not effective. The student does say he or she would have been personally convinced by certain parts, but it is to defend the essay, not his or her own perspective. Weaknesses in the article are also addressed, showing the student saw the argument's failings as well as its successes. In the Writing area, the introductory paragraph sets up the overall direction of the essay, which is supported by the rest of the paragraphs. The essay is not without any errors, but they do not distract from its overall strength. The conclusion paragraph is short, suggesting the student may have run out of time, but it does provide what the essay needs. Overall, the essay is strong and addresses all major score requirements of the 2016 SAT Essay.

NEW SAT CHALLENGE CORRELATION CHART

Use the following table to determine which SAT content you need to review most. Check to find out the areas of study covered by the questions you answered incorrectly. For example, if you missed a lot of Heart of Algebra questions, then you need to practice these skills.

Writing and Language Test	Question Number
Conventions of usage/Logical comparison	1
Conventions of punctuation/Unnecessary punctuation	2, 7
Conventions of punctuation/Nonrestrictive and parenthetical elements	3
Conventions of punctuation/Within-sentence punctuation	4, 12
Agreement/Pronoun-antecedent agreement	5
Organization/Introductions, conclusions, and transitions	6, 18
Organization/Logical sequence	8
Development/Focus	9
Effective language use/Style and tone	10
Development/Proposition	11
Effective language use/Precision	13, 22
Effective language use/Concision	14
Inappropriate shifts in construction/Verb tense, mood, and voice	15
Agreement/Subject-verb agreement	16
Sentence formation/Parallel structure	17
Sentence formation/Sentence boundaries	19
Effective language use/Syntax	20
Development/Quantitative information	21

Math Test—Calculator	Question Number
Heart of Algebra	1, 4, 7, 9, 13, 16
Problem Solving and Data Analysis	3, 5, 8, 10, 11, 15, 19
Passport to Advanced Math	2, 6, 12, 14
Additional Topics in Math	17, 18

Reading Test	Question Number
Determining the central idea	1, 11, 21
Analyzing details	1, 21
Rhetoric	2, 4, 9, 16, 24
Analyzing arguments	2, 9, 10, 12, 19, 22, 29
Analyzing reasoning	2
Information and ideas	3, 5, 7, 8, 11, 12, 13, 15, 17, 18, 19, 23, 25, 27, 28
Citing textual evidence	3, 7, 13, 17, 23, 27
Analyzing author's point of view	4, 24
Interpreting words and phrases in context	5, 8, 15, 16, 18, 25, 28
Determining implicit meaning	6, 10, 24, 26
Drawing inference based on evidence	6, 16, 20
Understanding relationships	10, 30
Reading closely	12, 19
Synthesis	14, 20
Analyzing verbal and graphic information	14, 20
Interpreting character motivations	22, 26, 29, 30

Math Test—No Calculator	Question Number
Heart of Algebra	1, 3, 6, 8
Problem Solving and Data Analysis	
Passport to Advanced Math	2, 4, 9, 10
Additional Topics in Math	5, 7

5 STRATEGIES FOR THE NEW SAT

Kaplan Methods
Writing & Language
Infographics
Math
Extended Thinking
Reading Comprehension

Using Kaplan Methods during your preparation, practice, and—most importantly—on Test Day will increase your efficiency and score! Below are five of Kaplan's tried and true Methods to help you build confidence and score higher. Make sure to incorporate these methods when you practice.

To get started, read each Kaplan Method and then apply it first to a question from *The New SAT Challenge* and then to an entirely new question. Be sure to continue practicing these methods until they become second nature. The additional practice test included in this book is a great resource to help you hone your skills and build your stamina for Test Day.

THE KAPLAN METHOD FOR WRITING & LANGUAGE

STEP 1
Read the passage and identify the issue

- If there's an infographic, apply the Kaplan Method for infographics

STEP 2
Eliminate answer choices that do not address the issue

STEP 3
Plug in the remaining answer choices and select the most correct, concise, and relevant one

APPLYING THE METHOD

Step 1 of the Kaplan Method for Writing & Language instructs you to read enough of the text to figure out what may be wrong with the underlined portion. Discarding wrong answer choices in Step 2 saves time and increases your chances of answering the question correctly. Plugging in the remaining answer choices in Step 3 reminds you to re-read the sentence to make sure the answer you choose is the most correct, concise, and relevant option.

The two questions below feature small portions of Writing & Language passages. On Test Day, be sure to read the entire passage without skipping any sentences, so you can better answer questions that ask about structure, organization, and the passage as whole.

First, let's try the Method on a Writing & Language question from *The New Sat Challenge*.

New SAT Challenge Q. 12

ARCTIC SEA ICE AND GLOBAL WARMING

Polar ice consists of sea-ice formed from frozen seawater as well as ice sheets and glaciers formed from the buildup and compaction of falling snow. The Earth is home to **12** two polar ice caps; high-latitude regions of a planet or natural satellite covered in ice.

12. (A) NO CHANGE
    (B) two polar ice caps high-latitude regions of a planet or natural satellite covered in ice.
    (C) two polar ice caps: high-latitude regions of a planet or natural satellite covered in ice.
    (D) two polar ice caps. High-latitude regions of a planet or natural satellite covered in ice.

Now, let's apply the Kaplan Method for Writing and Language to these questions. Remember, at first using the Kaplan Method may slow you down, but with practice it will help you become more efficient and, most importantly, more effective on Test Day!

STEP 1
Read the passage and identify the issue.
A semicolon is used to separate two independent clauses. "The Earth is home to two polar ice caps" is an independent clause, but "high-latitude regions of a planet or natural satellite covered in ice" is a dependent clause.
STEP 2
Eliminate answer choices that do not address the issue.
Since the underlined portion contains an error, you can immediately eliminate A. Choice B doesn't include the grammatically incorrect semicolon, but the lack of punctuation creates a run-on sentence.
STEP 3
Plug in the remaining answer choices and select the most correct, concise, and relevant one.
Plug C and D into the original sentence. A colon is used to separate an independent clause from a list or explanation. Choice C correctly uses a colon to separate an independent clause—*The Earth is home to two polar ice caps*—from an explanation—*high-latitude regions of a planet or natural satellite covered in ice*. A period, on the other hand, is used to separate two independent clauses. Choice D creates one correct sentence and one fragment. You can confidently choose (C) as the correct answer.

Now, let's apply the Kaplan Method to a new question..

Practice: Writing & Language

PREDICTING NATURE'S LIGHT SHOW

One of the most beautiful of nature's displays is the aurora borealis, commonly known as the Northern Lights. As ❶ their informal name suggests, the best place to view this phenomenon is in the north.

1. (A) NO CHANGE
   (B) an
   (C) its
   (D) that

STEP 1

Read the passage and identify the issue.

The word "their" is a pronoun, which means it needs to match its antecedent in gender and number. The antecedent, "this phenomenon," is gender-neutral and singular. The word "their" is gender-neutral but plural, so it is incorrect.

STEP 2

Eliminate answer choices that do not address the issue.

Since the underlined portion contains an error, you can immediately eliminate A. Choice B is not a pronoun, so you can eliminate it as an option.

STEP 3

Plug in the remaining answer choices and select the most correct, concise, and relevant one.

Plug C and D Into the original sentence. The sentence requires a singular gender-neutral possessive pronoun. Choice C correctly uses the pronoun *its*. Choice D offers a gender-neutral singular pronoun but one that is not possessive, so it is grammatically incorrect. Select (C), and you're done!

THE KAPLAN METHOD FOR INFOGRAPHICS

STEP 1 Read the question

STEP 2 Examine the infographic
- Circle parts of the infographic that diretly relate to the question
- Identify units, labels, and titles

STEP 3 Predict and answer

APPLYING THE METHOD

The Kaplan Method for Infographics dictates that you focus on the location and format of relevant information that will assist you in accurately answering questions about infographics. Step one zeroes in on what part of the infographic is relevant to answering the question. Step 2 is important in evaluating relevant trends and patterns that will assist you in completing Step 3: Making a prediction and selecting an answer choice based on that prediction.

First, let's try the Method on an Infographics question from *The New Sat Challenge*.

New SAT Challenge Q. 21

A careful review of this research reveals that

21 this drop occurred steadily over the twenty-year period, suggesting this temperature change was the result of an anomaly rather than a growing trend.

21. Which choice completes the sentence with accurate data based on the line graph?

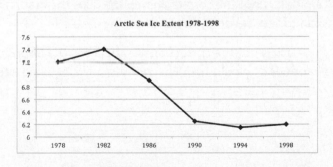

(A) NO CHANGE

(B) most of this drop occurred during only a portion of the 20-year period

(C) almost the entirety of this drop occurred during a period of only one year

(D) the reverse is true

Now, let's apply the Kaplan Method for Infographics to this question. Remember, at first using the Kaplan Method may slow you down, but with practice it will help you become more efficient and, most importantly, more effective on Test Day!

STEP 1 **Read the question** The question asks for the answer choice that accurately reflects the data presented in the line graph.

STEP 2
Examine the infographic
  • Circle parts of the infographic that diretly relate to the question
  • Identify units, labels, and titles
 	
The *Arctic Sea Ice Extent, 1978-1998* graph includes a span of 20 years in four-year increments along the *x*-axis and arctic sea ice extent on the *y*-axis. The graph includes an increase in arctic sea ice from 1978 to 1982. From 1982 to 1990, there is a steady decline. From 1990 to 1994, the arctic sea ice decreased, but at a slower rate. From 1994 to 1998, the arctic sea ice slightly increased. Overall, the arctic sea ice decreased from 7.2 in 1978 to 6.2 in 1998, but not at a constant decreasing rate.

STEP 3 **Predict and answer** Use the slope of the graph to evaluate each answer choice separately: Choice A is not the correct answer because as written, the text and the chart do not match. A steady 20-year decrease would be a straight downward sloping line while the line featured on the graph smooths out after a major decrease. Choice (B) accurately reflects the decrease from 7.4 in 1982 to just above 6.2 in 1990 and is therefore correct. Choice C is not the correct answer because the graph is broken up into four-year periods, so it is not possible to see the drop during a single year. Choice D is not the correct answer because the opposite of "this drop occurred steadily over the twenty-year period" would be a line without any steady decreases.

Now, let's apply the Kaplan Method to a new question.

Practice: Infographics

Scientists and interested amateurs in the Northern Hemisphere use tools readily available to all in order to predict the likelihood of seeing auroras in their location at a specific time. One such tool is the Kp Index, a number that determines the potential visibility of an aurora. The Kp Index measures the energy added to Earth's magnetic field from the sun on a scale of 0–9, with 1 representing a solar calm and 5 or more indicating a magnetic storm, or solar flare. The magnetic fluctuations are measured in three-hour intervals (12 am to 3 am, 3 am to 6 am, and so on) so that deviations can be factored in and accurate data can be presented.

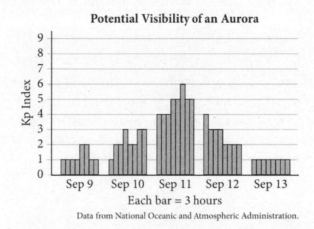

Data from National Oceanic and Atmospheric Administration.

2. Using the graphic and the information in the passage, identify the complete time period when a solar flare took place.

(A) 3 pm to 6 pm on September 11

(B) 12 am on September 11 to 3 am on September 12

(C) 9 am on September 10 to 12 pm on September 12

(D) 9 am on September 11 to 12 am on September 12

STEP 1

Read the question

The question asks you to use the bar graph to identify the complete time period when a solar flare took place.

STEP 2

Examine the infographic

- Circle parts of the infographic that diretly relate to the question
- Identify units, labels, and titles

The *Potential Visibility of an Aurora* bar graph includes five separate dates on the *x*-axis and the Kp index measure on the *y*-axis. Each bar is equal to three hours. September 11th includes the highest Kp Index measurements.

STEP 3

Predict and answer

The passage states that a solar flare is represented by any Kp Index of 5 or higher. Use that information to calculate the precise start and end time for the solar flare as indicated in the graphic. While there is one three-hour period in which the Kp Index reached 6, there is a consistent period in which the chart shows readings of level 5 or higher. Choice (D) is the correct answer because it gives the complete time period showing a reading of level 5 or higher, according to the graph.

THE KAPLAN METHOD FOR MATH

STEP 1   Read the question, identifying and organizing important information as you go

- What information are you given?
- How are the answer choices different?
- Should you label or draw a diagram?

STEP 2   Choose the best strategy to answer the question

- Look for patterns
- Pick numbers
- Use straightforward math

STEP 3   Check that you answered the *right* question

- Review the question stem
- Check units of measurement
- Double-check your work

APPLYING THE METHOD

The Kaplan Method for Math is your foundational approach for every question you see on the Math Test. Step 1 of the Kaplan Method for Math helps you focus on the relevant information in both the question stem and answer choices that will assist you in solving the question correctly. Step 2 reminds you to look for patterns and choose your approach before you begin any calculations, which helps eliminate unnecessary work. By checking that you answered the *right* question in Step 3, you can avoid wrong answer traps that are designed for test-takers who stop too soon when solving a question. As you work through the two questions below, pay close attention to how following this systematic approach increases your efficiency and accuracy.

First, let's try the Method on a Math question from *The New Sat Challenge*.

New SAT Challenge Q. 7

7. A commercial airline has calculated that the approximate fuel mileage for its 600-passenger airplane is 0.2 miles per gallon when the plane travels at an average speed of 500 miles per hour. Flight 818's fuel tank has 42,000 gallons of fuel at the beginning of an international flight. If the plane travels at an average speed of 500 miles per hour, which of the following functions *f* models the number of gallons of fuel remaining in the tank *t* hours after the flight begins?

(A) $f(t) = 42,000 - \dfrac{500t}{0.2}$

(B) $f(t) = 42,000 - \dfrac{0.2}{500t}$

(C) $f(t) = \dfrac{42,000 - 500t}{0.2}$

(D) $f(t) = \dfrac{42,000 - 0.2t}{500}$

Now, let's apply the Kaplan Method for Math to this question. Remember, at first using the Kaplan Method may slow you down, but with practice it will help you become more efficient and, most importantly, more effective on Test Day!

STEP 1

Read the question, identifying and organizing important information as you go

- What information are you given?
- How are the answer choices different?
- Should you label or draw a diagram?

The question stem describes an airplane with 42,000 gallons of fuel traveling at an average speed of 500 miles per hour. The plane's fuel mileage is 0.2 miles per gallon. You need to pick the answer choice that offers the correct algebraic expression that represents the number of gallons of fuel remaining in the tank t hours after the flight begins. For this question, there is no need to draw a diagram.

STEP 2

Choose the best strategy to answer the question

- Look for Patterns
- Pick numbers
- Use straightforward math

For this problem, straightforward math is the best strategy. Because the airplane is traveling at an average speed of 500 miles per hour and the plane's fuel mileage is 0.2 miles per gallon, the number of gallons of fuel used each hour can be found by $\dfrac{500 \text{ miles}}{1 \text{ hour}} \times \dfrac{1 \text{ gallon}}{0.2 \text{ miles}} = \dfrac{500}{0.2}$ gallons per hour. This means that in t hours, the plane uses $\dfrac{500}{0.2} \times t$, or $\dfrac{500t}{0.2}$, gallons of fuel.

STEP 3

Check that you answered the *right* question

- Review the question stem
- Check units of measurement

The plane's tank has 42,000 gallons of fuel at the beginning of the flight, so after t hours the amount of fuel remaining is $f(t) = 42{,}000 - \dfrac{500t}{0.2}$. The correct answer is (A).

Now, let's apply the Kaplan Method to a new question..

Practice: Math

3. According to the *Project on Student Debt* prepared by The Institute for College Access and Success, 7 out of 10 students graduating in 2012 from a four-year college in the United States had student loan debt. The average amount borrowed per student was $29,400, which is up from $18,750 in 2004. If student debt experiences the same total percent increase over the next eight years, approximately how much will a college student graduating in 2020 owe, assuming she takes out student loans to pay for her education?

   (A) $40,100

   (B) $44,300

   (C) $46,100

   (D) $48,200

STEP 1

Read the question, identifying and organizing important information as you go

- What information are you given?
- How are the answer choices different?
- Should you label or draw a diagram?

The question stem includes the average amount borrowed per student in 2004 and 2012. You can use the percent change formula to find the percent increase. Then, apply the same percent increase to the amount for 2012.

Percent change formula

$$\text{Percent change} = \frac{\text{actual change}}{\text{original amount}} \times 100\%$$

STEP 2

Choose the best strategy to answer the question

- Look for patterns
- Pick numbers
- Use straightforward math

Calculate the actual change by subtracting 29,400 from 18,750, which is 10,650. Then divide the actual change by the original amount: 10,650 ÷ 18,750 = 0.568. Multiply 0.568 by 100% to get 56.8%.

STEP 3

Check that you answered the *right* question

- Review the question stem
- Check units of measurement
- Double-check your work

If the total percent increase over the next 8 years is the same, the average student who borrowed money will have loans totaling 29,400 × 1.568 = 46,099.20, or about $46,100, which makes (C) the correct answer.

THE KAPLAN METHOD FOR EXTENDED THINKING

STEP 1   **Read the first part of the question, looking for clues**

STEP 2   **Identify and organize the information you need**
- What are you given?
- What are you solving for?

STEP 3   **Based on what you know, plan your steps to navigate the first part**
- What pieces are you missing?

STEP 4   **Solve, step-by-step, checking units as you go**

STEP 5   **Check that you answered the *right* question**

STEP 5   **Repeat for remaining sections, incorporating results from the previous parts**

APPLYING THE METHOD

Steps 1 through 5 of the Kaplan Method for Extended Thinking walk you through answering the first part of an Extended Thinking question accurately so that you can use the work you completed for that section to help you answer subsequent sections.

Looking for clues in the question stem during Step 1 is important in locating which information you will use to answer the first part of the question. Organizing the information provided as part of Step 2 makes it possible for you to create the plan you will develop in Step 3. Step 4 prompts you to check your units as you solve so you don't miss out on any points due to using the wrong units or forgetting to convert numbers. Step 5 prevents you from stopping your calculations too early, which is another way students fall into answer traps. Step 6 reminds you to use your calculations from the first part of the question to help you answer the other sections of an Extended Thinking question.

Tackling the questions below with the Kaplan Method is your first step to conquering this question type. Continue to practice using the Kaplan Method throughout your preparation to ensure test day success.

First, let's try the Method on some Extended Thinking questions from *The New Sat Challenge*.

New SAT Challenge Q. 19 & 20

19. Eli left his home in New York and traveled to Brazil on business. On Monday, he used his credit card to purchase these pewter vases as a gift for his wife.

For daily purchases totaling less than 200 U.S. dollars, Eli's credit card company charges a 2% fee. If the total charge on his credit card for the vases was $126.48, and no other purchases were made, what was the foreign exchange rate on Monday in Brazilian reais (R$) per U.S. dollar? If necessary, round your answer to the nearest hundredth.

20. On Wednesday, Eli bought a tourmaline ring that cost R$ 763. For daily purchases over $200, his credit card company charges the same 2% fee on the first $200 of the converted price and 3% on the portion of the converted price that is over $200. If the total charge on his credit card for the ring was $358.50, what was the amount of decrease, as a percentage, in the foreign exchange rate between Monday and Wednesday? Round your answer to the nearest whole percent.

Now, let's apply the Kaplan Method for Extended Thinking to these questions. Remember, at first using the Kaplan Method may slow you down, but with practice it will help you become more efficient and, most importantly, more effective on Test Day!

STEP 1
Read the first part of the question, looking for clues
Eli purchased three pewter vases that add up to 279 Brazilian reais.

STEP 2
Identify and organize the information you need
• What are you given?
• What are you solving for?
The charge amount of $126.48 represents the conversion of 128 + 66 + 85 = 279 Brazilian reais plus the 2% fee that Eli's credit card company charged him. You need to solve for the exchange rate of reais to U.S. dollars.

STEP 3
Based on what you know, plan your steps to navigate the first part
• What pieces are you missing?
You need to determine the original cost of the vases in U.S. dollars before you can calculate the exchange rate.

STEP 4

Solve, step-by-step, checking units as you go

To find the original cost, c, of the vases in U.S. dollars (before the 2% fee), write and solve the equation, $1.02c = 126.48$. Dividing both sides of the equation by 1.02 results in a cost of $c = \$124$. To find the foreign exchange rate, r, in Brazilian reais per U.S. dollar, let units guide you:

$$124 \text{ dollars} \times \frac{r \text{ reais}}{1 \text{ dollar}} = 279 \text{ reais} \;\rightarrow\; r = \frac{279}{124} = 2.25$$

STEP 5

Check that you answered the *right* question

The exchange rate on Monday was 2.25 Brazilian reais per U.S. dollar.

STEP 6

Repeat for remaining sections, incorporating results from the previous parts

If p represents the original price in U.S. dollars, then the total charge of \$358.50 represents $1.02(200) + 1.03(p - 200)$. Setting the total charge equal to this expression and solving for p yields:

$$358.5 = 1.02(200) + 1.03(p - 200)$$
$$358.5 = 204 + 1.03p - 206$$
$$358.5 = -2 + 1.03p$$
$$360.5 = 1.03p$$
$$350 = p$$

To calculate the exchange rate on Wednesday:

$$350 \text{ dollars} \times \frac{r \text{ reais}}{1 \text{ dollar}} = 763 \text{ reais} \;\rightarrow\; r = \frac{763}{350} = 2.18$$

To find the amount of decrease, as a percentage, in the exchange rates from Monday to Wednesday:

$$\frac{2.18 - 2.25}{2.25} = \frac{-0.07}{2.25} \approx -0.031, \text{ which represents a decrease of about 3\%.}$$

Now, let's apply the Kaplan Method to a new set of questions.

Practice: Extended Thinking

4. Daniel works for a pest control company and is spraying all the lawns in a neighborhood. The figure below shows the layout of the neighborhood and the times that Daniel started spraying the lawns at two of the houses. Each lawn in the neighborhood is approximately 0.2 acres in size and takes the same amount of time to spray.

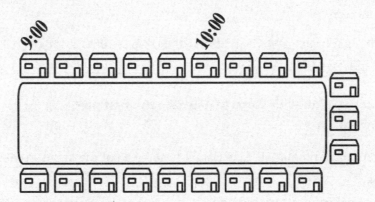

How many minutes will it take Daniel to spray all of the lawns in the neighborhood?

5. Daniel uses a mobile spray rig that holds 20 gallons of liquid. It takes 1 gallon to spray 2,500 square feet of lawn. How many times, including the first time, will Daniel need to fill the spray rig, assuming he fills it to the very top each time? [1 acre = 43,560 square feet]

STEP 1

Read the first part of the question, looking for clues

The figure shows the lawns in Daniel's neighborhood. He started spraying the first house at 9:00 and the sixth house at 10:00.

STEP 2

Identify and organize the information you need

- What are you given?
- What are you solving for?

Since Daniel started the first house at 9:00 and the sixth house at 10:00, it took him 1 hour, or 60 minutes, to spray 5 houses. This gives a unit rate of 60 ÷ 5 = 12 minutes per house.

STEP 3

Based on what you know, plan your steps to navigate the first part

- What pieces are you missing?

You need the total amount of time it will take Daniel to spray all of the lawns in the neighborhood.

STEP 4

Solve, step-by-step, checking units as you go

Count the houses in the figure—there are 21. Multiply the unit rate by the number of houses.

STEP 5

Check that you answered the *right* question

12 minutes per house × 21 houses = 252 minutes to spray all the lawns.

STEP 6

Repeat for remaining sections, incorporating results from the previous parts

The total acreage of all the lawns in the neighborhood is 21 × 0.2 = 4.2 acres. This is equivalent to 4.2 × 43,560 = 182,952 square feet. Each gallon of spray covers 2,500 square feet so divide to find that Daniel needs 182,952 ÷ 2,500 = 73.1808 gallons to spray all the lawns. The spray rig holds 20 gallons, so Daniel will need to fill it 4 times. After he fills it the fourth time and finishes all the lawns, there will be some spray left over.

THE KAPLAN METHOD FOR READING COMPREHENSION

STEP 1   Read Actively
- Ask questions as you read
- Take notes and circle keywords

STEP 2   Examine the question stem
- Identify keywords and line references

STEP 3   Predict and answer
- Predict an answer before looking at the answer choices
- Select the best match

APPLYING THE METHOD

Step 1 of the Kaplan Method for Reading Comprehension reduces the amount of time you spend reading because it prevents unnecessary tedious, line-by-line investigation. Circling keywords helps you identify the central idea of each paragraph, and your notes are designed to highlight the function of the passage structure. Examining the question stem in Step 2 makes predicting an answer choice, as part of Step 3, much easier since keywords and line references point you to the relevant parts of the passage that you can use to answer the question. Step 3 is a crucial part of avoiding wrong answer traps. Using support from the passage to predict an answer helps you focus on correct answers that reflect the tone and purpose of the passage.

First, let's try the Method on a Reading Comprehension question from *The New Sat Challenge.*

New SAT Challenge Q. 24

My father was a justice of the peace, and I supposed he possessed the power of life and death over all men and could hang anybody that offended him.
Line This was distinction enough for me as a general
(5) thing; but the desire to be a steamboatman kept intruding, nevertheless. I first wanted to be a cabin boy so that I could come out with a white apron on and shake a tablecloth over the side, where all my old comrades could see me. Later I thought I would
(10) rather be the deck hand who stood on the end of the stage plank with a coil of rope in his hand, because he was particularly conspicuous. But these were only daydreams—too heavenly to be contemplated as real possibilities. By and by one of
(15) the boys went away. He was not heard of for a long time. At last he turned up as an apprentice engineer or "striker" on a steamboat.

24. The author makes the statement that "I supposed he . . . offended him" (lines 1–3) primarily to suggest the

(A) power held by a justice of the peace in a frontier town.

(B) respect in which the townspeople held his father and how that influenced his thinking.

(C) somewhat naïve point of view he held about his father's importance.

(D) harsh environment in which he was brought up and how that influenced his point of view.

Now, let's apply the Kaplan Method for Reading Comprehension to this question. Remember, at first using the Kaplan Method may slow you down, but with practice it will help you become more efficient and, most importantly, more effective on Test Day!

STEP 1

Read Actively

- Ask questions as you read
- Take notes and circle keywords

This is a prose fiction passage, so you want to concentrate on characters and their feelings. As you read the first paragraph, focus on the narrator and his father. The narrator knows that his father's role as justice of the peace is important, but the narrator can't help himself from dreaming of being a steamboat man.

STEP 2

Examine the question stem

- Identify keywords and line references

Reread lines 1-3, paying specific attention to the author's tone.

STEP 3

Predict and answer

- Predict an answer before looking at the answer choices
- Select the best match

Lines 1–3 convey the author's boyish, naïve belief that his father was all-powerful in his role as justice of the peace; they help establish that all events described in the passage will reflect the point of view of a child. Choice (C) is correct.

Now, let's apply the Kaplan Method to a new question..

Practice: Reading Comprehension

Today's technology and resources enable people to educate themselves on any topic imaginable, and human health is one of particular interest to all.

Line From diet fads to exercise trends, sleep studies to
(5) nutrition supplements, people strive to adopt healthier lifestyles. And while some people may associate diets and gym memberships with sheer enjoyment, most of the population tends to think of personal healthcare as a necessary but time-consuming,
(10) energy-draining, less-than-fun aspect of daily life.

Yet for centuries, or perhaps for as long as conscious life has existed, sneaking suspicion has suggested that fun, or more accurately, *funniness*, is essential to human health. Finally, in recent years
(15) this notion, often phrased in the adage, "Laughter is the best medicine," has materialized into scientific evidence.

6. As used in line 15, "adage" most nearly means

   (A) remark

   (B) comment

   (C) cliché

   (D) proverb

STEP 1

Read Actively

- Ask questions as you read
- Take notes and circle keywords

This is a history/social studies passage. While reading the introductory paragraph, determine the topic, tone, and purpose of the passage. As you read the second paragraph, determine the main idea of the paragraph and how it relates to the passage as a whole.

STEP 2

Examine the question stem

- Identify keywords and line references

Reread the last sentence of the second paragraph.

STEP 3

Predict and answer

- Predict an answer before looking at the answer choices
- Select the best match

The phrase, "Laughter is the best medicine," is an adage, which is a short statement expressing a general truth. A proverb is a saying that includes a general truth or piece of advice. Choice (D) is correct.

How to Use this Practice Test

This Practice Test is a Kaplan-created exam, similar to the actual redesigned 2016 SAT. Before starting this test, find a quiet room where you can work uninterrupted for 3 hours (3 hours and 50 minutes if you take the optional Essay Test). Make sure you have a comfortable desk, your calculator, and several No. 2 pencils. Use the answer sheet to record your answers. Once you start the Practice Test, don't stop until you've finished. Remember, you can review any question within a subject test, but you may not jump from one subject test to another.

You'll find the answers and explanations immediately following the test.

READING TEST

65 Minutes—52 Questions

Turn to Section 1 of your answer sheet to answer the questions in this section.

Directions: Each passage or pair of passages below is followed by a number of questions. After reading each passage or pair, choose the best answer to each question based on what is stated or implied in the passage or passages and in any accompanying graphics (such as a table or graph).

Questions 1–10 are based on the following passage.

The following passage is adapted from Leo Tolstoy's 1873 novel, Anna Karenina *(translated from the original Russian by Constance Garnett). Prior to this excerpt, one of the major characters, Levin, has realized that he is in love with his longtime friend Kitty Shtcherbatsky.*

At four o'clock, conscious of his throbbing heart, Levin stepped out of a hired sledge at the Zoological Gardens, and turned along the path to the frozen
Line mounds and the skating ground, knowing that he
(5) would certainly find her there, as he had seen the Shtcherbatskys' carriage at the entrance.

It was a bright, frosty day. Rows of carriages, sledges, drivers, and policemen were standing in the approach. Crowds of well-dressed people, with hats
(10) bright in the sun, swarmed about the entrance and along the well-swept little paths between the little houses adorned with carving in the Russian style. The old curly birches of the gardens, all their twigs laden with snow, looked as though freshly decked in
(15) sacred vestments.

He walked along the path towards the skating-ground, and kept saying to himself—"You mustn't be excited, you must be calm. What's the matter with you? What do you want? Be quiet, stupid," he
(20) conjured his heart. And the more he tried to compose himself, the more breathless he found himself. An acquaintance met him and called him by his name, but Levin did not even recognize him. He went towards the mounds, whence came the clank
(25) of the chains of sledges as they slipped down or were dragged up, the rumble of the sliding sledges, and the sounds of merry voices. He walked on a few steps, and the skating-ground lay open before his

eyes, and at once, amidst all the skaters, he knew her.
(30) He knew she was there by the rapture and the terror that seized on his heart. She was standing talking to a lady at the opposite end of the ground. There was apparently nothing striking either in her dress or her attitude. But for Levin she was as easy to find
(35) in that crowd as a rose among nettles. Everything was made bright by her. She was the smile that shed light on all round her. "Is it possible I can go over there on the ice, go up to her?" he thought. The place where she stood seemed to him a holy shrine, unap-
(40) proachable, and there was one moment when he was almost retreating, so overwhelmed was he with terror. He had to make an effort to master himself, and to remind himself that people of all sorts were moving about her, and that he too might come there
(45) to skate. He walked down, for a long while avoiding looking at her as at the sun, but seeing her, as one does the sun, without looking.

On that day of the week and at that time of day people of one set, all acquainted with one another,
(50) used to meet on the ice. There were crack skaters there, showing off their skill, and learners clinging to chairs with timid, awkward movements, boys, and elderly people skating with hygienic motives. They seemed to Levin an elect band of blissful beings
(55) because they were here, near her. All the skaters, it seemed, with perfect self-possession, skated towards her, skated by her, even spoke to her, and were happy, quite apart from her, enjoying the capital ice and the fine weather.
(60) Nikolay Shtcherbatsky, Kitty's cousin, in a short jacket and tight trousers, was sitting on a garden seat with his skates on. Seeing Levin, he shouted to him:

GO ON TO THE NEXT PAGE ⟶

"Ah, the first skater in Russia! Been here long?
(65) First-rate ice—do put your skates on."

1. According to the passage, how did Levin first know
    that Kitty was at the Zoological Gardens?

    A) Kitty's carriage was parked near the
        entrance.

    B) Nikolay said he had been skating with Kitty
        earlier.

    C) He saw her talking with another woman
        near the pond.

    D) Kitty invited him to meet her there at a
        certain time.

2. As used in line 10, "swarmed" most nearly means

    A) invaded.

    B) gathered.

    C) flew.

    D) obstructed.

3. The passage most strongly suggests that which of
    the following is true of Levin?

    A) He worries about his appearance.

    B) He wishes he were more impressive.

    C) He is an extremely passionate person.

    D) He is wary of his surroundings.

4. Which choice provides the best evidence for the
    answer to the previous question?

    A) Lines 7–12 ("It was a bright, frosty
        day . . . in the Russian style")

    B) Lines 22–27 ("An acquaintance met
        him . . . merry voices")

    C) Lines 38–45 ("The place where . . . there to
        skate")

    D) Lines 48–53 ("On that day . . . hygienic
        motives")

5. What theme does the passage communicate
    through the experiences of Levin?

    A) Love is a powerful emotion.

    B) People long to have company.

    C) Life should be filled with joy.

    D) People are meant to work hard.

6. The passage most strongly suggests that which
    of the following is true of how Levin appears to
    others?

    A) People think that Levin looks agitated
        because of the way he is acting.

    B) People think that Levin is sick because he
        seems to be feverish.

    C) People think that Levin seems
        normal because he is doing nothing
        unusual.

    D) People think that Levin is in trouble because
        he is not protecting himself emotionally.

7. Which choice provides the best evidence for the
    answer to the previous question?

    A) Lines 1–6 ("At four o'clock . . . at the
        entrance")

    B) Lines 9–12 ("Crowds . . . the Russian style")

    C) Lines 23–29 ("He went . . . he knew her")

    D) Lines 60–65 ("Nikolay Shtcherbatsky . . .
        your skates on")

8. As used in line 20, "conjured" most nearly means

    A) begged.

    B) created.

    C) summoned.

    D) tricked.

9. The author's use of the word "throbbing" in line 1 implies that Levin

    A) has cut himself badly.

    B) has a sudden pain in his chest.

    C) is about to collapse.

    D) is in an agitated state.

10. Based on the tone of this passage, what emotion does the author wish the reader to feel about Levin?

    A) Empathy

    B) Cynicism

    C) Hostility

    D) Disgust

Questions 11–20 are based on the following passage.

This passage is adapted from a speech delivered by President Franklin Roosevelt on January 6, 1941, to the United States Congress. In the passage, Roosevelt reveals his intention to preserve and spread American ideals around the world.

The Nation takes great satisfaction and much strength from the things which have been done to make its people conscious of their individual stake
Line in the preservation of democratic life in America.
(5) Those things have toughened the fibre of our people, have renewed their faith and strengthened their devotion to the institutions we make ready to protect.

Certainly this is no time for any of us to stop thinking about the social and economic problems
(10) which are the root cause of the social revolution which is today a supreme factor in the world.

For there is nothing mysterious about the foundations of a healthy and strong democracy. The basic things expected by our people of their political and
(15) economic systems are simple. They are:

•   Equality of opportunity for youth and for others.

•   Jobs for those who can work.

•   Security for those who need it.

•   The ending of special privilege for the few.

(20) •   The preservation of civil liberties for all.

•   The enjoyment of the fruits of scientific progress in a wider and constantly rising standard of living.

These are the simple, basic things that must never be lost sight of in the turmoil and unbelievable com
(25) plexity of our modern world. The inner and abiding strength of our economic and political systems is dependent upon the degree to which they fulfill these expectations.

Many subjects connected with our social econo-
(30) my call for immediate improvement.

As examples:

•   We should bring more citizens under the coverage of old-age pensions and unemployment insurance.

•   We should widen the opportunities for adequate
(35) medical care.

•   We should plan a better system by which persons deserving or needing gainful employment may obtain it.

I have called for personal sacrifice. I am as-
(40) sured of the willingness of almost all Americans to respond to that call.

A part of the sacrifice means the payment of more money in taxes. In my Budget Message I shall recommend that a greater portion of this great de-
(45) fense program be paid for from taxation than we are paying today. No person should try, or be allowed, to get rich out of this program; and the principle of tax payments in accordance with ability to pay should be constantly before our eyes to guide our legislation.
(50) If the Congress maintains these principles, the voters, putting patriotism ahead of pocketbooks, will give you their applause.

In the future days, which we seek to make secure, we look forward to a world founded upon four
(55) essential human freedoms.

The first is freedom of speech and expression—everywhere in the world.

The second is freedom of every person to worship God in his own way—everywhere in the world.
(60) The third is freedom from want—which, translated into world terms, means economic

GO ON TO THE NEXT PAGE ⟩

understandings which will secure to every nation a healthy peacetime life for its inhabitants—everywhere in the world.

(65)   The fourth is freedom from fear—which, translated into world terms, means a world-wide reduction of armaments to such a point and in such a thorough fashion that no nation will be in a position to commit an act of physical aggression against

(70) any neighbor—anywhere in the world.

      That is no vision of a distant millennium. It is a definite basis for a kind of world attainable in our own time and generation. That kind of world is the very antithesis of the so-called new order of

(75) tyranny which the dictators seek to create with the crash of a bomb.

      To that new order we oppose the greater conception—the moral order. A good society is able to face schemes of world domination and

(80) foreign revolutions alike without fear.

      Since the beginning of our American history, we have been engaged in change—in a perpetual peaceful revolution—a revolution which goes on steadily, quietly adjusting itself to changing

(85) conditions—without the concentration camp or the quick-lime in the ditch. The world order which we seek is the cooperation of free countries, working together in a friendly, civilized society.

      This nation has placed its destiny in the hands

(90) and heads and hearts of its millions of free men and women; and its faith in freedom under the guidance of God. Freedom means the supremacy of human rights everywhere. Our support goes to those who struggle to gain those rights or keep them.

(95) Our strength is our unity of purpose. To that high concept there can be no end save victory.

11. Which phrase from the passage most clearly reflects President Roosevelt's purpose in making this speech?

   A) Lines 2–4 ("to make . . . democratic life")

   B) Lines 8–11 ("to stop thinking . . . the world")

   C) Lines 54–55 ("[to] look forward to . . . freedoms")

   D) Lines 79–80 ("to face . . . without fear")

12. Which choice provides the best evidence for the answer to the previous question?

   A) Lines 13–15 ("The basic things . . . are simple")

   B) Lines 29–30 ("Many subjects . . . improvement")

   C) Lines 50–52 ("If the Congress . . . applause")

   D) Lines 53–55 ("In the future days . . . freedoms")

13. As used in line 39, "sacrifice" most nearly means

   A) religious offerings to a deity.

   B) service in the military.

   C) losses of limbs in battle.

   D) surrender of interests to a greater good.

14. The passage most strongly suggests a relationship between which of the following phenomena?

   A) Protection of human rights abroad and military service

   B) Spread of freedom abroad and defense of democracy at home

   C) Defeat of tyrants abroad and establishment of democratic government at home

   D) Investment in global democracies abroad and strengthening of patriotism at home

GO ON TO THE NEXT PAGE ⇒

15. Which choice provides the best evidence for the answer to the previous question?

    A) Lines 23–28 ("These are . . . expectations")

    B) Lines 50–52 ("If the Congress . . . applause")

    C) Lines 71–76 ("That is no . . . of a bomb")

    D) Lines 92–95 ("Freedom means . . . unity of purpose")

16. In line 51, "pocketbooks" most nearly refers to

    A) local, state, and national taxes.

    B) war debt accumulated by the nation.

    C) citizens' individual monetary interests.

    D) Americans' personal investment in the defense industry.

17. In lines 71–73 ("That is no . . . generation"), President Roosevelt is most likely responding to what implicit counterclaim to his own argument?

    A) The spread of global democracy is idealistic and unrealistic.

    B) The defeat of tyrannical dictators in Europe is implausible.

    C) The commitment of the American people to the war effort is limited.

    D) The resources of the United States are insufficient to wage war abroad.

18. Which choice offers evidence that the spread of global democracy is achievable?

    A) Lines 46–47 ("No person . . . this program")

    B) Lines 54–55 ("we look forward . . . human freedoms")

    C) Lines 81–82 ("Since the beginning . . . in change")

    D) Line 95 ("Our strength . . . purpose")

19. In lines 60–64 ("The third is . . . world"), President Roosevelt sets a precedent by which he would most likely support which of the following policies?

    A) Military defense of political borders

    B) Investment in overseas business ventures

    C) Aid to nations struggling due to conflict and other causes

    D) Reduction of domestic services to spur job growth

20. The author refers to "the so-called new order of tyranny" primarily to

    A) connect the global conflict for human rights to citizens on a personal level.

    B) demonstrate the power of the global opposition to the United States.

    C) offer an alternative vision of the world without democracy.

    D) provide examples of the political and social revolutions underway.

GO ON TO THE NEXT PAGE ⟶

Questions 21–31 are based on the following passage and supplementary material.

The United States Constitution has been amended twenty-seven times since its ratification. Rights such as freedom of speech, religion, and press, for example, are granted by the First Amendment. This passage focuses on the Nineteenth Amendment, which gave women the right to vote.

The American political landscape is constantly shifting on a myriad of issues, but the voting process itself has changed over the years as well. Electronic
Line ballot casting, for example, provides the public with
(5) instantaneous results, and statisticians are more accurate than ever at forecasting our next president. Voting has always been viewed as an intrinsic American right and was one of the major reasons for the nation's secession from Britain's monarchical
(10) rule. Unfortunately, although all men were constitutionally deemed "equal," true equality of the sexes was not extended to the voting booths until 1920.

The American women's suffrage movement began in 1848, when Elizabeth Cady Stanton and Lucretia
(15) Mott organized the Seneca Falls Convention. The meeting, initially an attempt to have an open dialogue about women's rights, drew a crowd of nearly three hundred women and included several dozen men. Topics ranged from a woman's role in society
(20) to law, but the issue of voting remained a contentious one. A freed slave named Frederick Douglass spoke eloquently about the importance of women in politics and swayed the opinion of those in attendance. At the end of the convention, one hundred
(25) people signed the Seneca Falls Declaration, which listed "immediate admission to all the rights and privileges which belong to [women] as citizens of the United States."

Stanton and Mott's first victory came thirty years
(30) later when a constitutional amendment allowing women to vote was proposed to Congress in 1878. Unfortunately, election practices were already a controversial issue, as unfair laws that diminished the African-American vote had been passed during
(35) Reconstruction. Questionable literacy tests and a "vote tax" levied against the poor kept minority turnout to a minimum. And while several states al-

lowed women to vote, federal consensus was hardly as equitable. The rest of the world, however, was
(40) taking note—and women were ready to act.

In 1893, New Zealand allowed women the right to vote, although women could not run for office in New Zealand. Other countries began reviewing and ratifying their own laws as well. The United King-
(45) dom took small steps by allowing married women to vote in local elections in 1894. By 1902, all women in Australia could vote in elections, both local and parliamentary.

The suffrage movement in America slowly built
(50) momentum throughout the early twentieth century and exploded during World War I. President Woodrow Wilson called the fight abroad a war for democracy, which many suffragettes viewed as hypocritical. Democracy, after all, was hardly worth fighting for
(55) when half of a nation's population was disqualified based on gender. Public acts of civil disobedience, rallies, and marches galvanized pro-women advocates while undermining defenders of the status quo. Posters read "Kaiser Wilson" and called into ques-
(60) tion the authenticity of a free country with unjust laws. The cry for equality was impossible to ignore and, in 1919, with the support of President Wilson, Congress passed the Nineteenth Amendment to the Constitution. It was ratified one year later by two-
(65) thirds of the states, effectively changing the Constitution. Only one signatory from the original Seneca Falls Declaration lived long enough to cast her first ballot in a federal election.

America's election laws were far from equal for
(70) all, as tactics to dissuade or prohibit African Americans from effectively voting were still routinely employed. However, the suffrage movement laid the groundwork for future generations. Laws, like people's minds, could change over time. The civil
(75) rights movement in the mid- to late twentieth century brought an end to segregation and so-called Jim Crow laws that stifled African-American advancement. The Voting Rights Act of 1965 was the final nail in the coffin; what emerged was a free nation
(80) guided by elections determined not by skin color or gender, but by the ballot box.

GO ON TO THE NEXT PAGE ⟩

Women's Suffrage in the United States

1848 ➤| Seneca Falls Convention.

1878 ➤ 19th Amendment submitted; not ratified.

1911 ➤ Several states now grant women suffrage.

1914 ➤ Start of World War I.

1917 ➤ Picketing at the White House.

1918 ➤ Amendment passes in the House but fails in the Senate.

1919 ➤ Both the House and Senate pass the amendment.

1920 ➤| 19th Amendment ratified.

21. The stance the author takes in the passage is best described as that of

A) an advocate of women's suffrage proposing a constitutional amendment.

B) a legislator reviewing the arguments for and against women's suffrage.

C) a scholar evaluating the evolution and impact of the women's suffrage movement.

D) a historian summarizing the motivations of women's suffrage leaders.

22. Lines 69–70 ("America's election laws . . . equal for all") most clearly support which explicit claim?

A) The founders of the Constitution did not provide for free and fair elections.

B) The United States still had work to do to secure equal voting rights for some people.

C) Most women in the United States did not want suffrage and equal rights.

D) The women's suffrage movement perpetuated discriminatory voting laws.

23. Which choice provides the best evidence for the answer to the previous question?

A) Lines 13–14 ("The American . . . in 1848")

B) Lines 41–42 ("In 1893 . . . to vote")

C) Lines 63–64 ("Congress . . . the Constitution")

D) Lines 78–79 ("The Voting Rights Act . . . the coffin")

24. As used in line 57, "galvanized" most nearly means

A) displaced.

B) divided.

C) excited.

D) organized.

25. The main rhetorical effect of lines 73–74 ("Laws, like . . . could change") is to

A) connect the success of legislative reform with shifts in public sentiment.

B) dissuade reformers from focusing on grassroots activity rather than political campaigns.

C) evaluate the effectiveness of judicial rulings based on popular response to public polls.

D) reject the need for legal actions and court proceedings to attain social change.

GO ON TO THE NEXT PAGE ▷

26. As a whole, the passage most strongly suggests which conclusion?

   A) American government adapts to the changing needs and ideas of society.

   B) The best-organized reform movements are most likely to achieve their goals.

   C) The nation is more vulnerable to change during the confusion of wartime.

   D) The civil rights movement would not have happened without women suffragists.

27. Which choice provides the best evidence for the answer to the previous question?

   A) Lines 3–7 ("Electronic ballot casting . . . our next president")

   B) Lines 7–10 ("Voting has . . . monarchical rule")

   C) Lines 15–19 ("The meeting . . . dozen men")

   D) Lines 74–78 ("The civil rights . . . advancement")

28. The graphic most clearly illustrates which idea?

   A) The Nineteenth Amendment happened as a result of World War I.

   B) The states slowed reform of national voting rights laws.

   C) Women's suffrage resulted from a slow evolution of events.

   D) Acts of civil disobedience won support for suffrage in Congress.

29. In line 60, the word "authenticity" most nearly means

   A) reliability.

   B) realism.

   C) legitimacy.

   D) truth.

30. The passage suggests that President Wilson contributed to the success of the women's suffrage movement by

   A) circulating government propaganda in support of women's suffrage.

   B) framing the fight in World War I as a fight for democracy and freedom.

   C) engaging in a foreign war to distract the nation from political debate.

   D) working with legislators to write the Nineteenth Amendment.

31. The graphic helps support which statement referred to in the passage?

   A) Early women suffragists did not live to vote in national elections.

   B) The Nineteenth Amendment passed within a few years of its introduction.

   C) A majority of state representatives opposed women's suffrage in 1918.

   D) Many state governments approved suffrage before the federal government did.

Questions 32–42 are based on the following passages.

Passage 1

Coffee is a pillar of the world economy, generating both jobs and profits. The plant produced revenue to the tune of $15.4 billion in 2013 alone.
Line The coffee industry is also one of the world's largest
(5) employers, supporting 26 million employees. Because of the global importance of coffee, scientists at the University at Buffalo and their international colleagues were compelled to sequence the genome of the most popular coffee plant. In the genome lies
(10) the secrets of the bold flavor that people around the world have come to enjoy daily, as well as the caffeine kick that comes along with it. This new genetic information can be used to expand the market by creating new types of coffee varieties. The results of
(15) the study can also safeguard the existing industry. Scientists can now modify the genetic material of

GO ON TO THE NEXT PAGE

the coffee plant. Heartier strains of popular coffee types can be created so that they are resistant to
drought, disease, and bugs.

(20)   Researchers began their work by sequencing
the genome of the type of coffee that makes up
30 percent of all coffee production. The conclusions drawn from this study will help save money
and resources during the coffee production process.

(25) Researchers were able to isolate the genetic information of the enzymes in the coffee plant that produce
caffeine. With this information, it may be possible
to reduce or eliminate caffeine from coffee. This
would remove a costly step in the current process

(30) of extracting caffeine from the coffee beans, while
expanding the coffee market to people who avoid
caffeine for health reasons, such as high blood pres-
sure or pregnancy. The same research team plans
to sequence the genome of other types of coffee in

(35) the future. It is their hope that the information will
benefit the coffee producer, consumer, and also the
environment.

Passage 2

The Gibbon Genome Sequencing Consortium has
successfully sequenced the genome of the Northern

(40) white-cheeked gibbon. Both gibbons and humans
have DNA that changes during the course of their
lifetime. Some DNA changes in humans are the
result of mutations, which cause cancer and other
diseases. The changes in gibbons' DNA have resulted

(45) in many changes to the species over a very short
period of time. Although gibbons are close relatives
to humans, their DNA changes do not cause disease.
Understanding the pattern of the gibbon genome
might turn out to be very important to humans. If

(50) these changes in DNA can be understood, scientists
may be able to use the information to better understand human disease.

Cancer and other genetic diseases are caused by
faulty gene regulation. Scientists have sought to under-

(55) stand human biology through the lens of gibbon DNA
structures for some time. Until now, there has simply
been too much information to analyze. The endless re-
arrangements made it difficult to align gibbon DNA to
that of humans, but it has finally been accomplished.

(60) Scientists discovered a piece of DNA that is unique
to the gibbon species. Gibbons have a specific repeat

element, or a piece of DNA that copies itself multiple times throughout the genome. Repeat elements,
in both gibbons and humans, are related to the

(65) maintenance of genetic structures. Scientists hope
to be able to answer the question "Why can gibbon
DNA rearrange itself without causing diseases—
unlike humans' DNA?" If this complicated biological
question can be solved, scientists may be able to work

(70) backward in order to help stop cancer, heart failure,
and other human disease related to genetic repeats.

32. Which of the following best describes the central
     idea of Passage 1?

     A) Advancements in genome sequencing will
         lead to healthier food options worldwide.

     B) Genome sequencing of coffee can increase
         the profitability of coffee as a commodity.

     C) Removing caffeine from coffee will allow
         more people to drink and enjoy coffee.

     D) The coffee trade is an important sector of
         the global economy.

33. The author of Passage 2 would most likely agree that

     A) instead of studying nonhuman animals,
         scientists should look for a way to stop
         human DNA from changing when it repli-
         cates itself.

     B) sequencing the genome of other nonhuman
         primates could yield results that would be
         beneficial to people.

     C) the benefits of genome sequencing of gibbons
         and other nonhuman animals does not
         justify the great expense and resources used.

     D) scientists will be able to cure cancer once the
         mystery is solved of how the DNA of gibbons
         replicates itself without causing disease.

GO ON TO THE NEXT PAGE ▷

34. Passage 1 most strongly suggests that

    A) the coffee industry will fail without new developments stemming from genome sequencing.

    B) newly developed varieties of coffee plants are more expensive for consumers than are existing varieties.

    C) future research will lead to developments that could increase the profitability for coffee producers.

    D) genome sequencing of coffee plants could help scientists understand diseases that affect humans.

35. Which choice provides the best evidence for the answer to the previous question?

    A) Lines 5–9 ("Because of the global . . . coffee plant")

    B) Lines 16–17 ("Scientists can . . . coffee plant")

    C) Lines 20–22 ("Researchers began . . . coffee production")

    D) Lines 28–33 ("This would remove . . . pregnancy")

36. Passage 2 most strongly suggests which of the following?

    A) The genetic makeup of the Northern white-cheeked gibbon is more similar to that of humans than to other primates.

    B) More research is needed before the findings of scientists studying the DNA of gibbons can be used to cure disease in humans.

    C) Many diseases and illnesses that affect humans can only be understood by studying the DNA of plants and other animals.

    D) Cancer and other diseases can be eliminated completely if enough funding is given to scientific research.

37. Which choice provides the best evidence for the answer to the previous question?

    A) Lines 40–44 ("Both gibbons . . . diseases")

    B) Lines 54–56 ("Scientists have sought . . . some time")

    C) Lines 63–65 ("Repeat elements . . . genetic structures")

    D) Lines 68–71 ("If this . . . genetic repeats")

38. Which of the following best summarizes a shared purpose of the two authors?

    A) To explain how genome sequencing in animals and plants can benefit people in unexpected ways

    B) To summarize how genome sequencing has changed the field of medicine and the study of diseases

    C) To inform readers about how scientific research can be applied to improving the world economy

    D) To convince readers to support funding for research in genome sequencing of plants and animals

39. As used in line 8, "compelled" most nearly means

    A) forced.

    B) driven.

    C) required.

    D) constrained.

40. As used in line 65, "maintenance" most nearly means

    A) preservation.

    B) protection.

    C) organization.

    D) repair.

GO ON TO THE NEXT PAGE

41. Which point is the author of Passage 1 trying to make by using the phrase "a pillar of the world economy" in line 1 to refer to the coffee industry?

    A) Research into the coffee plant is important and should be continued.

    B) The coffee industry plays a significant role in global economics.

    C) Many jobs will be lost if the coffee industry goes into decline.

    D) The coffee industry provides financial stability for millions of people worldwide.

42. Which of the following can reasonably be inferred based on the information in both passages?

    A) Studying the genomes of animals closely related to humans can help scientists learn about diseases that affect humans.

    B) Expanding the customer base of the coffee industry will lead to higher profits and increase the stability of the global economy.

    C) The scientists who study coffee and those who study gibbons could learn more by collaborating.

    D) The genomes of other plants and nonhuman animals hold secrets that can benefit people and are worthy of exploration.

Questions 43–52 are based on the following passage and supplementary material.

In 1948, Swiss chemist George de Mestral was impressed with the clinging power of burrs snagged in his dog's fur and on his pant legs after he returned
Line from a hike. While examining the burrs under a
(5) microscope, he observed many hundreds of small fibers that grabbed like hooks. He experimented with replicas of the burrs and eventually invented Velcro,® a synthetic clinging fabric that was first marketed as "the zipperless zipper." In the 1960s,

(10) NASA used de Mestral's invention on space suits, and now, of course, we see it everywhere.

You might say that de Mestral was the father of biomimicry, an increasingly essential field that studies nature, looking for efficiencies in materials and
(15) systems, and asks the question "How can our homes, our electronics, our cities work better?" As one biomimetics company puts it: "Nature is the largest laboratory that ever existed and ever will."

Architecture is one field that is constantly
(20) exploring new ways to incorporate biomimicry. Architects have studied everything from beehives to beaver dams to learn how to best use materials, geometry, and physics in buildings. Termite mounds, for example, very efficiently regulate temperature,
(25) humidity, and airflow, so architects in Zimbabwe are working to apply what they've learned from termite mounds to human-made structures.

Says Michael Pawlyn, author of *Biomimicry in Architecture,* "If you look beyond the nice shapes
(30) in nature and understand the principles behind them, you can find some adaptations that can lead to new, innovative solutions that are radically more resource-efficient. It's the direction we need to take in the coming decades."

(35) Designers in various professional fields are drawing on biomimicry; for example, in optics, scientists have examined the surface of insect eyes in hopes of reducing glare on handheld device screens. Engineers in the field of robotics worked to replicate the
(40) property found in a gecko's feet that allows adhesion to smooth surfaces.

Sometimes what scientists learn from nature isn't more advanced, but simpler. The abalone shrimp, for example, makes its shell out of calcium carbonate,
(45) the same material as soft chalk. It's not a rare or complex substance, but the unique arrangement of the material in the abalone's shell makes it extremely tough. The walls of the shell contain microscopic pieces of calcium carbonate stacked like bricks,
(50) which are bound together using proteins just as concrete mortar is used. The result is a shell three thousand times harder than chalk and as tough as Kevlar® (the material used in bullet-proof vests).

GO ON TO THE NEXT PAGE

Often it is necessary to look at the nanoscale
(55) structures of a living material's exceptional properties
in order to re-create it synthetically. Andrew Parker,
an evolutionary biologist, looked at the skin of the
thorny devil (a type of lizard) under a scanning elec-
tron microscope, in search of the features that let the
(60) animal channel water from its back to its mouth.

Examples like this from the animal world abound.
Scientists have learned that colorful birds don't
always have pigment in their wings but are sometimes completely brown; it's the layers of keratin
(65) in their wings that produce color. Different colors,
which have varying wavelengths, reflect differently
through keratin. The discovery of this phenomenon
can be put to use in creating paints and cosmetics
that won't fade or chip. At the same time, paint for
(70) outdoor surfaces can be made tougher by copying
the structures found in antler bone. Hearing aids
are being designed to capture sound as well as the
ears of the *Ormia* fly do. And why can't we have a
self-healing material like our own skin? Researchers
(75) at the Beckman Institute at the University of Illinois
are creating just that; they call it an "autonomic
materials system." A raptor's feathers, a whale's fluke,
a mosquito's proboscis—all have functional features
we can learn from.

(80) The driving force behind these innovations, aside
from improved performance, is often improved
energy efficiency. In a world where nonrenewable energy resources are dwindling and carbon
emissions threaten the planet's health, efficiency has
(85) never been more important. Pawlyn agrees: "For
me, biomimicry is one of the best sources of inno-
vation to get to a world of zero waste because those
are the rules under which biological life has had to
exist."

(90) Biomimicry is a radical field and one whose prac-
titioners need to be radically optimistic, as Pawlyn
is when he says, "We could use natural products
such as cellulose, or even harvest carbon from the
atmosphere to create bio-rock."

Tiny florets in a sunflower's center are arranged in an
interlocking spiral, which inspired engineers in the
design of this solar power plant. Mirrors positioned
at the same angle as the florets bounce light toward
the power plant's central tower.

Adapted from David Ferris, "Innovate: Solar Designs
from Nature." © 2014 by Sierra Club.

43. The central idea of the passage is primarily concerned with

A) the field of biomimicry, the study of materials
and systems found in nature and replicated in
ways that benefit people.

B) the work of George de Mestral, the
Swiss chemist who invented Velcro® after
observing burrs under a microscope.

C) the ways in which architects use termite
mounds as models for human-made structures in Zimbabwe.

D) how scientists are seeking ways to improve
energy efficiency as nonrenewable energy
sources decline.

44. Which choice provides the best evidence for the
answer to the previous question?

A) Lines 1–6 ("In 1948 . . . hooks")

B) Lines 12–18 ("You might say . . . ever will'")

C) Lines 23–27 ("Termite mounds . . . structures")

D) Lines 80–85 ("The driving . . . more
important")

GO ON TO THE NEXT PAGE

45. The author includes a quote in paragraph 4 in order to

    A) explain why architects are looking to biomimicry for solutions in architecture.

    B) provide an argument for more scientists to study biomimicry.

    C) give an explanation as to why someone might choose a career in architecture.

    D) provide a counterargument to the author's central claim.

46. Based on the information in paragraph 6, how does the shell of an abalone shrimp compare with soft chalk?

    A) The essential building blocks are arranged in a similar manner, but the material that makes up the shell of an abalone shrimp is harder.

    B) Both are made from the same essential building blocks, but the shell of the abalone shrimp is much harder because of the manner in which the materials are arranged.

    C) The essential building blocks of both are the same, but the abalone shrimp shell is harder because the soft chalk lacks a protein binding the materials together.

    D) They are made from different essential building blocks, but they have a similar hardness because the materials are arranged in a similar manner.

47. In paragraph 9, what is the most likely reason that the author included the quote from Pawlyn about efficiency?

    A) To convince readers that Pawlyn is an expert in his field

    B) To prove that great strides are being made in creating products that do not generate waste

    C) To demonstrate the limits of what biomimicry can achieve

    D) To support the statement that energy efficiency "has never been more important"

48. In line 30, "principles" most nearly means

    A) sources.

    B) attitudes.

    C) standards.

    D) theories.

49. It can be reasonably inferred from the passage that

    A) more scientists will utilize solutions developed through biomimicry in the future.

    B) the field of biomimicry will eventually decline as more nonrenewable resources are discovered.

    C) scientists will leave the fields they are currently working in and begin research in biomimicry.

    D) doctors will create a self-healing skin called an "autonomic materials system" using methods based in biomimicry.

GO ON TO THE NEXT PAGE

50. Which choice provides the best evidence for the answer to the previous question?

    A) Lines 35–38 ("Designers . . . screens")

    B) Lines 54–56 ("Often it is . . . synthetically")

    C) Lines 61–79 ("Examples like . . . learn from")

    D) Lines 89–94 ("Biomimicry . . . bio-rock")

51. As used in line 90, "radical" most nearly means

    A) pervasive.

    B) drastic.

    C) essential.

    D) revolutionary.

52. The graphic and caption that accompany this passage help illustrate how biomimicry can be used to

    A) make a solar plant more attractive.

    B) decrease waste generated by energy sources.

    C) improve the efficiency of existing models.

    D) replicate a pattern common in nature.

WRITING AND LANGUAGE TEST

35 Minutes—44 Questions

Turn to Section 2 of your answer sheet to answer the questions in this section.

Directions: Each passage below is accompanied by a number of questions. For some questions, you will consider how the passage might be revised to improve the expression of ideas. For other questions, you will consider how the passage might be edited to correct errors in sentence structure, usage, or punctuation. A passage or a question may be accompanied by one or more graphics (such as a table or graph) that you will consider as you make revising and editing decisions.

Some questions will direct you to an underlined portion of a passage. Other questions will direct you to a location in a passage or ask you to think about the passage as a whole.

After reading each passage, choose the answer to each question that most effectively improves the quality of writing in the passage or that makes the passage conform to the conventions of standard written English. Many questions include a "NO CHANGE" option. Choose that option if you think the best choice is to leave the relevant portion of the passage as it is.

Questions 1–11 are based on the following passage.

The Age of the Librarian

When Kristen Harris ❶ is in college, she worked in her university's library and was constantly told, "You really should be studying to be a librarian; this is ❷ your home" however Harris was pursuing a bachelor's degree in elementary education at the time. Little did she realize that becoming a school librarian was indeed ❸ elective. During the 21st century, the age of information, what could be more necessary than an individual trained to gather, process, and disseminate information? So, after teaching children in the classroom, Harris went back to school to earn her Master of Library Science degree.

1. A) NO CHANGE
   B) has been
   C) was
   D) had been

2. A) NO CHANGE
   B) your home," however Harris
   C) your home."; However Harris
   D) your home." However, Harris

3. A) NO CHANGE
   B) imminent
   C) threatening
   D) optional

GO ON TO THE NEXT PAGE

Today, Harris is preparing a story time for a group of young students. As it has done with everything else, the technology revolution has elevated the school library to "Library 2.0," and Harris's tablet-integrated story time begins when she projects images for *The Very Cranky Bear* onto a projector screen. As a child, Harris got excited whenever a puppet appeared during story time, but now she uses an interactive app (application software) to enhance her own story time and ❹ <u>integrate</u> this next generation of children.

As she introduces the children to the problem of cheering up a cranky ❺ <u>bear, Harris sees Miguel</u> scouring the library shelves for another book by a popular author. ❻ <u>Miguel had said asking Harris for a book two weeks earlier "If you have any funny stories, I like those."</u>

4. A) NO CHANGE
    B) enervate
    C) energize
    D) elucidate

5. A) NO CHANGE
    B) bear; Harris sees Miguel
    C) bear: Harris sees Miguel
    D) bear Harris sees Miguel

6. A) NO CHANGE
    B) Miguel had said, "If you have any funny stories, I like those, "asking Harris for a book two weeks earlier.
    C) Asking Harris for a book two weeks earlier, Miguel had said, "If you have any funny stories, I like those."
    D) Miguel asked Harris for a book two weeks earlier had said, "If you have any funny stories, I like those."

GO ON TO THE NEXT PAGE

"It will always be satisfying," reflects Harris, "the act of finding books for students and having them return to say, 'I really liked that one. Are there any more by that author?'"

[7] These days, Harris would call herself a media mentor as much as a librarian because she regularly visits her favorite websites for reviews of apps and other digital tools to suggest to students and parents. Librarians have always been an important resource for families in a community, but this importance has grown exponentially because of the advent of technology. Librarians are offering guidance about new media to address the changing information needs in our communities. Furthermore, libraries are becoming increasingly technology driven, for example,

7. Which sentence could be added to the paragraph to most effectively establish its main idea?

A) Harris maintains active profiles on multiple social media networks to better connect with her students.

B) The role of the school librarian has changed rapidly to meet the needs of students who are digital citizens.

C) Librarians still perform many traditional tasks such as putting great literature in the hands of their students.

D) In the future, many school libraries are unlikely to have books on the shelves because students prefer electronic media.

8 enabling access to collections of other libraries, offering remote access to databases, or they house video production studios. So, in Harris's opinion, librarians must be masters of the digital world. **9**

Harris finishes her story time and heads across the library. A young student stops her and asks, "Ms. Harris, what's new in the library?"

8. A) NO CHANGE

B) by enabling access to collections of other libraries, offering remote access to databases, or by housing video production studios.

C) they enable access to collections of other libraries, offering remote access to databases, or they house video production studios.

D) enabling access to collections of other libraries, offering remote access to databases, or housing video production studios.

9. Which sentence would provide evidence to effectively support the main idea of the paragraph?

A) Harris sponsors a weekly "Fun Read" book discussion club that is well attended by many of the students at her school.

B) Librarians continue to help students and teachers locate the perfect book in the library's collection.

C) Teachers frequently ask Harris to recommend educational apps to support early literacy for their students.

D) Many parents are concerned with online safety and digital citizenship due to the proliferation of social media.

❿ <u>She chuckles</u> and thinks about the many collections, services, and programs their school library offers. "Have you seen the Trendy 10 list? You read the books on the list and blog **⓫** <u>your</u> ideas about them. I'll set you up with a password and username so you can blog," says Harris. In this library full of information, she's the gatekeeper.

Questions 12–22 are based on the following passage.

Unforeseen Consequences: The Dark Side of the Industrial Revolution

There is no doubt that the Industrial Revolution guided America through the nascent stages of independence **⓬** <u>and into being a robust economic powerhouse</u>. Inventions like the cotton gin revolutionized the textile industry, and the steam engine ushered in the advent of expeditious cross-country distribution.

The Industrial Revolution marked a shift from an agrarian to an industry-centered society. People eschewed farming in favor of **⓭** <u>more lucrative enterprises in urban areas which put a strain on</u> existing local resources. Necessary goods such as **⓮** <u>food crops, vegetables, and meat products</u> also had to be shipped in order to meet the dietary needs of a consolidated population. And because there were fewer people farming, food had to travel farther and in higher quantities to meet demand. Issues like carbon dioxide emissions, therefore, arose not only as byproducts of industrial production but also from the delivery of these products. As a result, booming metropolises needed additional lumber, metal, and coal shipped from rural areas to sustain population and industrial growth.

10. A) NO CHANGE
    B) He chuckles
    C) Harris chuckles
    D) They chuckle

11. A) NO CHANGE
    B) they're
    C) you're
    D) their

12. A) NO CHANGE
    B) and into the role of a robust economic powerhouse.
    C) and turned into a robust economic powerhouse.
    D) and then became a robust economic powerhouse.

13. A) NO CHANGE
    B) more lucrative enterprises in urban areas, which put a strain on
    C) more lucrative enterprises in urban areas; which put a strain on
    D) more lucrative enterprises in urban areas. Which put a strain on

14. A) NO CHANGE
    B) food
    C) food crops
    D) vegetables and meat products

GO ON TO THE NEXT PAGE ▷

15 [1] The negative effects of such expansion on humans were immediately apparent. Improper water sanitization led to cholera outbreaks in big cities. [2] Miners suffered from black lung after spending hours harvesting coal in dark caverns. [3] Combusted fossil fuels **16** released unprecedented amounts of human-made carbon dioxide into the air, resulting in respiratory ailments. [4] The fact remains that smog, now an internationally recognized buzzword, simply did not exist before the factories that produced it.

The critical impact on the environment must also **17** be taken into account. Proper regulations were either not in place or not enforced.

15. To effectively transition from paragraph 2, which sentence should begin paragraph 3?

A) Sentence 1

B) Sentence 2

C) Sentence 3

D) Sentence 4

16. Which graphic would best support the underlined claim?

A) A line graph plotting an increase in atmospheric carbon dioxide over time

B) A pie chart comparing the present percentages of carbon dioxide and other atmospheric gases

C) A timeline tracking carbon dioxide emissions testing dates

D) A bar graph showing levels of atmospheric carbon dioxide in different locations

17. Which choice most effectively combines the sentences at the underlined portion?

A) be taken into account, and proper regulations

B) be taken into account since without proper regulations

C) be taken into account, as proper regulations

D) be taken into account; however, proper regulations

Industrial waste was often disposed of in the nearest river or buried in landfills, where it ⓲ polluted groundwater essential for wildlife to thrive. Deforestation across the United States served the dual purpose of providing inhabitable land and wood, but it also caused animals to migrate or die out completely.

Although the Industrial Revolution heralded an age of consumer ease and excess, it also invited a cyclical process of destruction and reduced resources. ⓳ Greenhouse gases were released into the atmosphere. Numerous health problems caused by ⓴ depressing working conditions prevented rural emigrants from thriving. And the environment that had cradled humankind since its inception was slowly being ㉑ degraded. All in the name of progress. ㉒

18. A) NO CHANGE
    B) disturbed
    C) drained
    D) enhanced

19. Which choice should be added to the end of the underlined sentence to better support the claim in the preceding sentence?

    A) NO CHANGE
    B) while carbon dioxide-consuming trees were cut down to make way for new living spaces.
    C) and caused an increase in global temperatures as well as a rise in coastal sea levels.
    D) faster than they could be absorbed by the atmosphere's shrinking ozone layer.

20. A) NO CHANGE
    B) urban
    C) substandard
    D) developing

21. A) NO CHANGE
    B) degraded; all
    C) degraded! All
    D) degraded—all

GO ON TO THE NEXT PAGE ⟶

22. Which choice most effectively states the central idea of the essay on the previous page?

   A) The Industrial Revolution created a new consumer society that replaced the existing farming society.

   B) Politicians and historians today disagree about the true consequences of the Industrial Revolution.

   C) Although some analysts suggest that industrialization had many problems, its immense benefits outweigh these concerns.

   D) Unfortunately, progress came at the expense of environmental and ecological preservation and may well have ruined the future that once looked so bright.

Questions 23–33 are based on the following passage.

Remembering Freud

   Psychology has grown momentously over the past century, largely due to the influence of Sigmund Freud, a pioneer of the field. This Austrian-born neurologist founded the practice of psychoanalysis and **23** began scientific study of the unconscious mind. **24** Since his career which ended in the mid-twentieth century, Freud has remained a common cultural and scientific reference point.

23. A) NO CHANGE
    B) continued
    C) spearheaded
    D) led to

24. A) NO CHANGE

    B) Since his career, which ended in the mid-twentieth century, Freud has remained

    C) Since his career ending in the mid-twentieth century; Freud has remained

    D) Since his career (ending in the mid-twentieth century) Freud has remained

25 Even the abiding popularity of terms such as "id," "ego," or talking about a "Freudian slip" serves to indicate how this psychologist lingers powerfully in Western memory.

As neuroscience has progressed, many early practices and theories, including some of Freud's, have been dismissed as outdated, unscientific, or even harmful. Much of Freud's theory, clinical practice, and even lifestyle are now discredited. But when considered in his historical context, alongside the astounding progress catalyzed by his work, Freud's contribution was significant indeed.

26 Because he is now widely referred to as the Father of Psychoanalysis, Freud was among the first to develop the now-commonplace psychological method of inviting patients to freely speak. For Freud, this was both study and treatment. It helped doctors to understand patients, but more importantly it helped patients to understand themselves. Freud employed the classic (now largely outdated) psychiatric style in which the patient lies face-up on a clinical bed, allegedly enabling access to deep **27** parts of the mind. These recesses, better known as the unconscious or subconscious, fascinated Freud.

25. A) NO CHANGE
    B) Even the abiding popularity of terms such as the "id," "ego," or a "Freudian slip"
    C) Even the abiding popularity of terms such as talking about an "id," "ego," or "Freudian slip"
    D) Even the abiding popularity of terms such as "id," "ego," or "Freudian slip"

26. A) NO CHANGE
    B) Widely remembered as the Father of Psychoanalysis, Freud was among the first to develop the now-commonplace psychological method of inviting patients to freely speak.
    C) Freud was among the first to develop the now-commonplace psychological method of inviting patients to freely speak, which is why he is now widely remembered as the Father of Psychoanalysis.
    D) Although he is widely remembered as the Father of Psychoanalysis, Freud was among the first to develop the now-commonplace psychological method of inviting patients to freely speak.

27. A) NO CHANGE
    B) recesses
    C) places
    D) components

GO ON TO THE NEXT PAGE ▷

28 He believed that uncovering repressed memories, was necessary for recovery. For Freud, understanding the activity of the innermost mind was essential. **29** In dealing with the conditions of patients, like neurosis or other psychological trauma, he suspected that there was a great deal going on beneath the "surface" of the psyche. He thought it was possible to reunite external, or conscious, thought with the internal,

28. A) NO CHANGE

    B) He believed that uncovering repressed memories, being necessary for recovery.

    C) He believed that uncovering repressed memories was necessary for recovery.

    D) He believed that uncovering, repressed memories was necessary for recovery.

29. A) NO CHANGE

    B) In dealing with patients' conditions, like neurosis or other psychological trauma, he suspected that

    C) In dealing with patients like neurosis or other psychological trauma conditions he suspected that

    D) He suspected that, in dealing with patients' conditions like neurosis or other psychological trauma,

or unconscious. `30` Moreover, the method of inviting patients to speak and process their thoughts aloud remains central to today's psychological practice.

Freud altered the course of twentieth-century medicine by initiating what would become a grand, global conversation about the ❸ <u>still vastly mysterious human mind before Freud, medicine</u> had barely scratched the surface in understanding mental health. Patients were met with very few answers, let alone recovery protocols. ❸ <u>Through trial and error—scientific method in action—Freud's finding of a method that seemed to work.</u>

30. Which detail would provide the best support for the ideas presented in this section?

A) At the same time that Freud practiced, many people were interested in spiritualism.

B) Freud lived and worked mostly in London although he had originally trained in Austria.

C) While some of Freud's more unusual practices have been criticized or abandoned, his interest in the unconscious altered the trajectory of the field.

D) Psychologists today employ many theories, not just those developed by Freud.

31. A) NO CHANGE

B) still vastly mysterious human mind. Before Freud, medicine

C) still vastly mysterious human mind, before Freud, medicine

D) still vastly mysterious human mind before Freud. Medicine

32. A) NO CHANGE

B) Through trial and error—scientific method in action—Freud's finding a method that seems to work.

C) Through trial and error—scientific method in action—Freud finds a method that seemed to work.

D) Through trial and error—scientific method in action—Freud found a method that seemed to work.

GO ON TO THE NEXT PAGE ⟹

Since then, decades of ever-sharpening science have used his work as a launching pad. Therefore, as long as occasions arise to celebrate the progress of ❸❸ the field, Sigmund Freud will be remembered for groundbreaking work that enabled countless advances.

Questions 34–44 are based on the following passage and supplementary material.

Success in Montreal

The Montreal Protocol on Substances That Deplete the Ozone Layer is an international treaty that was created to ensure that steps would be taken to reverse damage to Earth's ozone layer and ❸❹ preventing future damage. ❸❺ It was signed in 1987. This document created restrictions on chemicals that were known to be dangerous to the protective barrier that the ozone layer offers Earth. Without the ozone layer, the sun's dangerous UV rays would alter our climate so drastically, life on land and in water would cease to exist.

33. A) NO CHANGE
     B) the field; Sigmund Freud will be remembered for ground-breaking work that
     C) the field Sigmund Freud will be remembered for ground-breaking work that
     D) the field Sigmund Freud will be remembered for ground-breaking work, and that

34. A) NO CHANGE
     B) to prevent
     C) prevented
     D) was preventing

35. Which choice most effectively combines the sentences in the underlined portion?
     A) Signed in 1987, this document
     B) Because it was signed in 1987, this document
     C) It was signed in 1987, and this document
     D) It was signed in 1987 so this document

A hole in Earth's ozone layer was discovered over Antarctica **36** as long as two years prior to the signing of the treaty. The discovery brought the human impact on the environment to the forefront of **37** international conversation, the massive hole was evidence that a global response was necessary and that large-scale action was needed. The Montreal Protocol became effective January 1, 1989, and nearly 100 gases deemed dangerous to the ozone layer have been phased out. As a result, **38** the size of the ozone hole decreased significantly during the 1990s.

Now that a substantial amount of time has passed since the treaty was put into place, the effects can begin to be **39** looked at. As a part of the treaty, the Montreal Protocol's Scientific Assessment Panel was created to gauge **40** their effect on the hole in the ozone layer.

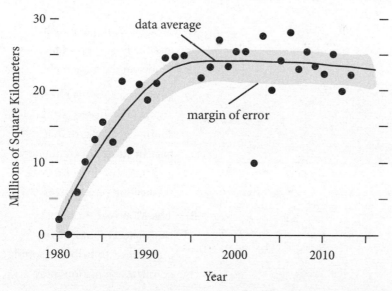

Size of Ozone Hole

Adapted from Ozone Hole Watch, NASA Goddard Space Flight Center.

36. A) NO CHANGE
    B) long ago, two years prior
    C) two years prior
    D) years prior

37. A) NO CHANGE
    B) international conversation, yet the massive hole
    C) international conversation. The massive hole
    D) international conversation, so the massive hole

38. Which choice completes the sentence with accurate data based on the graphic?
    A) NO CHANGE
    B) the average size of the ozone hole leveled off beginning in the 1990s.
    C) the average size of the ozone hole decreased beginning in the 2000s.
    D) the average size of the ozone hole increased beginning in the 1980s.

39. A) NO CHANGE
    B) controlled.
    C) measured.
    D) governed.

40. A) NO CHANGE
    B) its
    C) it's
    D) there

GO ON TO THE NEXT PAGE ▷

The Panel has since reported the results every four years. The Panel predicts that the ozone layer will return to its former state of health by 2060-2075. [41]

While the treaty is already an obvious success, work continues to ensure that human strides in technology and industry do not reverse the healing process. The Montreal Protocol's Multilateral Fund was established to help developing countries transition away from the consumption and production of harmful chemicals. So far, over $3 billion has been invested by the Fund. The developing countries are referred to as "Article 5 countries." [42]

41. Which choice could be added to paragraph 3 to most effectively convey its central idea?

A) It is the Panel's current estimation that the ozone layer is beginning to heal, but the rate of progress is slow.

B) The Panel meets once a year to assess the increase or decrease of each gas that has been identified as dangerous.

C) Of much concern to the Panel was the effect of ultraviolet radiation on the ozone layer.

D) The Panel has recently updated procedures for the nomination and selection of its membership.

42. Which sentence in paragraph 4 provides the least support for the central idea of the paragraph?

A) While the treaty is already an obvious success, work continues to ensure that human strides in technology and industry do not reverse the healing process.

B) The Montreal Protocol's Multilateral Fund was established to help developing countries transition away from the consumption and production of harmful chemicals.

C) So far, over $3 billion has been invested by the Fund.

D) The developing countries are referred to as "Article 5 countries."

GO ON TO THE NEXT PAGE

[1] The Montreal Protocol is a living document. [2] A current amendment proposition has been put forth by the United States, Mexico, and Canada jointly. [3] It aims to cut down on harmful gases that were put into use as an alternative to the gases specified in the original Montreal Protocol treaty. [4] It has been amended four times since its inception. [5] Combating the erosion of our ozone layer will take time and flexibility, but the research is clear: If humans stay conscious of what we emit into the atmosphere, we can not only stall the damage we have done in the past, but we can **43** <u>change</u> it. **44**

43. A) NO CHANGE
    B) switch
    C) invert
    D) reverse

44. For the sake of cohesion of this paragraph, sentence 4 should be placed

    A) where it is now.
    B) before sentence 1.
    C) after sentence 1.
    D) before sentence 3.

MATH TEST

25 Minutes—20 Questions

NO-CALCULATOR SECTION

Turn to Section 3 of your answer sheet to answer the questions in this section.

Directions: For this section, solve each problem and decide which is the best of the choices given. Fill in the corresponding oval on the answer sheet. You may use any available space for scratch work.

Notes:

1. Calculator use is NOT permitted.
2. All numbers used are real numbers.
3. All figures used are necessary to solving the problems that they accompany. All figures are drawn to scale EXCEPT when it is stated that a specific figure is not drawn to scale.
4. Unless stated otherwise, the domain of any function f is assumed to be the set of all real numbers x, for which $f(x)$ is a real number.

Information:

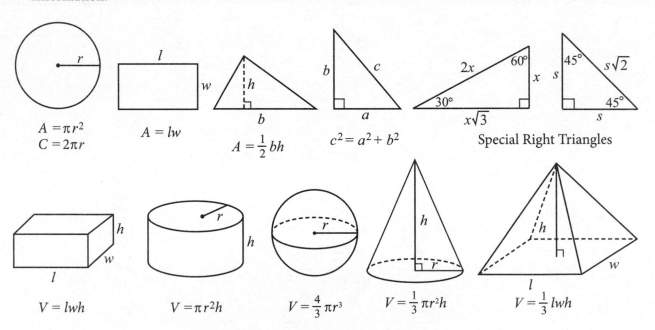

$A = \pi r^2$
$C = 2\pi r$

$A = lw$

$A = \frac{1}{2}bh$

$c^2 = a^2 + b^2$

Special Right Triangles

$V = lwh$

$V = \pi r^2 h$

$V = \frac{4}{3}\pi r^3$

$V = \frac{1}{3}\pi r^2 h$

$V = \frac{1}{3}lwh$

The sum of the degree measures of the angles in a triangle is 180.

The number of degrees of arc in a circle is 360.

The number of radians of arc in a cirlce is 2π.

GO ON TO THE NEXT PAGE

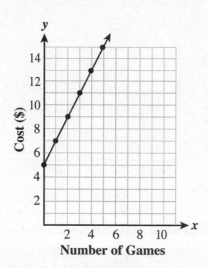

Number of Games

1. The graph above shows the amount that a new, high-tech video arcade charges its customers. What could the *y*-intercept of this graph represent?

    A) The cost of playing 5 games

    B) The cost per game, which is $5

    C) The entrance fee to enter the arcade

    D) The number of games that are played

$$\frac{3x}{x+5} \div \frac{6}{4x+20}$$

2. Which of the following is equivalent to the expression above, given that $x \neq -5$?

    A) $2x$

    B) $\dfrac{x}{2}$

    C) $\dfrac{9x}{2}$

    D) $2x + 4$

$$(x+3)^2 + (y+1)^2 = 25$$

3. The graph of the equation above is a circle. What is the area, in square units, of the circle?

    A) 4π

    B) 5π

    C) 16π

    D) 25π

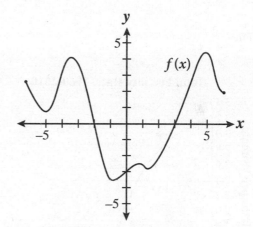

4. The figure above shows the graph of $f(x)$. For which value(s) of x does $f(x)$ equal 0?

    A) 3 only

    B) −3 only

    C) −2 and 3

    D) −3, −2, and 3

GO ON TO THE NEXT PAGE

$$\frac{4(d+3)-9}{8}=\frac{10-(2-d)}{6}$$

5. In the equation above, what is the value of *d*?

A) $\dfrac{23}{16}$

B) $\dfrac{23}{8}$

C) $\dfrac{25}{8}$

D) $\dfrac{25}{4}$

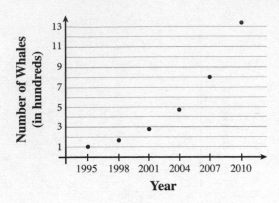

Total Fertility Rate, 1960-2010

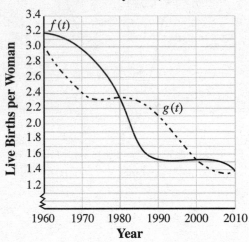

Source: Data from Eurostat.

6. One indicator of a declining economy is a continued decline in birth rates. In 2010, birth rates in Europe were at an all-time low, with the average number of children that a woman has in her lifetime at well below two. In the figure above, *f(t)* represents birth rates for Portugal between 1960 and 2010, and *g(t)* represents birth rates in Slovakia for the same time period. For which value(s) of *t* is *f(t)* > *g(t)*?

A) 1960 < *t* < 1980 only

B) 1980 < *t* < 2000 only

C) 1960 < *t* < 1980 and 1990 < *t* < 2000

D) 1960 < *t* < 1980 and 2000 < *t* < 2010

7. The blue whale is the largest creature in the world and has been found in every ocean in the world. A marine biologist surveyed the blue whale population in Monterey Bay, off the coast of California, every three years between 1995 and 2010. The figure above shows her results. If *w* is the number of blue whales present in Monterey Bay and *t* is the number of years since the study began in 1995, which of the following equations best represents the blue whale population of Monterey Bay?

A) $w = 100 + 2t$

B) $w = 100 + \dfrac{t^2}{4}$

C) $w = 100 \times 2^t$

D) $w = 100 \times 2^{\frac{t}{4}}$

GO ON TO THE NEXT PAGE

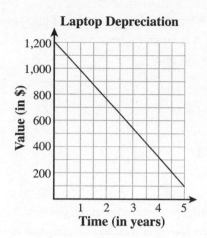

Laptop Depreciation

8. The figure above shows the straight-line deprecia-
    tion of a laptop computer over the first five years of
    its use. According to the figure, what is the average
    rate of change in dollars per year of the value of the
    computer over the five-year period?

    A) −1,100

    B) −220

    C) −100

    D) 100

9. What is the coefficient of x^2 when $6x^2 - \dfrac{2}{5}x + 1$ is
    multiplied by $10x + \dfrac{1}{3}$?

    A) −4

    B) −2

    C) 2

    D) 4

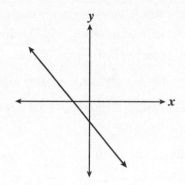

10. The graph above could represent which of the fol-
    lowing equations?

    A) $-6x - 4y = 5$

    B) $-6x - 4y = -5$

    C) $-6x + 4y = 5$

    D) $-6x + 4y = -5$

$$\frac{3}{4}x - \frac{1}{2}y = 12$$
$$kx - 2y = 22$$

11. If the system of linear equations above has no solu-
    tion, and k is a constant, what is the value of k?

    A) $-\dfrac{4}{3}$

    B) $-\dfrac{3}{4}$

    C) 3

    D) 4

GO ON TO THE NEXT PAGE

12. In Delray Beach, Florida, you can take a luxury golf cart ride around downtown. The driver charges $4 for the first $\frac{1}{4}$ mile, plus $1.50 for each additional $\frac{1}{2}$ mile. Which inequality represents the number of miles, m, that you could ride and pay no more than $10?

    A) $3.25 + 1.5m \le 10$

    B) $3.25 + 3m \le 10$

    C) $4 + 1.5m \le 10$

    D) $4 + 3m \le 10$

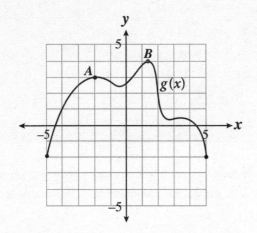

13. The graph of $g(x)$ is shown in the figure above. If $h(x) = -g(x) + 1$, which of the following statements is true?

    A) The range of $h(x)$ is $-3 \le y \le 3$.

    B) The minimum value of $h(x)$ is -4.

    C) The coordinates of point A on the function $h(x)$ are $(2, 4)$.

    D) The graph of $h(x)$ is increasing between $x = -5$ and $x = -2$.

14. If $a + bi$ represents the complex number that results from multiplying $3 + 2i$ times $5 - i$, what is the value of a?

    A) 2

    B) 13

    C) 15

    D) 17

$$\frac{1}{x} + \frac{4}{x} = \frac{1}{72}$$

15. In order to create safe drinking water, cities and towns use water treatment facilities to remove contaminants from surface water and groundwater. Suppose a town has a treatment plant but decides to build a second, more efficient facility. The new treatment plant can filter the water in the reservoir four times as quickly as the older facility. Working together, the two facilities can filter all the water in the reservoir in 72 hours. The equation above represents the scenario. Which of the following describes what the term $\frac{1}{x}$ represents?

    A) The portion of the water the older treatment plant can filter in 1 hour

    B) The time it takes the older treatment plant to filter the water in the reservoir

    C) The time it takes the older treatment plant to filter $\frac{1}{72}$ of the water in the reservoir

    D) The portion of the water the new treatment plant can filter in 4 hours

GO ON TO THE NEXT PAGE

Directions: For questions 16-20, solve the problem and enter your answer in the grid, as described below, on the answer sheet.

1. Although not required, it is suggested that you write your answer in the boxes at the top of the columns to help you fill in the circles accurately. You will receive credit only if the circles are filled in correctly.

2. Mark no more than one circle in any column.

3. No question has a negative answer.

4. Some problems may have more than one correct answer. In such cases, grid only one answer.

5. **Mixed numbers** such as $3\frac{1}{2}$ must be gridded as 3.5 or $\frac{7}{2}$. (If $3\frac{1}{2}$ is entered into the grid as $\boxed{3\,1\,/\,2}$, it will be interpreted as $\frac{31}{2}$, not $3\frac{1}{2}$).

6. **Decimal answers:** If you obtain a decimal answer with more digits than the grid can accommodate, it may be either rounded or truncated, but it must fill the entire grid.

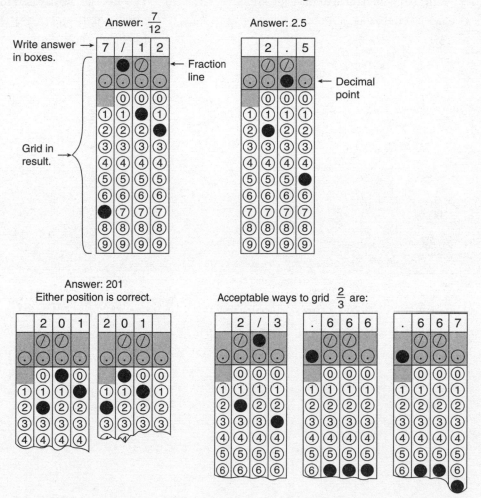

16. If $\dfrac{1}{4}x = 5 - \dfrac{1}{2}y$, what is the value of $x + 2y$?

$$x + 3y \leq 18$$
$$2x - 3y \leq 9$$

17. If (a, b) is a point in the solution region for the system of inequalities shown above and $a = 6$, what is the minimum possible value for b?

$$\dfrac{\sqrt{x} \cdot x^{\frac{5}{6}} \cdot x}{\sqrt[3]{x}}$$

18. If x^n is the simplified form of the expression above, what is the value of n?

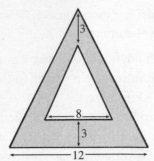

Note: Figure not drawn to scale.

19. In the figure above, the area of the shaded region is 52 square units. What is the height of the larger triangle?

20. If $y = ax^2 + bx + c$ passes through the points $(-3, 10)$, $(0, 1)$, and $(2, 15)$, what is the value of $a + b + c$?

MATH TEST

55 Minutes—38 Questions

CALCULATOR SECTION

Turn to Section 4 of your answer sheet to answer the questions in this section.

Directions: For this section, solve each problem and decide which is the best of the choices given. Fill in the corresponding oval on the answer sheet. You may use any available space for scratch work.

Notes:

1. Calculator use is permitted.
2. All numbers used are real numbers.
3. All figures used are necessary to solving the problems that they accompany. All figures are drawn to scale EXCEPT when it is stated that a specific figure is not drawn to scale.
4. Unless stated otherwise, the domain of any function f is assumed to be the set of all real numbers x, for which $f(x)$ is a real number.

Information:

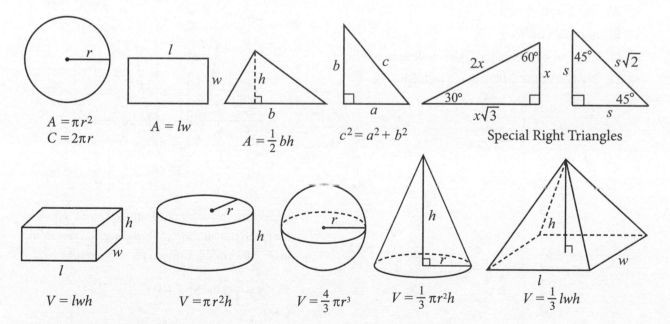

$A = \pi r^2$
$C = 2\pi r$

$A = lw$

$A = \frac{1}{2}bh$

$c^2 = a^2 + b^2$

Special Right Triangles

$V = lwh$

$V = \pi r^2 h$

$V = \frac{4}{3}\pi r^3$

$V = \frac{1}{3}\pi r^2 h$

$V = \frac{1}{3}lwh$

The sum of the degree measures of the angles in a triangle is 180.

The number of degrees of arc in a circle is 360.

The number of radians of arc in a cirlce is 2π.

GO ON TO THE NEXT PAGE ▷

1. Oceans, seas, and bays represent about 96.5% of Earth's water, including the water found in our atmosphere. If the volume of the water contained in oceans, seas, and bays is about 321,000,000 cubic miles, which of the following best represents the approximate volume, in cubic miles, of all the world's water?

   A) 308,160,000

   B) 309,765,000

   C) 332,642,000

   D) 334,375,000

2. An electrician charges a one-time site visit fee to evaluate a potential job. If the electrician accepts the job, he charges an hourly rate plus the cost of any materials needed to complete the job. The electrician also charges for tax, but only on the cost of the materials. If the total cost of completing a job that takes h hours is given by the function $C(h) = 45h + 1.06(82.5) + 75$, then the term $1.06(82.5)$ represents

   A) the hourly rate.

   B) the site visit fee.

   C) the cost of the materials, including tax.

   D) the cost of the materials, not including tax.

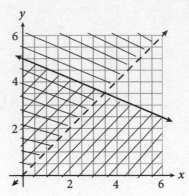

3. The figure above shows the solution set for the system $\begin{cases} y > x \\ y \le -\dfrac{3}{7}x + 5 \end{cases}$. Which of the following is not a solution to the system?

   A) $(0, 3)$

   B) $(1, 2)$

   C) $(2, 4)$

   D) $(3, 3)$

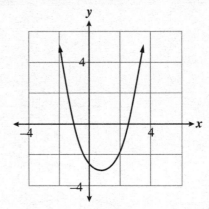

4. Each of the following quadratic equations represents the graph shown above. Which equation reveals the exact values of the x-intercepts of the graph?

   A) $y = \dfrac{1}{2}(2x - 5)(x + 1)$

   B) $y = x^2 - \dfrac{3}{2}x - \dfrac{5}{2}$

   C) $y + \dfrac{49}{16} = \left(x - \dfrac{3}{4}\right)^2$

   D) $y = \left(x - \dfrac{3}{4}\right)^2 - \dfrac{49}{16}$

GO ON TO THE NEXT PAGE

National Government Concerns

Average Annual Gas Prices

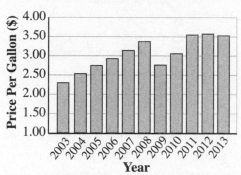

Data from U.S. Energy Information Administration.

5. Margo surveyed all the students in the government classes at her school to see what they thought should be the most important concern of a national government. The results of the survey are shown in the figure above. If the ratio of students who answered "Foreign Policy" to those who answered "Environment" was 5:3, what percentage of the students answered "Environment"?

    A) 16%

    B) 21%

    C) 24%

    D) 35%

6. Marco needs to buy several white dress shirts for his new job. He finds one he likes for $35 that is on sale for 40% off. He also likes a black tie that costs $21. Which of the following represents the total cost, not including tax, if Marco buys x of the white shirts that are on sale and two of the black ties?

    A) $C = 14x + 42$

    B) $C = 21x + 21$

    C) $C = 21x + 42$

    D) $C = 35x + 42$

7. The figure above shows the average annual gas prices in the United States from 2003 to 2013. Based on the information shown, which of the following conclusions is valid?

    A) A gallon of gas cost more in 2008 than in 2013.

    B) The price more than doubled between 2003 and 2013.

    C) The drop in price from 2008 to 2009 was more than $1.00 per gallon.

    D) The overall change in price was greater between 2003 and 2008 than it was between 2008 and 2013.

$$-2x + 5y = 1$$
$$7x - 10y = -11$$

8. If (x, y) is a solution to the system of equations above, what is the sum of x and y?

    A) $-\dfrac{137}{30}$

    B) -4

    C) $-\dfrac{10}{3}$

    D) -3

GO ON TO THE NEXT PAGE

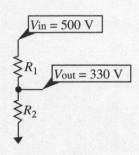

$V_{in} = 500$ V

R_1

$V_{out} = 330$ V

R_2

9. A voltage divider is a simple circuit that converts a large voltage into a smaller one. The figure above shows a voltage divider that consists of two resistors that together have a total resistance of 294 ohms. To produce the desired voltage of 330 volts, R_2 must be 6 ohms less than twice R_1. Solving which of the following systems of equations gives the individual resistance for R_1 and R_2?

A) $R_2 = 2R_1 - 6$
    $R_1 + R_2 = 294$

B) $R_1 = 2R_2 + 6$
    $R_1 + R_2 = 294$

C) $R_2 = 2R_1 - 6$
    $R_1 + R_2 = \dfrac{294}{330}$

D) $R_1 = 2R_2 + 6$
    $R_1 + R_2 = 330(294)$

10. If $\dfrac{2}{5}(5x) + 2(x-1) = 4(x+1) - 2$, what is the value of x?

A) $x = -2$

B) $x = 2$

C) There is no value of x for which the equation is true.

D) There are infinitely many values of x for which the equation is true.

11. Crude oil is being transferred from a full rectangular storage container with dimensions 4 meters by 9 meters by 10 meters into a cylindrical transportation container that has a diameter of 6 meters. What is the minimum possible length for a transportation container that will hold all of the oil?

A) 40π

B) $\dfrac{40}{\pi}$

C) 60π

D) $\dfrac{120}{\pi}$

12. The percent increase from 5 to 12 is equal to the percent increase from 12 to what number?

A) 16.8

B) 19.0

C) 26.6

D) 28.8

$$b = \dfrac{L}{4\pi d^2}$$

13. The brightness of a celestial body, like a star, decreases as you move away from it. In contrast, the luminosity of a celestial body is a constant number that represents its intrinsic brightness. The inverse square law, shown above, is used to find the brightness, b, of a celestial body when you know its luminosity, L, and the distance, d, in meters to the body. Which equation shows the distance to a celestial body, given its brightness and luminosity?

A) $d = \dfrac{1}{2}\sqrt{\dfrac{L}{\pi b}}$

B) $d = \sqrt{\dfrac{L}{2\pi b}}$

C) $d - \dfrac{\sqrt{L}}{2\pi b}$

D) $d = \dfrac{L}{2\sqrt{\pi b}}$

GO ON TO THE NEXT PAGE

Questions 14 and 15 refer to the following information.

Each month, the Bureau of Labor Statistics conducts a survey called the Current Population Survey (CPS) to measure unemployment in the United States. Across the country, about 60,000 households are included in the survey sample. These households are grouped by geographic region. A summary of the January 2014 survey results for male respondents in one geographic region is shown in the table below.

Age Group	Employed	Unemployed	Not in the Labor Force	Total
16 to 19	8	5	10	23
20 to 24	26	7	23	56
25 to 34	142	11	28	157
35 to 44	144	8	32	164
45 to 54	66	6	26	98
Over 54	65	7	36	152
Total	451	44	155	650

14. According to the data in the table, for which age group did the smallest percentage of men report that they were unemployed in January 2014?

    A) 20 to 24 years

    B) 35 to 44 years

    C) 45 to 54 years

    D) Over 54 years

15. If one unemployed man from this sample is chosen at random for a follow-up survey, what is the probability that he will be between the ages of 45 and 54?

    A) 6.0%

    B) 13.6%

    C) 15.1%

    D) 44.9%

GO ON TO THE NEXT PAGE ▷

16. Which of the following are solutions to the quadratic equation $(x-1)^2 = \dfrac{4}{9}$?

    A) $x = -\dfrac{5}{3},\ x = \dfrac{5}{3}$

    B) $x = \dfrac{1}{3},\ x = \dfrac{5}{3}$

    C) $x = \dfrac{5}{9},\ x = \dfrac{13}{9}$

    D) $x = 1 \pm \sqrt{\dfrac{2}{3}}$

17. Damien is throwing darts. He has a total of 6 darts to throw. He gets 5 points for each dart that lands in a blue ring and 10 points for each dart that lands in a red ring. If x of his darts land in a blue ring and the rest land in a red ring, which expression represents his total score?

    A) $10x$

    B) $10x + 5$

    C) $5x + 30$

    D) $60 - 5x$

18. Red tide is a form of harmful algae that releases toxins as it breaks down in the environment. A marine biologist is testing a new spray, composed of clay and water, hoping to kill the red tide that almost completely covers a beach in southern Florida. He applies the spray to a representative sample of 200 square feet of the beach. By the end of the week, 184 square feet of the beach is free of the red tide. Based on these results, and assuming the same general conditions, how much of the 10,000-square-foot beach would still be covered by red tide if the spray had been used on the entire area?

    A) 800 sq ft

    B) 920 sq ft

    C) 8,000 sq ft

    D) 9,200 sq ft

$$y = \dfrac{1}{2}x - 2$$
$$y = -x^2 + 1$$

19. If (a, b) is a solution to the system of equations above, which of the following could be the value of b?

    A) -3

    B) -2

    C) 1

    D) 2

20. Given the function $g(x) = \dfrac{2}{3}x + 7$, what domain value corresponds to the range value of 3?

    A) -6

    B) -2

    C) 6

    D) 9

21. A landscaper buys a new commercial-grade lawn mower that costs \$2,800. Based on past experience, he expects it to last about 8 years, and then he can sell it for scrap metal with a salvage value of about \$240. Assuming the value of the lawn mower depreciates at a constant rate, which equation could be used to find its approximate value after x years, given that $x < 8$?

    A) $y = -8x + 2{,}560$

    B) $y = -240x + 2{,}800$

    C) $y = -320x + 2{,}800$

    D) $y = 240x - 2{,}560$

GO ON TO THE NEXT PAGE

22. A microbiologist is studying the effects of a new antibiotic on a culture of 20,000 bacteria. When the antibiotic is added to the culture, the number of bacteria is reduced by half every hour. What kind of function best models the number of bacteria remaining in the culture after the antibiotic is added?

    A) A linear function

    B) A quadratic function

    C) A polynomial function

    D) An exponential function

23. An airline company purchased two new airplanes. One can travel at speeds of up to 600 miles per hour and the other at speeds of up to 720 miles per hour. How many more miles can the faster airplane travel in 12 seconds than the slower airplane?

    A) $\dfrac{1}{30}$

    B) $\dfrac{2}{5}$

    C) 2

    D) 30

State	Minimum Wage per Hour
Idaho	$7.25
Montana	$7.90
Oregon	$9.10
Washington	$9.32

24. When bordering states offer a higher minimum wage, workers often commute across state lines in order to earn a better living. The table above shows the 2014 minimum wages for several states that share a border. Assuming an average workweek of between 35 and 40 hours, which inequality represents how much more a worker who earns minimum wage can earn per week in Oregon than in Idaho?

    A) $x \geq 1.85$

    B) $7.25 \leq x \leq 9.10$

    C) $64.75 \leq x \leq 74$

    D) $253.75 \leq x \leq 364$

25. In the United States, the maintenance and construction of airports, transit systems, and major roads is largely funded through a federal excise tax on gasoline. Based on the 2011 statistics given below, how much did the average household pay per year in federal gasoline taxes?

    - The federal gasoline tax rate was 18.4 cents per gallon.
    - The average motor vehicle was driven approximately 11,340 miles per year.
    - The national average fuel economy for noncommercial vehicles was 21.4 miles per gallon.
    - The average American household owned 1.75 vehicles.

    A) $55.73

    B) $68.91

    C) $97.52

    D) $170.63

GO ON TO THE NEXT PAGE

Rescued Dolphin Recovery

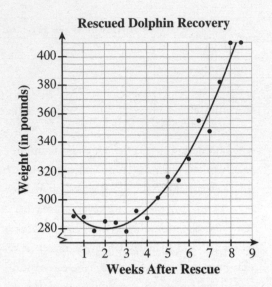

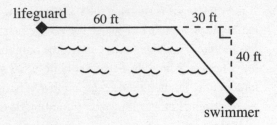

26. Following the catastrophic oil spill in the Gulf of Mexico in April of 2010, more than 900 bottlenose dolphins were found dead or stranded in the oil spill area. The figure above shows the weight of a rescued dolphin during its recovery. Based on the quadratic model fit to the data shown, which of the following is the closest to the average rate of change in the dolphin's weight between week 2 and week 8 of its recovery?

A) 4 pounds per week

B) 16 pounds per week

C) 20 pounds per week

D) 40 pounds per week

27. As shown in the figure above, a lifeguard sees a struggling swimmer who is 40 feet from the beach. The lifeguard runs 60 feet along the edge of the water at a speed of 12 feet per second. He pauses for 1 second to locate the swimmer again, and then dives into the water and swims along a diagonal path to the swimmer at a speed of 5 feet per second. How many seconds go by between the time the lifeguard sees the struggling swimmer and the time he reaches the swimmer?

A) 16

B) 22

C) 50

D) 56

28. What was the initial amount of gasoline in a fuel trailer, in gallons, if there are now x gallons, y gallons were pumped into a storage tank, and then 50 gallons were added to the trailer?

A) $x + y + 50$

B) $x + y - 50$

C) $y - x + 50$

D) $x - y - 50$

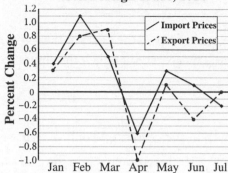

U.S. Foreign Trade, 2014

29. The figure above shows the net change, as a percentage, for U.S. import and export prices from January to July 2014 as reported by the Bureau of Labor Statistics. For example, U.S. import prices declined 0.2 percent in July while export prices remained unchanged for that month. Based on this information, which of the following statements is true for the time period shown in the figure?

A) On average, export prices increased more than import prices.

B) Import prices showed an increase more often than export prices.

C) Import prices showed the greatest change between two consecutive months.

D) From January to July, import prices showed a greater overall decrease than export prices.

$$\frac{3.86}{x} + \frac{180.2}{10x} + \frac{42.2}{5x}$$

30. The Ironman Triathlon originated in Hawaii in 1978. The format of the Ironman has not changed since then: it consists of a 3.86-km swim, a 180.2-km bicycle ride, and a 42.2-km run, all raced in that order and without a break. Suppose an athlete bikes 10 times as fast as he swims and runs 5 times as fast as he swims. The variable x in the expression above represents the rate at which the athlete swims, and the whole expression represents the number of hours that it takes him to complete the race. If it takes him 16.2 hours to complete the race, how many kilometers did he swim in 1 hour?

A) 0.85

B) 1.01

C) 1.17

D) 1.87

Directions: For questions 31-38, solve the problem and enter your answer in the grid, as described below, on the answer sheet.

1. Although not required, it is suggested that you write your answer in the boxes at the top of the columns to help you fill in the circles accurately. You will receive credit only if the circles are filled in correctly.

2. Mark no more than one circle in any column.

3. No question has a negative answer.

4. Some problems may have more than one correct answer. In such cases, grid only one answer.

5. **Mixed numbers** such as $3\frac{1}{2}$ must be gridded as 3.5 or $\frac{7}{2}$. (If $3\frac{1}{2}$ is entered into the grid as $\begin{array}{|c|c|c|c|}\hline 3 & 1 & / & 2 \\\hline \end{array}$, it will be interpreted as $\frac{31}{2}$, not $3\frac{1}{2}$).

6. **Decimal answers:** If you obtain a decimal answer with more digits than the grid can accommodate, it may be either rounded or truncated, but it must fill the entire grid.

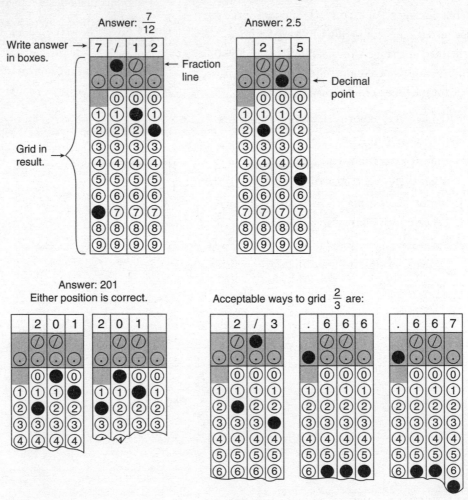

GO ON TO THE NEXT PAGE ⇨

31. What value of x satisfies the equation $\frac{2}{3}(5x+7)=8x$?

32. Some doctors base the dosage of a drug to be given to a patient on the patient's body surface area (BSA). The most commonly used formula for calculating BSA is $BSA = \sqrt{\dfrac{wh}{3,600}}$, where w is the patient's weight (in kg), h is the patient's height (in cm), and BSA is measured in square meters. How tall (in cm) is a patient who weighs 150 kg and has a BSA of $2\sqrt{2}$ m²?

33. If $-\dfrac{3}{2} < -2m+1 < -\dfrac{7}{5}$, what is one possible value of $10m - 5$?

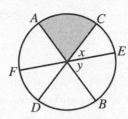

34. In the figure above, $\overline{AB}$, $\overline{CD}$, and $\overline{EF}$ are diameters of the circle. If $y = 2x - 12$, and the shaded area is $\dfrac{1}{5}$ of the circle, what is the value of x?

35. If the slope of a line is $-\dfrac{7}{4}$ and a point on the line is $(4, 7)$, what is the y-intercept of the line?

36. Rory left home and drove straight to the airport at an average speed of 45 miles per hour. He returned home along the same route, but traffic slowed him down and he only averaged 30 miles per hour on the return trip. If his total travel time was 2 hours and 30 minutes, how far is it, in miles, from Rory's house to the airport?

Questions 37 and 38 refer to the following information.

Chemical Makeup of One Mole of Chloroform

Element	Number of Moles	Mass per Mole (grams)
Carbon	1	12.011
Hydrogen	1	1.008
Chlorine	3	35.453

A chemical solvent is a substance that dissolves another to form a solution. For example, water is a solvent for sugar. Unfortunately, many chemical solvents are hazardous to the environment. One eco-friendly chemical solvent is chloroform, also known as trichloromethane ($CHCl_3$). The table above shows the chemical makeup of one mole of chloroform.

37. Carbon makes up what percent of the mass of one mole of chloroform? Round your answer to the nearest whole percent and ignore the percent sign when entering your answer.

38. If a chemist starts with 1,000 grams of chloroform and uses 522.5 grams, how many moles of chlorine are left?

IF YOU FINISH BEFORE TIME IS CALLED, YOU MAY CHECK YOUR WORK ON THIS SECTION ONLY. DO NOT TURN TO ANY OTHER SECTION IN THE TEST. **STOP**

ESSAY TEST (OPTIONAL)

50 minutes

The essay gives you an opportunity to show how effectively you can read and comprehend a passage and write an essay analyzing the passage. In your essay, you should demonstrate that you have read the passage carefully, present a clear and logical analysis, and use language precisely.

Your essay must be written on the lines provided in your answer booklet; except for the planning page of the answer booklet, you will receive no other paper on which to write. You will have enough space if you write on every line, avoid wide margins, and keep your handwriting to a reasonable size. Remember that people who are not familiar with your handwriting will read what you write. Try to write or print so that what you are writing is legible to those readers.

You have 50 minutes to read the passage and write an essay in response to the prompt provided inside this booklet.

1. Do not write your essay in this booklet. Only what you write on the lined pages of your answer booklet will be evaluated.

2. An off-topic essay will not be evaluated.

As you read the passage below, consider how Morris uses

-   evidence, such as facts or examples, to support claims.

-   reasoning to develop ideas and to connect claims and evidence.

-   stylistic or persuasive elements, such as word choice or appeals to emotion, to add power to the ideas expressed.

This passage is adapted from Elisabeth Woodbridge Morris's essay "The Tyranny of Things." In this portion, Morris paints a portrait of American consumerism in 1917 and offers a distinct perspective on the joy of freedom from "things, things, things."

Two fifteen-year-old girls stood eyeing one another on first acquaintance. Finally one little girl said, "Which do you like best, people or things?" The other little girl said, "Things." They were friends at once.

I suppose we all go through a phase when we like things best; and not only like them, but want to possess them under our hand. The passion for accumulation is upon us. We make "collections," we fill our rooms, our walls, our tables, our desks, with things, things, things.

Many people never pass out of this phase. They never see a flower without wanting to pick it and put it in a vase, they never enjoy a book without wanting to own it, nor a picture without wanting to hang it on their walls. They keep photographs of all their friends and Kodak albums of all the places they visit, they save all their theater programmes and dinner cards, they bring home all their alpenstocks.* Their houses are filled with an undigested mass of things, like the terminal moraine where a glacier dumps at length everything it has picked up during its progress through the lands.

But to some of us a day comes when we begin to grow weary of things. We realize that we do not possess them; they possess us. Our books are a burden to us, our pictures have destroyed every restful wall-space,

---

* alpenstocks: strong pointed poles used by mountain climbers

GO ON TO THE NEXT PAGE ⇨

our china is a care, our photographs drive us mad, our programmes and alpenstocks fill us with loathing. We feel stifled with the sense of things, and our problem becomes, not how much we can accumulate, but how much we can do without. We send our books to the village library, and our pictures to the college settlement. Such things as we cannot give away, and have not the courage to destroy, we stack in the garret, where they lie huddled in dim and dusty heaps, removed from our sight, to be sure, yet still faintly importunate.

Then, as we breathe more freely in the clear space that we have made for ourselves, we grow aware that we must not relax our vigilance, or we shall be once more overwhelmed. . . .

It extends to all our doings. For every event there is a "souvenir." We cannot go to luncheon and meet our friends but we must receive a token to carry away. Even our children cannot have a birthday party, and play games, and eat good things, and be happy. The host must receive gifts from every little guest, and provide in return some little remembrance for each to take home. Truly, on all sides we are beset, and we go lumbering along through life like a ship encrusted with barnacles, which can never cut the waves clean and sure and swift until she has been scraped bare again. And there seems little hope for us this side our last port.

And to think that there was a time when folk had not even that hope! When a man's possessions were burned with him, so that he might, forsooth, have them all about him in the next world! Suffocating thought! To think one could not even then be clear of things, and make at least a fresh start! That must, indeed, have been in the childhood of the race.

Once upon a time, when I was very tired, I chanced to go away to a little house by the sea. . . . There was nothing in the house to demand care, to claim attention, to cumber my consciousness with its insistent, unchanging companionship. There was nothing but a shelter, and outside, the fields and marshes, the shore and the sea. These did not have to be taken down and put up and arranged and dusted and cared for. They were not things at all, they were powers, presences. . . .

If we could but free ourselves once for all, how simple life might become! One of my friends, who, with six young children and only one servant, keeps a spotless house and a soul serene, told me once how she did it. "My dear, once a month I give away every single thing in the house that we do not imperatively need. It sounds wasteful, but I don't believe it really is. . . ."

Write an essay in which you explain how Morris builds an argument to persuade her audience that possessions are oppressive. In your essay, analyze how Morris uses one or more of the features listed in the box above (or features of your own choice) to strengthen the logic and persuasiveness of her argument. Be sure that your analysis focuses on the most relevant features of the passage.

Your essay should not explain whether you agree with Morris's claims, but rather explain how Morris builds an argument to persuade her audience.

ANSWER KEY
READING TEST

1. A	14. B	27. D	40. A
2. B	15. D	28. C	41. B
3. C	16. C	29. C	42. D
4. C	17. A	30. B	43. A
5. A	18. D	31. D	44. B
6. C	19. C	32. B	45. A
7. D	20. C	33. B	46. B
8. A	21. C	34. C	47. D
9. D	22. B	35. D	48. D
10. A	23. D	36. B	49. A
11. A	24. C	37. D	50. C
12. D	25. A	38. A	51. D
13. D	26. A	39. B	52. C

WRITING AND LANGUAGE TEST

1. C	12. B	23. C	34. B
2. D	13. B	24. B	35. A
3. B	14. B	25. D	36. C
4. C	15. A	26. B	37. C
5. A	16. A	27. B	38. B
6. C	17. C	28. C	39. C
7. B	18. A	29. B	40. C
8. D	19. B	30. C	41. A
9. C	20. C	31. B	42. D
10. C	21. D	32. D	43. D
11. A	22. D	33. A	44. C

MATH—NO CALCULATOR

1. C	6. D	11. C	16. 20
2. A	7. D	12. B	17. 1
3. D	8. B	13. A	18. 2
4. C	9. B	14. D	19. 14
5. B	10. A	15. A	20. 6

MATH—CALCULATOR

1. C	11. B	21. C	31. 1
2. C	12. D	22. D	32. 192
3. D	13. A	23. B	33. $7 < x < 7.5$
4. A	14. D	24. C	34. 40
5. B	15. B	25. D	35. 14
6. C	16. B	26. C	36. 45
7. D	17. D	27. A	37. 10
8. B	18. A	28. B	38. 12
9. A	19. A	29. B	
10. C	20. A	30. D	

ANALYZE YOUR PERFORMANCE

STEP 1

Calculate your percentage correct. Refer to the answer key to figure out the number right in each section. Enter the results in the chart:

Section	# Correct	Total # of Questions	% Correct
Reading		52	
Writing & Language		44	
Math w/out Calculator		20	
Math w/ Calculator		38	

STEP 2

Review the correlation.

Use the following table to determine which SAT content you need to review most. Check to find out the areas of study covered by the questions you answered incorrectly. For example, if you missed a lot of Development/Organization questions in the Writing and Language section, then you need to practice developing the skills required to answer that type of question.

Reading Test	Question Number
Analyzing details	1, 28
Command of evidence	4, 7, 12, 15, 23, 27, 35, 37, 44, 50
Determining the central idea	5, 32, 43
Drawing inference based on evidence	3, 6, 14, 19, 26, 30, 34, 36, 46, 49
Interpreting words and phrases in context	2, 8, 13, 16, 24, 29, 39, 40, 48, 51
Rhetoric	9, 10, 11, 17, 18, 20, 21, 22, 25, 33, 38, 41, 45, 47
Synthesis	31, 42, 52

Writing and Language Test	Question Number
Agreement/Pronoun-antecedent agreement	11, 40
Usage/Ambiguous pronoun	10
Conventions of punctuation/Nonrestrictive and parenthetical elements	5
Conventions of punctuation/Unnecessary punctuation	28
Conventions of punctuation/ Within-sentence punctuation	2, 13, 24

Writing and Language Test	Question Number
Development/Focus	22
Development/Organization	19, 26, 30, 41, 42, 44
Development/Proposition	7, 9
Development/Quantitative information	16, 38
Effective language use/Concision	14, 35, 36
Effective language use/Precision	18, 20, 23, 27
Effective language use/Style and tone	3, 4, 39, 43
Inappropriate shifts in construction/Verb tense, mood, and voice	1
Organization/Introductions, conclusions, and transitions	15
Effective language use/Syntax	17, 21
Sentence formation/Modifiers	29
Sentence formation/Parallel structure	6, 8, 12, 25, 34
Sentence formation/Sentence boundaries	31, 33, 37
Sentence formation/Verb tense	32

Math Test —Calculator	Question Number
Additional Topics in Math	11, 27, 34
Heart of Algebra	2, 3, 6, 8, 9, 10, 17, 21, 24, 28, 31, 33, 35
Passport to Advanced Math	4, 13, 16, 19, 20, 30, 32
Problem Solving and Data Analysis	1, 5, 7, 12, 14, 15, 18, 22, 23, 25, 26, 29, 36, 37, 38

Math Test—No Calculator	Question Number
Additional Topics in Math	3, 14, 19
Heart of Algebra	1, 5, 8, 10, 11, 12, 16, 17
Passport to Advanced Math	2, 4, 6, 7, 9, 13, 15, 18, 20

ANSWERS AND EXPLANATIONS

READING TEST

Anna Karenina

1. A
Difficulty: Easy

Category: Reading / Detail

Strategic Advice: Make sure to read the passage closely so events are clearly understood.

Getting to the Answer: The first paragraph explicitly states how Levin knew that Kitty was there. Choice (A) matches the information stated in the passage.

2. B
Difficulty: Medium

Category: Reading / Vocab-in-Context

Strategic Advice: Use context clues to help you distinguish the shades of meaning each word has.

Getting to the Answer: Two of the answer choices have a somewhat negative connotation. The author is not describing the scene in a negative way. In this passage, the word "swarmed" means "gathered." Therefore, (B) is the correct answer. The other words' connotations do not fit with the context of the sentence.

3. C
Difficulty: Hard

Category: Reading / Inference

Strategic Advice: Look for clues in the text that suggest what Levin is like.

Getting to the Answer: Emotionally charged phrases, such as "the rapture and the terror that seized on

his heart," help reveal Levin's personality. Choice (C) reflects the depiction of Levin as a passionate person.

4. C
Difficulty: Hard

Category: Reading / Command of Evidence

Strategic Advice: Eliminate answer choices that don't include a description of Levin.

Getting to the Answer: Because the excerpt focuses on Levin's feelings toward Kitty, evidence of the kind of person he is will probably reflect this. Choice (C) provides the best evidence.

5. A
Difficulty: Medium

Category: Reading / Global

Strategic Advice: The central theme of a passage is the insight about life that the author is trying to get across to the reader. Eliminate any themes that are not revealed by the experiences of Levin.

Getting to the Answer: Though you may personally agree with more than one of the themes presented, (A) is only one answer choice that is supported by details in the passage. Levin's feelings and actions support this theme.

6. C
Difficulty: Medium

Category: Reading / Inference

Strategic Advice: Examine the passage to see what other characters do in response to Levin.

Getting to the Answer: The other skaters go about their business. Most take little notice of Levin. Therefore, (C) is the correct answer.

7. D

Difficulty: Medium

Category: Reading / Command of Evidence

Strategic Advice: Reread each quote in the context of the passage. This will help you decide the correct answer.

Getting to the Answer: Of all the answer choices, Nikolay's way of greeting Levin is the strongest evidence that people think Levin seems normal. Choice (D) is the correct answer.

8. A

Difficulty: Medium

Category: Reading / Vocab-in-Context

Strategic Advice: The context of the passage can help reveal the meaning of the word. Insert each choice in the sentence to see which one makes the most sense.

Getting to the Answer: Levin speaks directly to his heart, asking it to behave. Choice (A), "begged," comes closest to meaning the same thing as "conjured" in this context.

9. D

Difficulty: Medium

Category: Reading / Rhetoric

Strategic Advice: Think about the entire scene described in the passage and decide why the author chose to describe Levin's heart as "throbbing."

Getting to the Answer: Choice (D) is the correct answer. The author chose this word to capture Levin's agitated state.

10. A

Difficulty: Hard

Category: Reading / Rhetoric

Strategic Advice: Eliminate answer choices that are clearly not representative of the author's feelings, or attitude, about Levin.

Getting to the Answer: The author presents Levin's situation as one that is painful. The passage's tone suggests that Levin is worthy of the reader's empathy. Choice (A) fits this tone.

Franklin Delano Roosevelt Speech

11. A

Difficulty: Hard

Category: Reading / Rhetoric

Strategic Advice: Watch out for choices that indicate broad supporting goals. The correct answer will reflect the specific intent of President Roosevelt in giving this address.

Getting to the Answer: The introduction to the passage states that President Roosevelt reveals his intention to preserve and spread American democratic ideals. Roosevelt's remarks regarding taxation, patriotism, and sacrifice suggest that he wishes to gain the support of the American people for these goals and to persuade them to connect the fight for global democracy with their own democratic interests. Choice (A) makes clear the president's purpose in winning citizens' support for the battles abroad.

12. D

Difficulty: Hard

Category: Reading / Command of Evidence

Strategic Advice: Be careful of choices that do not provide direct evidence to support the president's purpose. The correct answer will relate specifically to the stated purpose, or intent, of the passage.

Getting to the Answer: President Roosevelt makes clear that his intention is to provide support for global efforts to end tyranny and spread democracy and to garner the support of the American people for these goals. In the previous question, his stated purpose is "to make its people conscious of their individual stake in the preservation of democratic life in America." The two elements of that purpose are the American people and the preservation of democratic life. Only (D) provides direct evidence for the previous question.

13. D

Difficulty: Easy

Category: Reading / Vocab-in-Context

Strategic Advice: All answer choices are alternate meanings of the word "sacrifice." The correct answer will relate directly to the context of the passage.

Getting to the Answer: Despite the fact that Roosevelt gave the speech on the eve of America's involvement in World War II, neither B nor C is the meaning he's after. Choice (D), "surrender of interests to a greater good," is the correct answer.

14. B

Difficulty: Hard

Category: Reading / Inference

Strategic Advice: Keep in mind that you're looking for a relationship that is suggested, not stated. To reach the correct answer, you must infer, or make a logical guess, based on information in the passage.

Getting to the Answer: The correct answer will provide support for the stated purpose of the passage while demonstrating a logical relationship. Choice (B) provides support for the stated goal of winning support among U.S. citizens for the spread of democracy abroad. It does so by suggesting that the security of U.S. democracy depends on the advancement of human rights and freedoms globally.

15. D

Difficulty: Medium

Category: Reading / Command of Evidence

Strategic Advice: Avoid answers that provide evidence for incorrect answers to the previous question. The correct answer will use language reflective of the correct answer above to demonstrate a relationship.

Getting to the Answer: Principles and ideas such as democracy, freedom, and protection of human rights are used interchangeably throughout Roosevelt's

speech. The lines in (D) draw the connection between freedom at home and freedom everywhere.

16. C

Difficulty: Easy

Category: Reading / Vocab-in-Context

Strategic Advice: Substitute each answer choice for the word in question and decide which one fits the context provided in the passage.

Getting to the Answer: In the context of the passage, (C) works best. It draws a distinction between individual citizens' monetary interests, or their pocketbooks, and the cause of patriotism, or the greater good.

17. A

Difficulty: Medium

Category: Reading / Rhetoric

Strategic Advice: Keep in mind that the correct answer will relate directly to the meaning of the elements in the identified lines.

Getting to the Answer: President Roosevelt is arguing against those who would oppose the overarching goal of his speech, namely to recruit American public support for the war effort and the spread of democracy overseas. Choice (A) fits best; Roosevelt asserts that his goals are realistic and attainable, not just idealistic visions, as his opponents might claim.

18. D

Difficulty: Medium

Category: Reading / Rhetoric

Strategic Advice: Be wary of answers like A and B that seem to offer specific advice or state specific goals relevant to the purpose of the passage without suggesting how those goals might be achieved. The correct answer will offer a tool, a condition, or another asset for achieving the passage's claim—in this case, the spread of democracy.

Getting to the Answer: The previous question identifies that President Roosevelt considers the spread of global democracy achievable. This question asks you to identify how the president envisions achieving that purpose. Choice (D) matches the intent. In this line, President Roosevelt identifies "our unity of purpose" as an asset that will help achieve his goal.

19. C
Difficulty: Hard

Category: Reading / Inference

Strategic Advice: Be careful of answers that cite other policies that the president might support that are not related to the lines quoted. The correct answer will relate directly to the specific lines in question.

Getting to the Answer: In this speech, Roosevelt identifies four freedoms that he views the United States as obligated to defend. The freedom from want signifies a commitment to helping struggling populations at home and abroad. Choice (C) fits. The president urges economic understandings among nations to help those in need.

20. C
Difficulty: Medium

Category: Reading / Rhetoric

Strategic Advice: Be careful of answers like A that offer other viable uses of rhetoric within the larger passage. The correct answer will relate specifically to the text cited in the question.

Getting to the Answer: Roosevelt suggests that the preservation of American freedoms cannot exist without the preservation of human rights on a global scale. To cement this connection, he contrasts democratic movements with tyrannical movements occurring in the world. Choice (C) is the correct answer. President Roosevelt references "the so-called new order of tyranny" in order to show what might happen should the United States and the American people not support other nations in their fight against such tyranny.

Women's Suffrage

21. C
Difficulty: Medium

Category: Reading / Rhetoric

Strategic Advice: Keep in mind that the "stance" of an author refers to his or her perspective or attitude toward the topic written about.

Getting to the Answer: The passage is written by a secondary source, such as a scholar or a historian, who is looking back on the events that led to the adoption of the Nineteenth Amendment. It is not written by a primary source, such as a legislator or an advocate in the midst of the movement's events. For this reason, (C) is the correct answer. The author of the passage is most clearly a scholar evaluating not just the motivation of women's suffrage leaders but the key events and impact of the movement as a whole.

22. B
Difficulty: Hard

Category: Reading / Rhetoric

Strategic Advice: Avoid answers like (A) that refer to related issues not relevant to the passage's purpose and answers like (D) that go too far. The correct answer will identify a claim made explicitly in the quote.

Getting to the Answer: In the quote, the author notes that election laws following passage of the Nineteenth Amendment did not secure equal voting rights for all. From this statement, it is fairly clear that other groups of people still needed support for their voting rights. Answer (B) is correct.

23. D
Difficulty: Medium

Category: Reading / Command of Evidence

Strategic Advice: Reread the line quoted in the previous question and notice that it occurs in the passage after ratification of the Nineteenth Amendment. Therefore, the evidence you're looking for will refer to an event that came later.

Getting to the Answer: The author suggests that the Nineteenth Amendment did not win equal voting rights for all citizens but that it did serve as an important step on the way to free and fair elections. Choice (D) demonstrates that a later event expanded voting rights further, to citizens regardless not only of gender but also of race.

24. C
Difficulty: Easy

Category: Reading / Vocab-in-Context

Strategic Advice: Consider the events that are being described in the paragraph in which the word appears. This will help you choose the best answer.

Getting to the Answer: It's clear in this paragraph that the women's suffrage movement was gaining momentum at this time. Events and tactics excited those who supported the movement and attracted more supporters. Therefore, (C) reflects the correct meaning of "galvanized."

25. A
Difficulty: Hard

Category: Reading / Rhetoric

Strategic Advice: Carefully review the paragraph in which the line appears before choosing the best answer.

Getting to the Answer: Choice (A) demonstrates the connection between successfully changing one element (people's minds) in order to change the other (laws).

26. A
Difficulty: Hard

Category: Reading / Inference

Strategic Advice: Be wary of answers like D that go too far in asserting unsubstantiated causal relationships. The correct answer will reference an idea or a relationship that is supported by the content of the passage.

Getting to the Answer: Choice (A) expresses the idea implicit in the passage that the American government responds, sometimes slowly, to the changing needs and sentiments of the American people.

27. D
Difficulty: Hard

Category: Reading / Command of Evidence

Strategic Advice: Watch for answers like A and C that cite specific changes or examples that might seem to support the implicit meaning but do not go far enough. The correct answer will reflect the full relationship or idea described in the implicit meaning.

Getting to the Answer: The correct answer to the previous question states the idea implicit in the passage that the government responds and adapts to changes in U.S. society. This suggests a change that takes place over time. Choice (D) demonstrates the idea that both society and the government have changed over time as the civil rights movement of the late twentieth century overcame social and legal inequalities inherited from earlier in the nation's history.

28. C
Difficulty: Medium

Category: Reading / Detail

Strategic Advice: Be careful of answers that aren't backed by sufficient evidence in the graphic.

Getting to the Answer: The graphic shows proof that women's suffrage unfolded through a series of events over a long period of time. Choice (C) is the correct answer.

29. C

Difficulty: Medium

Category: Reading / Vocab-in-Context

Strategic Advice: Read the sentence in which the word appears. The correct answer should be interchangeable with the word.

Getting to the Answer: The passage states that "Posters . . . called into question the authenticity of a free country with unjust laws." Choice (C) is the correct answer, as "legitimacy" refers to something that is in accordance with established rules or principles.

30. B

Difficulty: Medium

Category: Reading / Inference

Strategic Advice: Be cautious about answers that state true events but that do not directly relate to the content of the question.

Getting to the Answer: Choice (B) is the correct answer. Wilson's framing of the conflict abroad as a fight for democracy and freedom helped women suffragists draw attention to the fact that the U.S. government was fighting for justice abroad while denying justice at home.

31. D

Difficulty: Medium

Category: Reading / Synthesis

Strategic Advice: A question like this is asking you to compare information provided in the graphic with information provided in the passage text. Consider each answer choice as you make your comparison.

Getting to the Answer: Choice (D) is the correct answer. Both the graphic and the passage indicate that women's suffrage gained early victories in several states quite a few years before becoming law at the federal level through passage of the Nineteenth Amendment.

Paired Passages—Genomes

32. B

Difficulty: Medium

Category: Reading / Global

Strategic Advice: Look for the answer choice that describes an idea supported throughout the passage rather than a specific detail.

Getting to the Answer: Collectively, the details in the passage support the idea that the coffee market can be expanded and the profits generated from coffee sales can be increased by applying information gained in sequencing the genome of coffee plants. Choice (B) is the correct answer.

33. B

Difficulty: Hard

Category: Reading / Rhetoric

Strategic Advice: Avoid answers that are not directly supported by evidence in the passage.

Getting to the Answer: Eliminate answers such as A and C, which are not supported by the main idea of the passage. In contrast, there is evidential support for (B). The author would most likely agree that studying other nonhuman primates could be beneficial to people.

34. C

Difficulty: Medium

Category: Reading / Inference

Strategic Advice: Watch out for answer choices that seem plausible but are not directly implied by the evidence in the passage.

Getting to the Answer: Choice (C) is the correct answer. In the last paragraph, the author discusses how research that is currently being conducted could impact the future of coffee production.

35. D

Difficulty: Medium

Category: Reading / Command of Evidence

Strategic Advice: Look back at the previous question. Find the lines from the passage that describe research that could increase the profitability of coffee for producers.

Getting to the Answer: Choice (D) is the correct answer. In the last paragraph, the author describes how current research could lead to a way to produce coffee plants without caffeine in a more cost-effective manner.

36. B

Difficulty: Hard

Category: Reading / Inference

Strategic Advice: Eliminate any answer choices that may sound plausible but take the information presented in the passage too far.

Getting to the Answer: The passage states that the research being conducted on the DNA of gibbons could provide scientists with a way to start figuring out how to prevent cancer and other human ailments. Choice (B) is the correct answer.

37. D

Difficulty: Medium

Category: Reading / Command of Evidence

Strategic Advice: Look at your answer for the previous question. Skim the passage to find the paragraph you used to select your answer.

Getting to the Answer: Choice (D) is the quote from the passage that directly supports the idea that more research would be needed before current findings could be applied to curing diseases in humans.

38. A

Difficulty: Medium

Category: Reading / Rhetoric

Strategic Advice: Remember that you're looking for a statement that expresses the purposes of both passages, not just one.

Getting to the Answer: Both passages discuss how sequencing the genome of a nonhuman organism can benefit people. Therefore, (A) is the correct answer.

39. B

Difficulty: Medium

Category: Reading / Vocab-in-Context

Strategic Advice: Be careful of answer choices that are synonyms for "compelled" but do not make sense in the context in which they're used in the passage.

Getting to the Answer: Choice (B) makes the most sense in context. The scientists felt driven to pursue genome sequencing of the coffee plant.

40. A

Difficulty: Easy

Category: Reading / Vocab-in-Context

Strategic Advice: Replace the word in the sentence with each answer choice and eliminate those that do not make sense in context.

Getting to the Answer: In the context, (A) makes the most sense. "Maintenance" most nearly means "preservation."

41. B
Difficulty: Hard

Category: Reading / Rhetoric

Strategic Advice: Be careful of answer choices that are not directly related to the phrase being considered.

Getting to the Answer: The author of Passage 1 is making a generalization about the coffee industry in order to introduce the main topic to the reader. The author uses the phrase a "pillar of the world economy" to show that the coffee industry plays a vital role in the world economy. Choice (B) is the correct answer.

42. D
Difficulty: Hard

Category: Reading / Synthesis

Strategic Advice: Be careful of answer choices that make inferences based on only one of the passages.

Getting to the Answer: Each passage describes a way that genome sequencing of an organism other than a human has benefited people. Therefore, (D) is the correct answer.

Biomimicry Passage

43. A
Difficulty: Medium

Category: Reading / Global

Strategic Advice: Look for the answer choice that describes an idea supported throughout the passage rather than a specific detail.

Getting to the Answer: The passage cites several examples of biomimicry, the study of how materials and systems found in nature can be replicated to benefit humans. Therefore, (A) is the best summary of the central idea of the passage.

44. B
Difficulty: Medium

Category: Reading / Command of Evidence

Strategic Advice: Think back to why you chose your answer to the previous question. This will help you pick the correct quote as evidence.

Getting to the Answer: Choice (B) is the correct answer because it provides evidence for the central idea that the author presents about the field of biomimicry.

45. A
Difficulty: Hard

Category: Reading / Rhetoric

Strategic Advice: Think about the main idea of the quote. Eliminate any answer choices that don't support this main idea.

Getting to the Answer: The quote explains why architects turn to biomimicry for solutions in their work. Choice (A) is the correct answer.

46. B
Difficulty: Medium

Category: Reading / Inference

Strategic Advice: Reread the paragraph that the question is asking about. Look for specific details about the abalone shrimp shell and soft chalk.

Getting to the Answer: The passage clearly states that the abalone shrimp shell is harder than soft chalk because of the way the basic material composing each is arranged, so (B) is the correct answer.

47. D
Difficulty: Medium

Category: Reading / Rhetoric

Strategic Advice: In order to understand why an author includes a quote from another person, examine the surrounding sentences. This often makes clear the author's reason for including the quotation.

Getting to the Answer: The author includes the quote from Pawlyn to support and strengthen his or her own view that energy efficiency "has never been more important." Therefore, (D) is the correct answer.

48. D
Difficulty: Easy

Category: Reading / Vocab-in-Context

Strategic Advice: Replace the word in question with each of the answer choices. This will help you eliminate the ones that don't make sense in the context.

Getting to the Answer: Choice (D), "theories," is the only answer choice that makes sense in this context.

49. A
Difficulty: Medium

Category: Reading / Inference

Strategic Advice: Keep in mind that you're being asked to make an inference, a logical guess based on information in the passage. Therefore, the correct answer is not stated in a passage.

Getting to the Answer: The variety of examples of biomimicry mentioned in the passage make it reasonable to infer that more scientists will utilize solutions developed through biomimicry in the future. Choice (A) is the correct answer.

50. C
Difficulty: Medium

Category: Reading / Command of Evidence

Strategic Advice: Reread each quotation in the context of the passage. Consider which one is the best evidence to support the inference made in the previous question.

Getting to the Answer: The examples cited in (C) provide strong evidence for the inference that more scientists will probably make use of biomimicry in years to come.

51. D
Difficulty: Medium

Category: Reading / Vocab-in-Context

Strategic Advice: Eliminate answer choices that are synonyms for the word in question but do not work in the context of the sentence.

Getting to the Answer: Because biomimicry is such an innovative approach, it makes sense that the meaning of "radical" in this context is closest to (D), "revolutionary."

52. C
Difficulty: Hard

Category: Reading / Synthesis

Strategic Advice: Remember that a graphic might not refer to something explicitly stated in the passage. Instead, it often provides a visual example of how an important concept discussed in the passage works.

Getting to the Answer: The graphic and its caption help illustrate an example of biomimicry not mentioned in the passage: that of a solar power plant designed to mimic the arrangement of petals in a sunflower. This directs more energy toward the power plant's central tower and improves the efficiency of the power plant. Choice (C) is the correct answer.

WRITING AND LANGUAGE TEST

The Age of the Librarian

1. C
Difficulty: Easy

Category: Writing & Language / Shifts in Construction

Strategic Advice: Examine the verb tense in the rest of the sentence. This will help you find the correct answer.

Getting to the Answer: As written, the sentence switches verb tense midsentence. Other verbs in the sentence, "worked" and "was," indicate that the events happened in the past. Choice (C) is the correct choice because it correctly uses the past tense of the target verb.

2. D
Difficulty: Medium

Category: Writing & Language / Punctuation

Strategic Advice: Pay attention to the quotation marks. Make sure a complete sentence is properly punctuated within the quotation marks.

Getting to the Answer: Reading through the sentence and the answer choices shows that two issues might need correcting. The sentence inside the quotation marks is a complete sentence. The correct answer needs to punctuate that sentence before closing the quote. Additionally, "however" is being used as a connector or transition word and needs to be followed by a comma after beginning the new sentence. Choice (D) appropriately uses a period prior to the end quotes and correctly inserts a comma after the transition "However."

3. B
Difficulty: Medium

Category: Writing & Language / Effective Language Use

Strategic Advice: Watch out for choices that distort the tone of the passage.

Getting to the Answer: The passage suggests that people expected or anticipated that Harris would become a librarian. Evidence for this idea is found in the statement that she was "constantly told" that she "should be studying to be a librarian." Harris was certainly aware that people anticipated this course of study for her, but the presence of the phrase "Little did she realize" tells you that she didn't expect to become one. The correct choice is (B), "imminent," meaning that becoming a librarian was about to occur despite her own expectations.

4. C
Difficulty: Hard

Category: Writing & Language / Effective Language Use

Strategic Advice: Read the sentence carefully for context clues. Also, think about the tone of what is being described. This will help you choose the best answer.

Getting to the Answer: Given the phrasing of the sentence, the answer must be close in meaning to "excited," which is used earlier in the sentence. Therefore, (C) is the correct answer.

5. A
Difficulty: Medium

Category: Writing & Language / Punctuation

Strategic Advice: Determine whether a clause is independent or dependent to decide between a comma and a semicolon.

Getting to the Answer: Choice (A) is the correct answer. The sentence is correctly punctuated as written because it uses a comma at the end of the introductory clause.

6. C

Difficulty: Medium

Category: Writing & Language / Sentence Formation

Strategic Advice: Read the sentence carefully. The sentence sounds clunky and awkward. Look for an answer choice that makes the sentence clear and easy to understand. Notice that the word "asking" is part of a participial phrase that modifies "Miguel."

Getting to the Answer: A participial phrase should be placed as close as possible to the noun it modifies. When a participial phrase begins a sentence, it should be set off with a comma.

Choice (C) is correct. The placement of commas and modifiers makes the content easy to understand, and the sentence is free of grammatical or punctuation errors.

7. B

Difficulty: Medium

Category: Writing & Language / Development

Strategic Advice: Read the entire paragraph carefully and predict the main idea. Then look for a close match with your prediction.

Getting to the Answer: The paragraph discusses how the role of librarian has changed due to an increased use of technology. Choice (B) is the correct answer, as it explicitly addresses the changing role of the librarian due to technology.

8. D

Difficulty: Medium

Category: Writing & Language / Sentence Formation

Strategic Advice: Read the sentence and note the series of examples. A series should have parallel structure.

Getting to the Answer: The sentence is not correct as written. The items in the series switch forms from participial phrases beginning with "enabling" and "offering" to "they house." All of the items need to fit the same pattern or form. Choice (D) is correct because it appropriately begins each item in the series with a participle.

9. C

Difficulty: Hard

Category: Writing & Language / Development

Strategic Advice: Don't be fooled by answer choices that are true statements but do not directly support the main idea of the paragraph.

Getting to the Answer: The paragraph concerns how the role of librarian has changed due to an increased use of technology. The correct answer needs to support the idea that librarians work with technology in new ways. Choice (C) works best. It offers a specific example of how teachers look to the librarian to be a "media mentor" and illustrates this new role for school librarians.

10. C

Difficulty: Easy

Category: Writing & Language / Usage

Strategic Advice: Read the sentence prior to the pronoun and determine whom the pronoun is referencing. Pronouns should not be ambiguous, and they must match the verb in number.

Getting to the Answer: The sentence is ambiguous as written. "She" would presumably refer back to the "young student" but it seems unlikely that the student would be laughing and thinking about the collections in the library after asking the librarian a question. Choice (C) is the best choice. It clearly indicates the subject of the sentence (Harris) and avoids ambiguity.

11. A

Difficulty: Medium

Category: Writing & Language / Usage

Strategic Advice: Figure out whom the pronoun refers to and make sure it matches the antecedent in number. Watch out for confusing contractions and possessives.

Getting to the Answer: The pronoun in the sentence needs to indicate who will have the ideas. Harris is talking to a single student, so you will need a singular possessive pronoun.

Choice (A) is correct. As it is, the sentence correctly uses a singular possessive pronoun.

Unforeseen Consequences: The Dark Side of the Industrial Revolution

12. B

Difficulty: Medium

Category: Writing & Language / Sentence Formation

Strategic Advice: Be careful of answers that sound correct when they stand alone but do not conform to the structure of the sentence as a whole.

Getting to the Answer: The existing text is incorrect, as it does not maintain parallel structure. Choice (B) is the correct answer, as it maintains the parallel structure of preposition ("into") + noun ("the role").

13. B

Difficulty: Easy

Category: Writing & Language / Punctuation

Strategic Advice: Eliminate answers that confuse the usage of commas and semicolons.

Getting to the Answer: Choice (B) is correct. Without the comma, the following clause modifies "urban areas" when it should modify the entire preceding clause.

14. B

Difficulty: Medium

Category: Writing & Language / Effective Language Use

Strategic Advice: Avoid choices that are redundant and imprecise. The correct answer will use the clearest, most concise terminology to communicate the idea.

Getting to the Answer: Choice (B) is correct. It is the most concise—and clearest—word choice. The other choices use more words than necessary to convey meaning.

15. A

Difficulty: Medium

Category: Writing & Language / Organization

Strategic Advice: The first sentence should function as a transition between ideas in the previous paragraph and ideas in the current paragraph.

Getting to the Answer: Choice (A) makes sense. This choice connects ideas from the previous paragraph with the content of paragraph 3. The sentences that follow provide details to support that introductory idea.

16. A

Difficulty: Hard

Category: Writing & Language / Development

Strategic Advice: Eliminate answers like B that fail to directly support the cited sentence.

Getting to the Answer: The underlined sentence references "unprecedented amounts of human-made carbon dioxide into the air." This suggests an increase in the amount of carbon dioxide in the atmosphere over time. Therefore, (A) is the correct answer.

17. C
Difficulty: Medium

Category: Writing & Language / Effective Language Use

Strategic Advice: Choose the answer that presents the correct relationship between ideas.

Getting to the Answer: Choice (C) is correct. It shows the causal relationship without adding unnecessary verbiage.

18. A
Difficulty: Easy

Category: Writing & Language / Effective Language Use

Strategic Advice: Plug in the answer choices and select the one that reflects a specific meaning relevant to the sentence.

Getting to the Answer: The paragraph focuses on the negative effects of industrialization and waste production. Therefore, (A) is the correct answer.

19. B
Difficulty: Hard

Category: Writing & Language / Development

Strategic Advice: Be careful of choices that relate to the underlined portion of the text without showing clearly how the underlined portion supports the full implication of the preceding sentence.

Getting to the Answer: The paragraph explains that industrialization resulted in the destruction of resources. The correct answer, (B), serves as clear evidence of the "process of destruction and reduced resources."

20. C
Difficulty: Medium

Category: Writing & Language / Effective Language Use

Strategic Advice: Be careful of answers that make sense but do not fully support the meaning of the content. The correct answer will not only flow logically but will also reflect the precise purpose and meaning of the larger sentence and paragraph.

Getting to the Answer: Choice (C) is the correct answer. "Substandard" communicates clearly that the working conditions were the cause of the health problems.

21. D
Difficulty: Medium

Category: Writing & Language / Sentence Formation

Strategic Advice: Eliminate choices that result in sentence fragments or fragmented clauses. The correct answer will maintain appropriate syntax without misusing punctuation.

Getting to the Answer: Choice (D) is correct. It sets off the dependent clause without using incorrect punctuation to signal a hard break before an independent clause or second complete sentence.

22. D
Difficulty: Hard

Category: Writing & Language / Development

Strategic Advice: Avoid answers that draw on similar ideas but combine those ideas in a way that communicates a proposition not supported by the essay as a whole. The correct answer will make sense within the larger context of the essay.

Getting to the Answer: The central idea of the entire essay is that industrialization and progress came at a cost that made the promise of a bright future difficult to fulfill. Choice (D) is the correct answer.

Remembering Freud

23. C
Difficulty: Hard

Category: Writing & Language / Effective Language Use

Strategic Advice: Consider the fact that there may be a choice that helps make the meaning of the sentence very precise.

Getting to the Answer: Choice (C) most accurately indicates that Freud led a whole movement.

24. B
Difficulty: Medium

Category: Writing & Language / Punctuation

Strategic Advice: Plug in each answer choice and select the one that seems most correct.

Getting to the Answer: Choice (B) makes it clear to the reader that this is extra information modifying the word "career."

25. D
Difficulty: Medium

Category: Writing & Language / Sentence Formation

Strategic Advice: Remember that in a list, all things listed should be presented with the same grammatical structure.

Getting to the Answer: "Id," "ego," and "Freudian slip" are all nouns. Choice (D) is the correct answer because it uses a parallel structure for all three nouns.

26. B
Difficulty: Hard

Category: Writing & Language / Development

Strategic Advice: Notice that the underlined sentence is the first sentence in the paragraph. Think about which choice would make the best topic sentence, given the content of the rest of the paragraph.

Getting to the Answer: Choice (B) correctly makes the free-speaking technique the focus of the paragraph's topic sentence, while suggesting that the technique was radical enough to earn Freud his title.

27. B
Difficulty: Medium

Category: Writing & Language / Effective Language Use

Strategic Advice: Eliminate any choices that don't seem as precise as others.

Getting to the Answer: Choice (B) is correct. The word "recesses" is more precise; it connotes smaller parts of the brain and a sense of being hidden.

28. C
Difficulty: Easy

Category: Writing & Language / Punctuation

Strategic Advice: Try reading the sentence in question aloud. This often helps you get a good sense of whether or not a comma is needed.

Getting to the Answer: Choice (C) would fit here. The sentence eliminates the unneeded comma and is a correct sentence.

29. B
Difficulty: Hard

Category: Writing & Language / Sentence Formation

Strategic Advice: Remember that a modifier should be adjacent to the noun it is modifying and set off by punctuation.

Getting to the Answer: Choice (B) is correct. The modifier "like neurosis or other psychological trauma" should come directly after "conditions."

30. C

Difficulty: Hard

Category: Writing & Language / Development

Strategic Advice: Consider how this sentence relates to the one before it and the one that follows it. Does it offer strong support of the connecting ideas?

Getting to the Answer: This section discussed the development and lasting influence of Freud's ideas. The best supporting sentence will provide details connecting these concepts. Choice (C) is correct. It emphasizes that Freud developed new ideas that have had a lasting influence on psychological practices.

31. B

Difficulty: Medium

Category: Writing & Language / Sentence Formation

Strategic Advice: Notice that you are dealing with a run-on sentence. Identify the point in the run-on where it appears two sentences have been fused together.

Getting to the Answer: Choice (B) is correct. This choice splits the run-on sentence into two separate, grammatical sentences.

32. D

Difficulty: Easy

Category: Writing & Language / Sentence Formation

Strategic Advice: Eliminate answer choices that are not complete sentences or do not maintain the correct verb tense.

Getting to the Answer: Choice (D) correctly changes the phrase "Freud's finding of a method" to "Freud found a method," making the sentence complete. It also corrects the verb tense.

33. A

Difficulty: Hard

Category: Writing & Language / Sentence Formation

Strategic Advice: Recall that when a dependent clause precedes an independent clause, it should be set off with a comma.

Getting to the Answer: Choice (A) is the best choice. Although lengthy, the dependent clause in the sentence ("So as long as occasions arise . . . ") is correctly combined with its independent clause ("Sigmund Freud will be remembered . . . ") by use of a comma.

Success in Montreal

34. B

Difficulty: Easy

Category: Writing & Language / Sentence Formation

Strategic Advice: Always check whether two or more verbs that serve the same function have a parallel structure.

Getting to the Answer: Choice (B) is correct. "To prevent" is in the infinitive form like the first verb in the sentence, "to reverse."

35. A

Difficulty: Hard

Category: Writing & Language / Effective Language Use

Strategic Advice: Look for the choice that most concisely and correctly joins the two sentences.

Getting to the Answer: Choice (A) is the best fit. This option joins the sentences concisely and correctly.

36. C

Difficulty: Medium

Category: Writing & Language / Effective Language Use

Strategic Advice: Remember that the best answer is the most concise and effective way of stating the information while ensuring that the information is complete.

Getting to the Answer: Choice (C) works best here. It uses the fewest necessary words to convey the complete information.

37. C
Difficulty: Medium

Category: Writing & Language / Sentence Formation

Strategic Advice: Eliminate any choices that use transition words inappropriately.

Getting to the Answer: Two complete thoughts should be separated into two different sentences. Therefore, (C) is the best choice.

38. B
Difficulty: Hard

Category: Writing & Language / Quantitative

Strategic Advice: Examine the graphic for details that suggest which answer is correct.

Getting to the Answer: Choice (B) accurately reflects the information in the graphic. Beginning in the 1990s, the size of the ozone hole began to level off.

39. C
Difficulty: Medium

Category: Writing & Language / Effective Language Use

Strategic Advice: Check each word to see how it fits with the context of the sentence.

Getting to the Answer: While all of the words have similar meanings, only one fits the context of the paragraph. Choice (C), "measured," has a connotation that corresponds to "gauge" in the following sentence.

40. B
Difficulty: Easy

Category: Writing & Language / Usage

Strategic Advice: Remember that the possessive form must agree with its antecedent.

Getting to the Answer: The correct answer will reflect the gender and number of its antecedent; in this case, the word "treaty." Therefore, (B) is correct.

41. A
Difficulty: Hard

Category: Writing & Language / Development

Strategic Advice: To find the central idea of a paragraph, identify important details and then summarize them in a sentence or two. Then find the choice that is the closest to your summary.

Getting to the Answer: Choice (A) most clearly states the paragraph's central idea.

42. D
Difficulty: Medium

Category: Writing & Language / Development

Strategic Advice: To find the correct answer, first determine the central idea of the paragraph.

Getting to the Answer: Choice (D) is the least essential sentence in the paragraph, so it is the correct answer.

43. D
Difficulty: Medium

Category: Writing & Language / Effective Language Use

Strategic Advice: Context clues tell which word is appropriate in the sentence. Check to see which word fits best in the sentence.

Getting to the Answer: The word "reverse," (D), fits with the context of the sentence and connotes a more precise action than does "change."

44. C

Difficulty: Hard

Category: Writing & Language / Organization

Strategic Advice: Examine the entire paragraph. Decide whether the sentence provides more information about a topic mentioned in one of the other sentences.

Getting to the Answer: This sentence provides more information related to sentence 1, "The Montreal Protocol is a living document"; it describes how the document is "living." Choice (C) is the correct answer.

MATH TEST: NO-CALCULATOR SECTION

1. C

Difficulty: Easy

Category: Heart of Algebra / Linear Equations

Strategic Advice: To determine what the y-intercept could mean in the context of a word problem, examine the labels on the graph and note what each axis represents.

Getting to the Answer: According to the labels, the y-axis represents cost, and the x-axis represents the number of games played. The y-intercept, $(0, 5)$, has an x-value of 0, which means zero games were played, yet there is still a cost of $5. The cost must represent a flat fee that is charged before any games are played, such as an entrance fee to enter the arcade.

2. A

Difficulty: Easy

Category: Passport to Advanced Math / Exponents

Strategic Advice: To divide one rational expression by another, multiply the first expression by the reciprocal (the flip) of the second expression.

Getting to the Answer: Rewrite the division as multiplication, factor any factorable expressions, and then simplify if possible.

$$\frac{3x}{x+5} \div \frac{6}{4x+20} = \frac{3x}{x+5} \cdot \frac{4x+20}{6}$$
$$= \frac{3x}{\cancel{x+5}} \cdot \frac{4\cancel{(x+5)}}{6}$$
$$= \frac{12x}{6}$$
$$= 2x$$

Note that the question also states that $x \neq -5$. This doesn't affect your answer—it is simply stated because the denominators of rational expressions cannot equal 0.

3. D

Difficulty: Easy

Category: Additional Topics in Math / Geometry

Strategic Advice: When the equation of a circle is written in the form $(x - h)^2 + (y - k)^2 = r^2$, the point (h, k) represents the center of the circle on a coordinate plane, and r represents the length of the radius.

Getting to the Answer: To find the area of a circle, use the formula, $A = \pi r^2$. In the equation given in the question, r^2 is the constant on the right-hand side (25)—you don't even need to solve for r because the area formula involves r^2, not r. So, the area is $\pi(25)$ or 25π.

4. C

Difficulty: Easy

Category: Passport to Advanced Math / Functions

Strategic Advice: When using function notation, $f(x)$ is simply another way of saying y, so this question is asking you to find the values of x for which $y = 0$, or in other words, where the graph crosses the x-axis.

Getting to the Answer: The graph crosses the x-axis at the points $(-2, 0)$ and $(3, 0)$, so the values of x for which $f(x) = 0$ are -2 and 3.

5. B

Difficulty: Medium

Category: Heart of Algebra / Linear Equations

Strategic Advice: Choose the best strategy to answer the question. You could start by cross-multiplying to get rid of the denominators, but simplifying the numerators first will make the calculations easier.

Getting to the Answer:

$$\frac{4(d+3)-9}{8} = \frac{10-(2-d)}{6}$$
$$\frac{4d+12-9}{8} = \frac{10-2+d}{6}$$
$$\frac{4d+3}{8} = \frac{8+d}{6}$$
$$6(4d+3) = 8(8+d)$$
$$24d+18 = 64+8d$$
$$16d = 46$$
$$d = \frac{46}{16} = \frac{23}{8}$$

6. D

Difficulty: Medium

Category: Passport to Advanced Math / Functions

Strategic Advice: This is a crossover question, so quickly skim the first couple of sentences. Then look for the relevant information in the last couple of sentences. It may also help to circle the portions of the graph that meet the given requirement.

Getting to the Answer: Because *greater* means *higher* on a graph, the statement $f(t) > g(t)$ translates to "Where is $f(t)$ above $g(t)$?" The solid curve represents f and the dashed curve represents g, so $f > g$ between the years 1960 and 1980 and again between the years 2000 and 2010. Look for these time intervals in the answer choices: $1960 < t < 1980$ and $2000 < t < 2010$.

7. D

Difficulty: Medium

Category: Passport to Advanced Math / Scatterplots

Strategic Advice: Use the shape of the data to predict the type of equation that might be used as a model. Then, use specific values from the graph to choose the correct equation.

Getting to the Answer: According to the graph, the population of the whales grew slowly at first and then more quickly. This means that an exponential model is probably the best fit, so you can eliminate A (linear) and B (quadratic). The remaining equations are both exponential, so choose a data point and see which equation is the closest fit. Be careful—the vertical axis represents *hundreds* of whales, and the question states that *t* represents the number of years since the study began, so $t = 0$ for 1995, $t = 3$ for 1998, and so on. If you use the data for 1995, which is the point (0, 100), the results are the same for both equations, so choose a different point. Using the data for 2007, $t = 2007 - 1995 = 12$, and the number of whales was 800. Substitute these values into C and D to see which one is true. Choice C is not true because $800 \neq 100 \times 2^{12}$. Choice (D) is correct because $800 = 100 \times 2^{\frac{12}{4}} = 100 \times 2^3 = 100 \times 8$ is true.

8. B

Difficulty: Medium

Category: Heart of Algebra / Linear Equations

Strategic Advice: Average rate of change is the same as slope, so use the slope formula.

Getting to the Answer: To find the average rate of change over the 5-year period, find the slope between the starting point (0, 1,200) and the ending point (5, 100).

$$m = \frac{y_2 - y_1}{x_2 - x_1} = \frac{100 - 1,200}{5 - 0} = \frac{-1,100}{5} = -220$$

The average rate of change is negative because the laptop decreases in value over time.

Note: Because the question involves *straight-line* depreciation, you could have used any two points on the graph to find the slope. As a general rule, however, you should use the endpoints of the given time interval.

9. B

Difficulty: Medium

Category: Passport to Advanced Math / Exponents

Strategic Advice: When multiplying polynomials, carefully multiply each term in the first factor by each term in the second factor. This question doesn't ask for the entire product, so check to make sure you answered the right question (the coefficient of x^2).

Getting to the Answer:

$$6x^2 - \frac{2}{5}x + 1 \left(10x + \frac{1}{3} \right)$$

$$= 6x^2 \left(10x + \frac{1}{3} \right) - \frac{2}{5}x \left(10x + \frac{1}{3} \right) + 1 \left(10x + \frac{1}{3} \right)$$

$$= 60x^3 \underline{+ 2x^2 - 4x^2} - \frac{2}{15}x + 10x + \frac{1}{3}$$

The coefficient of x^2 is 2 + (–4) = –2.

10. A

Difficulty: Medium

Category: Heart of Algebra / Linear Equations

Strategic Advice: Notice that there are no grid lines and no numbers on the axes. This is a great clue that the numbers in the equations don't actually matter.

Getting to the Answer: The line is decreasing, so the slope (*m*) is negative. The line crosses the *y*-axis below 0, so the *y*-intercept (*b*) is also negative. Put each answer choice in slope-intercept form, one at a time, and examine the signs of *m* and *b*. Begin with A:

$$-6x - 4y = 5$$
$$-4y = 6x + 5$$
$$y = \frac{6x}{-4} + \frac{5}{-4}$$
$$y = -\frac{3}{2}x - \frac{5}{4}$$

You don't need to check any of the other equations. Choice (A) has a negative slope and a negative *y*-intercept, so it is the correct equation.

11. C

Difficulty: Hard

Category: Heart of Algebra / Systems of Linear Equations

Strategic Advice: Graphically, a system of linear equations that has no solution indicates two parallel lines or, in other words, two lines that have the same slope. So, write each of the equations in slope-intercept form ($y = mx + b$) and set their slopes (*m*) equal to each other to solve for *k*. Before finding the slopes, multiply the top equation by 4 to make it easier to manipulate.

Getting to the Answer:

$$4 \left(\frac{3}{4}x - \frac{1}{2}y = 12 \right) \to 3x - 2y = 48 \to y = \frac{3}{2}x - 24$$

$$kx - 2y = 22 \to -2y = -kx + 22 \to y = \frac{k}{2}x - 11$$

The slope of the first line is $\frac{3}{2}$, and the slope of the second line is $\frac{k}{2}$. Set them equal and solve for *k*.

$$\frac{3}{2} = \frac{k}{2}$$
$$2(3) = 2(k)$$
$$6 = 2k$$
$$3 = k$$

12. B

Difficulty: Hard

Category: Heart of Algebra / Inequalities

Strategic Advice: Pay careful attention to units, particularly when a question involves rates. The $4.00 for the first $\frac{1}{4}$ mile is a flat fee. Before you write the inequality, you need to find the per-mile rate for the remaining miles.

Getting to the Answer: The driver charges $4.00 for the first $\frac{1}{4}$ mile, which is a flat fee, so write 4. The additional charge is $1.50 per $\frac{1}{2}$ mile, or 1.50 times 2 = $3.00 per mile. The number of miles after the first $\frac{1}{4}$ mile is $m - \frac{1}{4}$, so the cost of the trip, not including the first $\frac{1}{4}$ mile, is $3\left(m - \frac{1}{4}\right)$. This means the cost of the whole trip is $4 + 3\left(m - \frac{1}{4}\right)$. The clue "no more than $10" means that much or less, so use the symbol ≤. The inequality is $4 + 3\left(m - \frac{1}{4}\right) \leq 10$, which simplifies to $3.25 + 3m \leq 10$.

13. A

Difficulty: Hard

Category: Passport to Advanced Math / Functions

Strategic Advice: Think about how the transformations affect the graph of $g(x)$ and draw a sketch of $h(x)$ on the same grid. Compare the new graph to each of the answer choices until you find one that is true.

Getting to the Answer: The graph of $h(x) = -g(x) + 1$ is a vertical reflection of $g(x)$, over the x-axis, that is then shifted up 1 unit. The graph looks like the dashed line in the following graph:

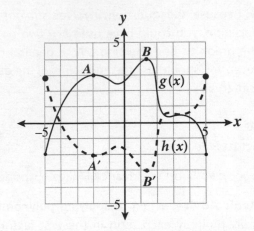

Now, compare the dashed line to each of the answer choices: the range of $h(x)$ is the set of y-values from lowest to highest (based on the dashed line). The lowest point occurs at point B' and has a y-value of –3; the highest value occurs at both ends of the graph and is 3, so the range is $-3 \leq y \leq 3$. This means (A) is correct and you can move on to the next question. Don't waste valuable time checking the other answer choices unless you are not sure about the range. (Choice B: The minimum value of $h(x)$ is –3, not –4. Choice C: The coordinates of point A on $h(x)$ are (–2, –2), not (2, 4). Choice D: the graph of $h(x)$ is decreasing, not increasing, between $x = -5$ and $x = -2$.)

14. D

Difficulty: Medium

Category: Additional Topics in Math / Imaginary Numbers

Strategic Advice: Multiply the two complex numbers just as you would two binomials (using FOIL). Then, combine like terms and use the definition $i^2 = -1$ to simplify the result.

Getting to the Answer:

$$(3+2i)(5-i) = 3(5-i) + 2i(5-i)$$
$$= 15 - 3i + 10i - 2i^2$$
$$= 15 + 7i - 2(-1)$$
$$= 15 + 7i + 2$$
$$= 17 + 7i$$

The question asks for a in $a + bi$, so the correct answer is 17.

15. A
Difficulty: Hard

Category: Passport to Advanced Math / Exponents

Strategic Advice: Think of the rate given in the question in terms of the constant term you see on the right-hand side of the equation. Working together, the two treatment plants can filter the water in 72 hours. This is equivalent to saying that they can filter $\frac{1}{72}$ of the water in 1 hour.

Getting to the Answer: If $\frac{1}{72}$ is the portion of the water the two treatment plants can filter *together*, then each term on the left side of the equation represents the portion that each plant can filter *individually* in 1 hour. Because the new facility is 4 times as fast as the older facility, $\frac{4}{x}$ represents the portion of the water the new plant can filter in 1 hour, and $\frac{1}{x}$ represents the portion of the water the older plant can filter in 1 hour.

16. 20
Difficulty: Medium

Category: Heart of Algebra / Linear Equations

Strategic Advice: Only one equation is given, and it has two variables. This means that you don't have enough information to solve for either variable. Instead, look for the relationship between the variable terms in the equation and those in the expression that you are trying to find, $x + 2y$.

Getting to the Answer: First, move the y-term to the left side of the equation to make it look more like the expression you are trying to find. The expression doesn't have fractions, so clear the fractions in the equation by multiplying both sides by 4. This yields the expression that you are looking for, $x + 2y$, so no further work is required—just read the value on the right-hand side of the equation. The answer is 20.

$$\frac{1}{4}x = 5 - \frac{1}{2}y$$
$$\frac{1}{4}x + \frac{1}{2}y = 5$$
$$4\left(\frac{1}{4}x + \frac{1}{2}y\right) = 4(5)$$
$$x + 2y = 20$$

17. 1
Difficulty: Medium

Category: Heart of Algebra / Inequalities

Strategic Advice: This question is extremely difficult to answer unless you draw a sketch. It doesn't have to be perfect—you just need to get an idea of where the solution region is. Don't forget to flip the inequality symbol when you graph the second equation.

Getting to the Answer: Sketch the system.

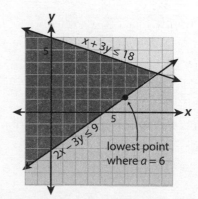

If (a, b) is a solution to the system, then a is the x-coordinate of any point in the darkest shaded region and b is the corresponding y-coordinate. When $a = 6$, the minimum possible value for b lies on the lower boundary line, $2x - 3y \leq 9$. It looks like the y-coordinate is 1, but to be sure, substitute $x = 6$ into the equation and solve for y. You can use = in the equation, instead of the inequality symbol, because you are finding a point on the boundary line.

$$2x - 3y = 9$$
$$2(6) - 3y = 9$$
$$12 - 3y = 9$$
$$-3y = -3$$
$$y = 1$$

18. 2
Difficulty: Hard

Category: Passport to Advanced Math / Exponents

Strategic Advice: Rewrite the radicals as fraction exponents: $\sqrt{x} = x^{\frac{1}{2}}$ and $\sqrt[3]{x} = x^{\frac{1}{3}}$.

Getting to the Answer: Write each factor in the expression in exponential form. Then use the rules of exponents to simplify the expression. Add the exponents of the factors that are being multiplied and subtract the exponent of the factor that is being divided:

$$\frac{\sqrt{x} \cdot x^{\frac{5}{6}} \cdot x}{\sqrt[3]{x}} = \frac{x^{\frac{1}{2}} \cdot x^{\frac{5}{6}} \cdot x^{1}}{x^{\frac{1}{3}}}$$

$$= x^{\frac{1}{2} + \frac{5}{6} + \frac{1}{1} - \frac{1}{3}}$$

$$= x^{\frac{3}{6} + \frac{5}{6} + \frac{6}{6} - \frac{2}{6}}$$

$$= x^{\frac{12}{6}} = x^2$$

Because n is the power of x, the value of n is 2.

19. 14
Difficulty: Hard

Category: Additional Topics in Math / Geometry

Strategic Advice: The shaded region is the area of the larger triangle minus the area of the smaller triangle. Set up and solve an equation using the information from the figure. Before you grid in your answer, check that you answered the right question (height of larger triangle).

Getting to the Answer: You don't know the height of the smaller triangle, so call it h. You do know the area of the shaded region—it's 52 square units.

Larger triangle: base = 12; height = $h + 3 + 3$

Smaller triangle: base = 8; height = h

Shaded area = large area − small area

$$52 = \frac{1}{2}(12)(h+6) - \frac{1}{2}(8)(h)$$

$$52 = 6(h+6) - 4h$$
$$52 = 6h + 36 - 4h$$
$$52 = 2h + 36$$
$$16 = 2h$$
$$8 = h$$

The question asks for the height of the *larger* triangle, so the correct answer is $8 + 3 + 3 = 14$.

20. 6
Difficulty: Hard

Category: Passport to Advanced Math / Quadratics

Strategic Advice: The highest power of x in the equation is 2, so the function is quadratic. Writing quadratic equations can be tricky and time-consuming. If you know the roots, you can use factors to write the equation. If you don't know the roots, you need to create a system of equations to find the coefficients of the variable terms.

Getting to the Answer: You don't know the roots of this equation, so start with the point that has the easiest values to work with, (0, 1), and substitute them into the equation $y = ax^2 + bx + c$.

$$1 = a(0)^2 + b(0) + c$$

$$1 = c$$

Now your equation looks like $y = ax^2 + bx + 1$. Next, use the other two points to create a system of two equations in two variables.

$$(-3, 10) \rightarrow 10 = a(-3)^2 + b(-3) + 1 \rightarrow 9 = 9a - 3b$$

$$(2, 15) \rightarrow 15 = a(2)^2 + b(2) + 1 \rightarrow 14 = 4a + 2b$$

You now have a system of equations to solve. None of the variables has a coefficient of 1, so use elimination to solve the system. If you multiply the top equation by 2 and the bottom equation by 3, the b-terms will eliminate each other.

$$2[9a - 3b = 9] \rightarrow 18a - 6b = 18$$
$$3[4a + 2b = 14] \rightarrow \underline{12a + 6b = 42}$$
$$30a = 60$$
$$a = 2$$

Now, find b by substituting $a = 2$ into either of the original equations. Using the top equation, you get:

$$9(2) - 3b = 9$$
$$18 - 3b = 9$$
$$-3b = -9$$
$$b = 3$$

The value of $a + b + c$ is $2 + 3 + 1 = 6$.

MATH TEST: CALCULATOR SECTION

1. C
Difficulty: Easy

Category: Problem Solving and Data Analysis / Rates, Ratios, Proportions, and Percentages

Strategic Advice: You can use the formula $\text{Percent} = \dfrac{\text{Part}}{\text{Whole}} \times 100\%$ whenever you know two out of the three quantities.

Getting to the Answer: The clue "all" tells you that the "whole" is what you don't know. The percent is 96.5, and the part is 321,000,000.

$$96.5 = \frac{321,000,000}{w} \times 100\%$$
$$96.5w = 32,100,000,000$$
$$w = \frac{32,100,000,000}{96.5}$$
$$w = 332,642,487$$

The answer choices are rounded to the nearest thousand, so the answer is 332,642,000.

2. C
Difficulty: Easy

Category: Heart of Algebra / Linear Equations

Strategic Advice: A *one-time* fee does not depend on the variable and is therefore a constant. A unit rate, however, is always multiplied by the independent variable.

Getting to the Answer: The total cost consists of the site visit fee (a constant), an hourly cost (which depends on the number of hours), and the cost of the materials (which are taxed). The constant in the equation is 75 and is therefore the site visit fee; 45 is being multiplied by h (the number of hours), so $45 must be the hourly rate. That leaves the remaining term, 1.06(82.5), which must be the cost of the materials ($82.50) plus a 6% tax.

3. D

Difficulty: Easy

Category: Heart of Algebra / Inequalities

Strategic Advice: The intersection (overlap) of the two shaded regions is the solution to the system of inequalities. Check each point to see whether it lies in the region with the darkest shading. Don't forget to check that you answered the right question—you are looking for the point that is *not* a solution to the system.

Getting to the Answer: Each of the first three points clearly lies in the overlap. The point (3, 3) looks like it lies on the dashed line, which means it is *not* included in the solution. To check this, plug (3, 3) into the easier inequality: $3 \not> 3$ (3 is equal to itself, not greater than itself), so (D) is correct.

4. A

Difficulty: Easy

Category: Passport to Advanced Math / Quadratics

Strategic Advice: Quadratic equations can be written in several forms, each of which reveals something special about the graph. For example, the vertex form of a quadratic equation gives the minimum or maximum value of the function, while the standard form reveals the *y*-intercept.

Getting to the Answer: The factored form of a quadratic equation reveals the solutions to the equation, which graphically represent the *x*-intercepts. Choice (A) is the only equation written in this form and therefore must be correct. You can set each factor equal to 0 and solve to find that the *x*-intercepts of the graph are $x = \dfrac{5}{2}$ and $x = -1$.

5. B

Difficulty: Easy

Category: Problem Solving and Data Analysis / Rates, Ratios, Proportions, and Percentages

Strategic Advice: Break the question into steps. Before you can use the ratio, you need to find the percent of the students who answered either "Foreign Policy" or "Environment."

Getting to the Answer: The ratio given in the question is 5:3, so write this as 5 parts "Foreign Policy" and 3 parts "Environment." You don't know how big a *part* is, so call it *x*. This means that $5x + 3x =$ the percent of the students who answered either "Foreign Policy" or "Environment," which is 100% – all the other answers:

$$100 - (16 + 14 + 9 + 5) = 100 - 44 = 56$$
$$5x + 3x = 56$$
$$8x = 56$$
$$x = 7$$

Each part has a value of 7, and 3 parts answered "Environment," so the correct percentage is 3(7) = 21%.

6. C

Difficulty: Easy

Category: Heart of Algebra / Linear Equations

Strategic Advice: Don't peek at the answers. They may confuse you because the numbers look different from the ones given in the question. Instead, write your own equation in words first and then translate from English to math.

Getting to the Answer: Keep in mind that the shirts are on sale but the tie is not. The shirts are 40% off, which means that Marco only pays 100 – 40 = 60% of the price, or 0.6(35).

Cost = (Shirt price times how many) plus (Tie price times how many)

$$C = 0.6(35)x + 21(2)$$

This is not one of the answer choices, so simplify to get $C = 21x + 42$.

There are variables in the answer choices, so you could also use the Picking Numbers strategy to answer this question.

7. D

Difficulty: Easy

Category: Problem Solving and Data Analysis / Statistics and Probability

Strategic Advice: Your only choice for this question is to compare each statement to the figure. Don't waste time trying to figure out the exact value for each bar—an estimate is good enough to determine whether each statement is true.

Getting to the Answer: Choice A is incorrect because the price in 2008 was slightly less (not more) than $3.50, while the price in 2013 was right around $3.50. Choice B is incorrect because the price in 2003 was more than $2.00, and the price in 2013 was not more than twice that ($4.00). Choice C is incorrect because the price in 2008 was about $3.25 and the price in 2009 was about $2.75—this is not a difference of more than $1.00. This means (D) must be correct. You don't have to check it—just move on. (Between 2003 and 2008, the change in price was about $3.40 − $2.30 = $1.10; between 2008 and 2013, the change in price was only about $3.50 − $3.40 = $0.10; the change in price was greater between 2003 and 2008.)

8. B

Difficulty: Medium

Category: Heart of Algebra / Systems of Linear Equations

Strategic Advice: Because none of the variable terms has a coefficient of 1, solve the system of equations using elimination by addition (combining the equations). Before you choose an answer, check that you answered the right question (the sum of x and y).

Getting to the Answer: Multiply the top equation by 2 to eliminate the terms that have y's in them.

$$
\begin{array}{l}
2[-2x+5y=1] \to -4x+10y=2 \\
7x-10y=-11 \to \underline{7x-10y=-11} \\
 3x = -9 \\
 x = -3
\end{array}
$$

Now, substitute the result into either of the original equations and simplify to find y:

$$
\begin{aligned}
-2x+5y &= 1 \\
-2(-3)+5y &= 1 \\
6+5y &= 1 \\
5y &= -5 \\
y &= -1
\end{aligned}
$$

The question asks for the *sum*, so add x and y to get $-3 + (-1) = -4$.

9. A

Difficulty: Medium

Category: Heart of Algebra / Systems of Linear Equations

Strategic Advice: Take a quick peek at the answers just to see what variables are being used, but don't study the equations. Instead, write your own system using the same variables as given in the answer choices.

Getting to the Answer: One of the equations in the system should represent the sum of the two resistors ($R_1 + R_2$), which is equal to 294. This means you can eliminate C and D. The second equation needs to satisfy the condition that R_2 is 6 less than twice R_1, or $R_2 = 2R_1 - 6$. This means (A) is correct.

10. C

Difficulty: Medium

Category: Heart of Algebra / Linear Equations

Strategic Advice: Use the distributive property to simplify each of the terms that contains parentheses. Then use inverse operations to solve for x.

Getting to the Answer:

$$\frac{2}{\cancel{5}}\left(\cancel{5}x\right)+2(x-1)=4(x+1)-2$$

$$2x+2x-2=4x+4-2$$

$$4x-2=4x+2$$

$$-2\neq 2$$

All of the variable terms cancel out, and the resulting numerical statement is false (because negative 2 does not equal positive 2), so there is no solution to the equation. Put another way, there is no value of x for which the equation is true.

11. B

Difficulty: Medium

Category: Additional Topics in Math / Geometry

Strategic Advice: Think about this question logically before you start writing things down—after it's transferred, the volume of the oil in the cylindrical container will be the same volume as the rectangular container, so you need to set the two volumes equal and solve for h.

Getting to the Answer: The volume of the rectangular container is $4 \times 9 \times 10$, or 360 cubic meters. The volume of a cylinder equals the area of its base times its height, or $\pi r^2 h$. Because the diameter is 6 meters, the radius, r, is half that, or 3 meters. Now we're ready to set up an equation and solve for h (which is the height of the cylinder, or in this case, the length of the transportation container):

Volume of oil $=$ Volume of rectangular container

$$\pi(3)^2 h = 360$$

$$9\pi h = 360$$

$$h = \frac{360}{9\pi} = \frac{40}{\pi}$$

12. D

Difficulty: Medium

Category: Problem Solving and Data Analysis / Rates, Ratios, Proportions, and Percentages

Strategic Advice: Even though this question uses the word *percent*, you are never asked to find the actual percent itself. Set this question up as a proportion to get the answer more quickly. Remember, percent change equals amount of change divided by the original amount.

Getting to the Answer:

$$\frac{12-5}{5}=\frac{x-12}{12}$$

$$\frac{7}{5}=\frac{x-12}{12}$$

$$12(7)=5(x-12)$$

$$84=5x-60$$

$$144=5x$$

$$28.8=x$$

13. A

Difficulty: Medium

Category: Passport to Advanced Math / Exponents

Strategic Advice: Don't spend too much time reading the scientific explanation of the equation. Focus on the question at the very end—it's just asking you to solve the equation for d.

Getting to the Answer: First, cross-multiply to get rid of the denominator. Then, divide both sides of the equation by $4\pi b$ to isolate d^2. Finally, take the square root of both sides to find d.

$$b(4\pi d^2) = L$$

$$\frac{\cancel{b}(\cancel{4\pi}d^2)}{\cancel{4\pi}\cancel{b}} = \frac{L}{4\pi b}$$

$$d^2 = \frac{L}{4\pi b}$$

$$\sqrt{d^2} = \sqrt{\frac{L}{4\pi b}}$$

$$d = \sqrt{\frac{L}{4\pi b}}$$

Unfortunately, this is not one of the answer choices, so you'll need to simplify further. You can take the square root of 4 (it's 2), but be careful—it's in the denominator of the fraction, so it comes out of the square root as $\frac{1}{2}$. The simplified equation is $d = \frac{1}{2}\sqrt{\frac{L}{\pi b}}$.

14. D

Difficulty: Easy

Category: Problem Solving and Data Analysis / Statistics and Probability

Strategic Advice: You do not need to use all of the information presented in the table to find the answer. Read the question carefully to make sure you use only what you need.

Getting to the Answer: To calculate the percentage of men in each age group who reported being unemployed in January 2014, divide the number in *that* age group who were unemployed by the total number in *that* age group. There are six age groups but only four answer choices, so don't waste time on the age groups that aren't represented. Choice (D) is correct because $7 \div 152 \approx 0.046 = 4.6\%$, which is a lower percentage than that for any other age group (20 to 24 = 12.5%; 35 to 44 = 4.9%; 45 to 54 = 6.1%).

15. B

Difficulty: Medium

Category: Problem Solving and Data Analysis / Statistics and Probability

Strategic Advice: The follow-up survey targets only those respondents who said they were unemployed, so focus on that column in the table.

Getting to the Answer: There were 6 respondents out of 44 unemployed males who were between the ages of 45 and 54, so the probability is $\frac{6}{44} = 0.1\overline{36}$, or about 13.6%.

16. B

Difficulty: Medium

Category: Passport to Advanced Math / Quadratics

Strategic Advice: Taking the square root is the inverse operation of squaring, and both sides of the equation are already perfect squares, so take their square roots. Then solve the resulting equations. Remember, there will be two equations to solve.

Getting to the Answer:

$$(x-1)^2 = \frac{4}{9}$$

$$\sqrt{(x-1)^2} = \sqrt{\frac{4}{9}}$$

$$x - 1 = \pm\frac{\sqrt{4}}{\sqrt{9}}$$

$$x = 1 \pm \frac{2}{3}$$

Now, simplify each equation: $x = 1 + \frac{2}{3} = \frac{3}{3} + \frac{2}{3} = \frac{5}{3}$ and $x = 1 - \frac{2}{3} = \frac{3}{3} - \frac{2}{3} = \frac{1}{3}$.

17. D

Difficulty: Medium

Category: Heart of Algebra / Linear Equations

Strategic Advice: The key to answering this question is to determine how many darts land in each color ring. If there are 6 darts total and x land in a blue ring, the rest, or $6 - x$, must land in a red ring.

Getting to the Answer: Write the expression in words first: points per blue ring (5) times number of darts in blue ring (x), plus points per red ring (10) times number of darts in red ring ($6 - x$). Now, translate the words into numbers, variables, and operations: $5x + 10(6 - x)$. This is not one of the answer choices, so simplify the expression by distributing the 10 and then combining like terms: $5x + 10(6 - x) = 5x + 60 - 10x = 60 - 5x$.

18. A

Difficulty: Medium

Category: Problem Solving and Data Analysis / Statistics and Probability

Strategic Advice: This is a science crossover question. Read the first two sentences quickly—they are simply describing the context of the question. The last two sentences pose the question, so read those more carefully.

Getting to the Answer: In the sample, 184 out of 200 square feet were free of red tide after applying the spray. This is $\frac{184}{200} = 0.92 = 92\%$ of the area. For the whole beach, $0.92(10,000) = 9,200$ square feet should be free of the red tide. Be careful—this is *not* the answer. The question asks how much of the beach would still be covered by red tide, so subtract to get $10,000 - 9,200 = 800$ square feet.

19. A

Difficulty: Medium

Category: Passport to Advanced Math / Quadratics

Strategic Advice: The solution to a system of equations is the point(s) where their graphs intersect. You can solve the system algebraically by setting the equations equal to each other, or you can solve it graphically using your calculator. Use whichever method gets you to the answer more quickly.

Getting to the Answer: Both equations are given in calculator-friendly format ($y = \ldots$), so graphing them is probably the more efficient approach. The graph looks like:

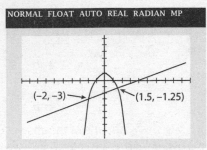

The solution point in the question is given as (a, b), so b represents the y-coordinate of the solution. The y-coordinates of the points of intersection are -3 and -1.25, so choice (A) is correct.

20. A

Difficulty: Medium

Category: Passport to Advanced Math / Functions

Strategic Advice: Don't answer this question too quickly—you may be tempted to substitute 3 for x, but 3 is the output (range), not the input (domain).

Getting to the Answer: The given range value is an output value, so substitute 3 for $g(x)$ and use inverse operations to solve for x, which is the corresponding domain value.

$$g(x) = \frac{2}{3}x + 7$$
$$3 = \frac{2}{3}x + 7$$
$$-4 = \frac{2}{3}x$$
$$-12 = 2x$$
$$-6 = x$$

You could also graph the function and find the value of x (the domain value) for which the value of y (the range value) is 3. The point on the graph is $(-6, 3)$.

21. C

Difficulty: Medium

Category: Heart of Algebra / Linear Equations

Strategic Advice: Don't peek at the answers. Write your own equation using the initial cost and the rate of change in the value of the lawn mower. Remember —when something changes at a constant rate, it can be represented by a linear equation.

Getting to the Answer: When a linear equation in the form $y = mx + b$ is used to model a real-world scenario, m represents the constant rate of change, and b represents the starting amount. Here, the starting amount is easy—it's the purchase price, $2,800. To find the rate of change, think of the initial cost as the value at 0 years, or the point (0, 2,800), and the salvage amount as the value at 8 years, or the point (8, 240). Substitute these points into the slope formula to find that $m = \dfrac{y_2 - y_1}{x_2 - x_1} = \dfrac{240 - 2,800}{8 - 0} = \dfrac{-2,560}{8} = -320$, so the equation is $y = -320x + 2,800$.

22. D

Difficulty: Medium

Category: Problem Solving and Data Analysis / Functions

Strategic Advice: Determine whether the change in the number of bacteria is a common difference (linear function) or a common ratio (exponential function) or if the number of bacteria changes direction (quadratic or polynomial function).

Getting to the Answer: The question tells you that the number of bacteria is reduced by half every hour after the antibiotic is applied. The microbiologist started with 20,000, so after one hour, there are 10,000 left, or $20,000 \times \dfrac{1}{2}$. After 2 hours, there are 5,000 left, or $20,000 \times \dfrac{1}{2} \times \dfrac{1}{2}$, and so on. The change in the number of bacteria is a common ratio $\dfrac{1}{2}$,

so the best model is an exponential function of the form $y = a\left(\dfrac{1}{2}\right)^x$. In this scenario, a is 20,000.

23. B

Difficulty: Medium

Category: Problem Solving and Data Analysis / Rates, Ratios, Proportions, and Percentages

Strategic Advice: Let the units in this question guide you to the solution. The speeds of the airplanes are given in miles per hour, but the question asks about the number of miles each airplane can travel in 12 seconds, so convert miles per hour to miles per second.

Getting to the Answer:

Slower airplane:

$$\dfrac{600 \text{ mi}}{\text{hr}} \times \dfrac{1 \text{ hr}}{60 \text{ min}} \times \dfrac{1 \text{ min}}{60 \text{ sec}} \times 12 \text{ sec} = 2 \text{ mi}$$

Faster airplane:

$$\dfrac{720 \text{ mi}}{\text{hr}} \times \dfrac{1 \text{ hr}}{60 \text{ min}} \times \dfrac{1 \text{ min}}{60 \text{ sec}} \times 12 \text{ sec} = 2.4 \text{ mi}$$

The faster plane can travel $2.4 - 2 = 0.4$ miles farther, which is the same as $\dfrac{2}{5}$ miles.

24. C

Difficulty: Medium

Category: Heart of Algebra / Inequalities

Strategic Advice: The best way to answer this question is to pretend you are the worker. How much more would you earn for one hour in Oregon than in Idaho? If you worked 35 hours per week, how much more would this be? If you worked 40 hours per week, how much more would this be?

Getting to the Answer: Based on the data in the table, a worker would earn $9.10 − $7.25 = $1.85 more for one hour of work in Oregon than in Idaho.

If he worked 35 hours per week, he would earn 35(1.85) = $64.75 more. If he worked 40 hours per week, he would earn 40(1.85) = $74 more. So, the worker would earn somewhere between $64.75 and $74 more per week, which can be expressed as the compound inequality $64.75 \leq x \leq 74$.

25. D

Difficulty: Medium

Category: Problem Solving and Data Analysis / Rates, Ratios, Proportions, and Percentages

Strategic Advice: This is another question where the units can help you find the answer. Use the number of vehicles owned to find the total number of miles driven to find the total number of gallons of gas used to find the total tax paid. Phew!

Getting to the Answer:

$$1.75 \ \cancel{\text{vehicles}} \times \frac{11{,}340 \text{ miles}}{\cancel{\text{vehicle}}} = 19{,}845 \text{ miles}$$

$$19{,}845 \ \cancel{\text{miles}} \times \frac{1 \text{ gallon of gas}}{21.4 \ \cancel{\text{miles}}} = 927.336 \text{ gallons}$$

$$927.336 \ \cancel{\text{gallons}} \times \frac{\$0.184}{\cancel{\text{gallon}}} = \$170.63$$

26. C

Difficulty: Medium

Category: Problem Solving and Data Analysis / Scatterplots

Strategic Advice: The average rate of change of a function over a given interval, from a to b, compares the change in the outputs, $f(b) - f(a)$, to the change in the inputs, $b - a$. In other words, it is the slope of the line that connects the endpoints of the interval, so you can use the slope formula.

Getting to the Answer: Look at the quadratic model, not the data points, to find that the endpoints of the given interval, week 2 to week 8, are (2, 280) and (8, 400). The average rate of change is $\frac{400 - 280}{8 - 2} = \frac{120}{6} = 20$.

On average, the dolphin's weight increased by 20 pounds per week.

27. A

Difficulty: Hard

Category: Additional Topics in Math / Geometry

Strategic Advice: In this question, information is given in both the diagram and the text. You need to relate the text to the diagram, one piece of information at a time, to calculate how long the lifeguard ran along the beach and how long he swam. Before you find the swim time, you need to know how *far* he swam.

Getting to the Answer: Whenever you see a right triangle symbol in a diagram, you should think Pythagorean theorem or, in this question, special right triangles. All multiples of 3-4-5 triangles are right triangles, so the length of the lifeguard's swim is the hypotenuse of a 30-40-50 triangle, or 50 feet. Add this number to the diagram. Now calculate the times using the distances and the speeds given. Don't forget the 1 second that the lifeguard paused.

Run time = $60 \ \cancel{\text{ft}} \times \dfrac{1 \sec}{12 \ \cancel{\text{ft}}} = \dfrac{60}{12} = 5 \sec$

Pause time = 1 sec

Swim time = $50 \ \cancel{\text{ft}} \times \dfrac{1 \sec}{5 \ \cancel{\text{ft}}} = \dfrac{50}{5} = 10 \sec$

Total time = 5 + 1 + 10 = 16 seconds

28. B

Difficulty: Hard

Category: Heart of Algebra / Linear Equations

Strategic Advice: Write an equation in words first and then translate from English to math. Finally, rearrange your equation to find what you're interested in, which is the initial amount of gasoline.

Getting to the Answer: Call the initial amount A. After you've written your equation, solve for A.

Amount now (x) = Initial amount (A) minus y, plus 50

$$x = A - y + 50$$
$$x + y - 50 = A$$

The initial amount was $x + y - 50$ gallons. Note that you could also use Picking Numbers to answer this question.

29. B
Difficulty: Hard

Category: Problem Solving and Data Analysis / Statistics and Probability

Strategic Advice: When a question involves reading data from a graph, it is sometimes better to skip an answer choice if it involves long calculations. Skim the answer choices for this question—A involves finding two averages, each of which is composed of 7 data values. Skip this choice for now.

Getting to the Answer: Start with (B). Be careful—you are not looking for places where the line segments are increasing. The y-axis already represents the change in prices, so you are simply counting the number of positive values for the imports (5) and for the exports (4). There are more for the imports, so (B) is correct and you don't need to check any of the other statements. Move on to the next question.

30. D
Difficulty: Hard

Category: Passport to Advanced Math / Exponents

Strategic Advice: The key to answering this question is deciding what you're trying to find. The question tells you that x represents the athlete's swim rate and you are looking for the number of kilometers he swam in one hour—these are the same thing. If you find x (in kilometers per hour), you will know how many kilometers he swam in one hour.

Getting to the Answer: Set the equation equal to the total time, 16.2, and solve for x. To do this, write the variable terms over a common denominator, $10x$, and combine them into a single term. Then cross-multiply and go from there.

$$16.2 = \frac{10}{10} \cdot \frac{3.86}{x} + \frac{180.2}{10x} + \frac{2}{2} \cdot \frac{42.2}{5x}$$
$$16.2 = \frac{38.6}{10x} + \frac{180.2}{10x} + \frac{84.4}{10x}$$
$$16.2 = \frac{303.2}{10x}$$
$$10x(16.2) = 303.2$$
$$162x = 303.2$$
$$x = \frac{303.2}{162} \approx 1.87$$

31. 1
Difficulty: Easy

Category: Heart of Algebra / Linear Equations

Strategic Advice: Choose the best strategy to answer the question. If you distribute the $\frac{2}{3}$, it creates messy calculations. Instead, clear the fraction by multiplying both sides of the equation by 3. Then use the distributive property and inverse operations to solve for x.

Getting to the Answer:

$$\frac{2}{3}(5x + 7) = 8x$$
$$\cancel{3} \cdot \frac{2}{\cancel{3}}(5x + 7) = 3 \cdot 8x$$
$$2(5x + 7) = 24x$$
$$10x + 14 = 24x$$
$$14 = 14x$$
$$1 = x$$

32. 192
Difficulty: Medium

Category: Passport to Advanced Math / Exponents

Strategic Advice: This looks like a word problem, but don't let it intimidate you. Once you read it, you'll see that it boils down to substituting a few given values for the variables and solving the equation.

Getting to the Answer: Before you start substituting values, quickly check that the units given match the units required to use the equation—they do, so proceed. The patient's weight (w) is 150 and the patient's BSA is $2\sqrt{2}$, so the equation becomes $2\sqrt{2} = \sqrt{\dfrac{150h}{3,600}}$. The only variable left in the equation is h, and you are trying to find the patient's height, so you're ready to solve the equation. To do this, square both sides of the equation and then continue using inverse operations. Be careful when you square the left side—you must square both the 2 and the root 2.

$$2\sqrt{2} = \sqrt{\dfrac{150h}{3,600}}$$

$$\left(2\sqrt{2}\right)^2 = \sqrt{\dfrac{150h}{3,600}}^{\,2}$$

$$2^2\left(\sqrt{2}\right)^2 = \dfrac{150h}{3,600}$$

$$4(2) = \dfrac{150h}{3,600}$$

$$28,800 = 150h$$

$$192 = h$$

33. Any value greater than 7 and less than 7.5
Difficulty: Medium

Category: Heart of Algebra / Inequalities

Strategic Advice: You could solve the compound inequality for m and substitute the result into the expression $10m - 5$, but there is a quicker way to answer this question. Look for a relationship between what you're given, the possible values of $-2m + 1$, and what you're looking for, the possible values of $10m - 5$.

Getting to the Answer: Notice that $10m - 5$ is -5 times the expression $-2m + 1$. This means you can answer the question by multiplying all three pieces of the inequality by -5. (Don't forget to flip the inequality symbols because you are multiplying by a negative number.) Then write the inequality with increasing values from left to right.

$$-5 -\dfrac{3}{2} < -5(-2m+1) < -5 -\dfrac{7}{5}$$

$$\dfrac{15}{2} > 10m - 5 > 7$$

$$7 < 10m - 5 < 7.5$$

You can enter any value between (but not including) 7 and 7.5, such as 7.1 or 7.2.

34. 40
Difficulty: Hard

Category: Additional Topics in Math / Geometry

Strategic Advice: Since $\overline{AB}$, $\overline{CD}$, and $\overline{EF}$ are diameters, the sum of x, y, and the interior angle of the shaded region is 180 degrees. The question tells you that the shaded region is $\dfrac{1}{5}$ of the circle, so the interior angle must equal $\dfrac{1}{5}$ of the degrees in the whole circle, or $\dfrac{1}{5}$ of 360.

Getting to the Answer: Use what you know about y (that it is equal to $2x - 12$) and what you know about the shaded region (that it is $\dfrac{1}{5}$ of 360 degrees) to write and solve an equation.

$$x + y + \dfrac{1}{5}(360) = 180$$

$$x + (2x - 12) + 72 = 180$$

$$3x + 60 = 180$$

$$3x = 120$$

$$x = 40$$

35. 14
Difficulty: Hard

Category: Heart of Algebra / Linear Equations

Strategic Advice: When you know the slope and one point on a line, you can use $y = mx + b$ to write the equation. Substitute the slope for m and the coordinates of the point for x and y and then solve for b, the y-intercept of the line.

Getting to the Answer: The slope is given as $-\dfrac{7}{4}$, so substitute this for m. The point is given as $(4, 7)$, so $x = 4$ and $y = 7$. Now, find b.

$$y = mx + b$$

$$7 = -\dfrac{7}{\cancel{4}}(\cancel{4}) + b$$

$$7 = -7 + b$$

$$14 = b$$

The *y*-intercept of the line is 14.

You could also very carefully graph the line using the given point and the slope. Start at (4, 7) and move toward the *y*-axis by rising 7 and running *to the left* 4 (because the slope is negative). You should land at the point (0, 14).

36. 45
Difficulty: Hard

Category: Problem Solving and Data Analysis / Rates, Ratios, Proportions, and Percentages

Strategic Advice: Make a chart that represents rate, time, and distance and fill in what you know. Then use your table to solve for distance. If it took Rory *t* hours to get to the airport, and the total trip took 2 hours and 30 minutes (or 2.5 hours), how long (in terms of *t*) did the return trip take?

Getting to the Answer:

	Rate	Time	Distance
To airport	45 mph	t	d
Back to home	30 mph	$2.5 - t$	d

Now use the formula $d = r \times t$ for both parts of the trip: $d = 45t$ and $d = 30(2.5 - t)$. Because both are equal to *d*, you can set them equal to each other and solve for *t*:

$$45t = 30(2.5 - t)$$
$$45t = 75 - 30t$$
$$75t = 75$$
$$t = 1$$

Now plug back in to solve for *d*:

$$d = 45t$$
$$d = 45(1)$$
$$d = 45$$

37. 10
Difficulty: Medium

Category: Problem Solving and Data Analysis / Rates, Ratios, Proportions, and Percentages

Strategic Advice: You don't need to know chemistry to answer this question. All the information you need is in the table. Use the formula $Percent = \dfrac{Part}{Whole} \times 100\%$.

Getting to the Answer: To use the formula, find the part of the mass represented by the carbon; there is 1 mole of carbon, and it has a mass of 12.011 grams. Next, find the whole mass of the mole of chloroform; 1 mole carbon (12.011 g) + 1 mole hydrogen (1.008 g) + 3 moles chlorine (3 × 35.453 = 106.359 g) = 12.011 + 1.008 + 106.359 = 119.378. Now use the formula:

$$Percent = \frac{12.011}{119.378} \times 100\%$$
$$= 0.10053 \times 100\%$$
$$= 10.053\%$$

Before you grid in your answer, make sure you follow the directions—round to the nearest whole percent, which is 10.

38. 12
Difficulty: Hard

Category: Problem Solving and Data Analysis / Rates, Ratios, Proportions, and Percentages

Strategic Advice: This part of the question contains several steps. Think about the units given in the question and how you can use what you know to find what you need.

Getting to the Answer: Start with grams of chloroform; the chemist starts with 1,000 and uses 522.5, so there are 1,000 − 522.5 = 477.5 grams left. From the previous question you know that 1 mole of chloroform has a mass of 119.378 grams, so there are 477.5 ÷ 119.378 = 3.999, or about 4 moles of chloroform left. Be careful—you're not finished yet. The question asks for the number of moles of *chlorine*, not chloroform. According to the table, each mole of chloroform contains 3 moles of chlorine, so there are 4 × 3 = 12 moles of chlorine left.

ESSAY TEST RUBRIC

The Essay Demonstrates...

4—Advanced	• **(Reading)** A strong ability to comprehend the source text, including its central ideas and important details and how they interrelate; and effectively use evidence (quotations, paraphrases, or both) from the source text.
	• **(Analysis)** A strong ability to evaluate the author's use of evidence, reasoning, and/or stylistic and persuasive elements, and/or other features of the student's own choosing; make good use of relevant, sufficient, and strategically chosen support for the claims or points made in the student's essay; and focus consistently on features of the source text that are most relevant to addressing the task.
	• **(Writing)** A strong ability to provide a precise central claim; create an effective organization that includes an introduction and conclusion, as well as a clear progression of ideas; successfully employ a variety of sentence structures; use precise word choice; maintain a formal style and objective tone; and show command of the conventions of standard written English so that the essay is free of errors.
3—Proficient	• **(Reading)** Satisfactory ability to comprehend the source text, including its central ideas and important details and how they interrelate; and use evidence (quotations, paraphrases, or both) from the source text.
	• **(Analysis)** Satisfactory ability to evaluate the author's use of evidence, reasoning, and/or stylistic and persuasive elements, and/or other features of the student's own choosing; make use of relevant and sufficient support for the claims or points made in the student's essay; and focus primarily on features of the source text that are most relevant to addressing the task.
	• **(Writing)** Satisfactory ability to provide a central claim; create an organization that includes an introduction and conclusion, as well as a clear progression of ideas; employ a variety of sentence structures; use precise word choice; maintain an appropriate formal style and objective tone; and show control of the conventions of standard written English so that the essay is free of significant errors.
2—Partial	• **(Reading)** Limited ability to comprehend the source text, including its central ideas and important details and how they interrelate; and use evidence (quotations, paraphrases, or both) from the source text.
	• **(Analysis)** Limited ability to evaluate the author's use of evidence, reasoning, and/or stylistic and persuasive elements, and/or other features of the student's own choosing; make use of support for the claims or points made in the student's essay; and focus on relevant features of the source text.
	• **(Writing)** Limited ability to provide a central claim; create an effective organization for ideas; employ a variety of sentence structures; use precise word choice; maintain an appropriate style and tone; or show control of the conventions of standard written English, resulting in certain errors that detract from the quality of the writing.

1—Inadequate	• **(Reading)** Little or no ability to comprehend the source text or use evidence from the source text.
	• **(Analysis)** Little or no ability to evaluate the author's use of evidence, reasoning, and/or stylistic and persuasive elements; choose support for claims or points; or focus on relevant features of the source text.
	• **(Writing)** Little or no ability to provide a central claim, organization, or progression of ideas; employ a variety of sentence structures; use precise word choice; maintain an appropriate style and tone; or show control of the conventions of standard written English, resulting in numerous errors that undermine the quality of the writing.

SAMPLE ESSAY RESPONSE #1 (ADVANCED SCORE)

As anyone knows who has had to help their family move house, find a textbook in a cluttered room, or even just clean a crowded apartment, possessions can have a huge amount of power over people. Far from being simply objects that we enjoy or that bring us pleasure, it can sometimes feel that our possessions oppress us. This is the point Morris eloquently makes in her essay "The Tyranny of Things." By using anecdotes, examples, reasoning, and powerful imagery, Morris argues that the very things we cherish are nearly crushing the life out of us.

The author begins by relating an anecdote about two teenagers becoming fast friends over their love of things. It is a touching moment, one to which readers can easily relate; even Morris herself says that we all probably go through this phase. This helps establish her credibility with readers, because her examples make sense to them. Gradually, however, Morris makes it clear that this touching moment has a sinister side—the love of things will only result in resentment.

Morris reasons that while it's natural to go through a phase of wanting objects, it is unhealthy to remain in this state. "Many people never pass out of this phase," she writes ominously. "They never see a flower without wanting to pick it . . . they bring home all their alpenstocks." It begins to sound obsessive, this need to control things. Morris goes on to develop her argument by suggesting that possessions are metaphorically suffocating us. She makes the idea of too many possessions sound repulsive by describing them as "an undigested mass of things." The things almost take on a kind of life force, according to Morris: "they possess us." They "have destroyed" our empty spaces and we feel "stifled."

Another way Morris supports her argument is by giving examples of the unnecessary "tokens" associated with social occasions. She describes how at events, luncheons, and parties, gifts are given and received. She then uses powerful negative imagery to describe the effects of these gifts, comparing the recipient to a "ship encrusted with barnacles" that needs to be "scraped bare again." This language suggests that the gifts are burdensome and even harmful.

By contrast, the imagery Morris uses to describe a simple life filled with fewer things is imagery of ease and relaxation. "We breathe more freely in the clear space that we have made for ourselves," she writes. It is not just that we have literally regained control from our possessions and are now acting rather than being acted upon; it is that we are physically more at ease.

In her conclusion, Morris longs for a day when we can live more simply, with fewer possessions. She describes a "house by the sea" that was simple and empty; it did not "demand care" or "claim attention" or otherwise act upon her. Her wish is that "we could but free ourselves" from the tyranny of things that she feels is draining us of our freedom. And at this point, it is likely the reader's wish, too.

SAMPLE ESSAY RESPONSE #2 (PROFICIENT SCORE)

Although as people we like to think of ourselves as owners of things, in fact it can sometimes feel like the things we own end up owning us. At least this is what Morris argues in her essay "The Tyranny of Things." Through her use of evidence, reasoning, and word choice, she makes a strong argument that we should own fewer things if we ever want to be truly happy.

Morris tells a story about two teenage girls who instantly know they will be friends because they both like things. They are not happy just to be. They have to own things. It's like their own experiences aren't enough for them. But Morris says that this is bad for people, because they will end up feeling like their possessions own them.

Morris's reasoning is that we can basically get control back over our own lives if we stop needing things so much. If we have too many things, "they possess us." So we have to get rid of things, and then we can feel better. At least these days we aren't buried with our things anymore, like they were in the olden days.

The word choices in the essay are interesting. She talks about the way things become a problem for us: "our books are a burden to us, our pictures have destroyed every restful wall-space, our china is a care." By using a lot of repetition, it shows how powerful things are.

Morris's essay encourages people to free themselves from their things. If they do so, they will be happier. Through her personal anecdotes, reasoning, and repetitive word choices, she makes her essay very powerful.